D0113958

MUDDY CUP

A Dominican Family Comes of Age
in a New America

BARBARA FISCHKIN

SCRIBNER

SCRIBNER
1230 Avenue of the Americas
New York, NY 10020

Designed by Colin Joh
Set in Bembo

Manufactured in the United States of America

1 3 5 7 9 10 8 6 4 2

Library of Congress Cataloging-in-Publication Data
Fischkin, Barbara.
Muddy Cup : a Dominican family comes of age in a new America / Barbara Fischkin.
p. cm.
1. Dominican Americans—New York (State)—New York—Biography.
2. Dominican Americans—New York (State)—New York—Social conditions.
3. Almonte family. I. Title.
E184.D6F57 1997
974.7'1004687293—dc21 97-3196
CIP
The author gratefully acknowledges permission to reprint the following:
Portions of this book based upon a series of newspaper articles by Barbara Fischkin
which appeared in Newsday from 1986–1987. © Newsday, Inc. 1986–1987.
"A Muddy Cup" from John Montague: Collected Poems.
Wake Forest University Press © 1995.
Lines from "Amen to Butterflies" (First Movement) from Countersong to
Walt Whitman & Other Poems by Pedro Mir. Translated by Jonathan Cohen and
Donald D. Walsh. Bilingual edition copyright © 1993, Azul Editions.

ISBN 0-684-80704-1

For Jim

CONTENTS

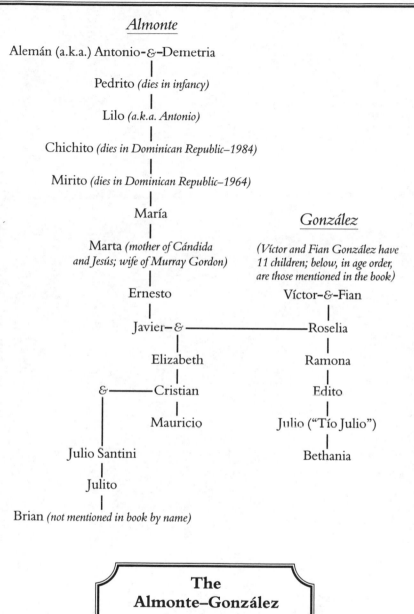

Almonte

Alemán (a.k.a.) Antonio-&-Demetria

Pedrito *(dies in infancy)*

Lilo *(a.k.a. Antonio)*

Chichito *(dies in Dominican Republic–1984)*

Mirito *(dies in Dominican Republic–1964)*

María

Marta *(mother of Cándida and Jesús; wife of Murray Gordon)*

González

(Víctor and Fian González have 11 children; below, in age order, are those mentioned in the book)

Ernesto

Víctor-&-Fian

Javier-&————————————Roselia

Elizabeth

Ramona

&————Cristian

Edito

Mauricio

Julio ("Tío Julio")

Julio Santini

Bethania

Julito

Brian *(not mentioned in book by name)*

The Almonte–González Family Tree

BEGINNING

Roselia, the mother, does not usually speak first. But now she must. This story, she says, begins on the day in 1986 when she was told she could not bring two of her three children to America. It cannot begin any other way.

Javier, Roselia's husband, says his wife still makes too much of what turned out to be a small dilemma. El Jefe was our real problem, insists Javier, the family's oral historian. El Jefe made all of us want to leave, although he did keep order. Start with him. Or better, start with Columbus.

Elizabeth is the eldest of the couple's children. She begins when she was five years old and her grandfather Víctor flipped over his pickup truck. Elizabeth, riding in the back, was pinned under it, although she was barely hurt. Elizabeth is often self-absorbed and spends a lot of time shopping for clothes. But she is correct to believe it was a miracle the truck did not kill her.

Mauricio, the youngest Almonte child, starts with the first time he slashed open a sweet coconut by himself and cut off the tip of his finger. Mauricio is now studying for a master's degree in Spanish literature. He says that everything changed after he slashed open that coconut at the age of eight, although the missing skin from his finger grew back.

Cristian, the middle child, will begin anywhere you want her to begin. She lives a difficult life, which she created for herself, and says that the beginning is not important. What is important, she says, is that *her* story is about love, not immigration.

"They are all wrong," interrupts Tía Marta, who is Javier's sister. She is in her sixties, but as contrary and emotive as a restless young woman. "The story has to start with me. Without me there would be no story. I am La Cabeza, the head of this family. Javier used to think it was Víctor. But Víctor is a González. The Almontes need their own head and it is me. I am the true *cabeza.*"

Víctor is Javier's father-in-law. But Víctor is not the last character and certainly not the last relative. The Almontes' story is chock-full of relatives. It is, after all, a story about immigration.

"Víctor pushed me out of Camú, although he didn't know he was doing it," Javier says. "It was a good push. I needed to go for Mauricio's sake. For all the children. Víctor could have pushed me without Marta. But I would have had nowhere to go. I would have been pushed into nothing. So, it is true that I got to America because of Marta. But she is not my beginning. Víctor is not my beginning. Mauricio isn't even my beginning, although my other children say that Mauricio is my world. We each have our own reasons for choosing where we begin. Bárbara, I am sure, will tell our story with a beginning of her own."

I have known Javier Almonte for a decade now and have found him to be wise and often correct. *My* story about a family of Dominicans who move to New York in the 1980s begins in the Ukraine during the winter of 1919. It begins, of course, with my own relatives.

Chaya Manya Siegel was my mother's name until she was six years old. She lived with her parents and her younger brother and sister in a small wooden hut in the Jewish section of the village of Felshteen, the shtetl. The changes that would revolutionize her life began on a February afternoon when her father, Ozzie, out of breath and his fur hat askew, ran into their hut and announced that they had to find a place to hide. "I was at the market and it was empty," her father, who was the village watchmaker, shouted at my grandmother. "Take the children and come! If we hide the children, they might not all die."

As the Felshteen pogrom began, my mother ran with her parents and her brother and sister away from their home and their snowy garden where large sunflowers grew in the spring. They ran down the hill, toward the synagogue; the entire shtetl seemed to be running with them. In the confusion my mother lost sight of her parents. Then, she felt herself being lifted by her uncle Motye, her father's brother, a handsome bachelor who told stories about their cousins in America. Vowing to be brave like those cousins and not cry, my mother let her uncle carry her until they were in the cellar of the town hall, one of the few buildings in the village made from brick.

"The tyrant's soldiers won't hurt us here," Motye said, as he set her down into a crowd of people crouched on the floor. "Brick will not burn."

When the tyrant's men set the brick hall on fire, my mother ran through the smoke, searching for the door. She lost her uncle, felt herself being pushed toward the flames and pushed back until she could breathe cold air. When she was sure she was outdoors, she ran as quickly as she could away from the burning house.

She ploughed through snowdrifts that were up to her waist until she found herself in the countryside. There, she spotted another place to hide—a haystack. She began pulling out clumps of hay with her hands; she had large hands for a little girl. When the hole she made was wide enough, she climbed in and tried to cover herself with the hay she had removed.

She heard gunshots, men's voices, a horse's neighs. A heavy weight pressed quickly on her back. She felt more weights and decided that the soldiers' horses were riding over her. Then it was quiet. But she was afraid to move. She waited, fell asleep, and woke with the feeling that she had been gone for a long time. She dug herself out and, in the darkness, saw a light coming from a farmhouse in the distance. As she walked closer, dogs surrounded her and began barking. A woman opened the door, a man stood behind the woman. My mother's teeth were chattering. She knew the farmers were gentile and she only spoke Yiddish, but she had to say something. "I am the watchmaker's daughter," she whispered. "Ozzie Siegel's daughter."

She spent the night at the farm, not knowing what had happened to her family. In Felshteen, her father believed that she was dead. He did not find out that she was alive until the next night, when the farmer came looking for him. When my grandfather went to fetch my mother, she was already waiting for him in the field outside the farmhouse, within sight of her haystack.

He reassured her that her mother, brother, and sister were alive. But her uncle Motye was dead; hundreds of people had been killed. "Petlyura the Tyrant did this because he thinks the Jews are all Bolsheviks," her father explained. He carried her back to Felshteen and my mother saw piles of bodies wherever she looked, although she could not recognize any of them. So many houses had burned, even the brick houses. Animals were loose and running in misshapen circles. "I want Mama," she told her father and he took her to a neighbor's house, where her mother grabbed her and wailed louder than any baby. Their hut had been so badly looted that they could not go home.

More attacks followed. My mother and her family hid in cellars again that winter. Then a messenger arrived, sent by Felshteeners who now lived in America. My grandfather was handed a piece of paper with the address of his brother in Brooklyn, New York.

My mother and her family walked, hitched buggy rides, and shivered in fear aboard trains as they made their way across Europe. My grandfather traded gold watches, paid bribes, and begged. Eventually, the family reached a ship that was sailing to New York from the Scottish coast. My grandfather added a year to each child's age, in case America didn't welcome small children. But it did. My mother was so grateful to the immigration officer at Ellis Island that she did not say a word, even when he told her that in America her name would be Ida.

Within two years after the Felshteen pogrom, my mother and her family were living in an apartment in downtown Brooklyn. My grandfather borrowed money from his American relatives and opened a small jewelry shop. He was a terrible businessman but a great patriot. During World War II, anyone who walked into Ozzie Siegel's shop wearing a military uniform could get his watch fixed for free.

My grandfather used the modest amount of money he did save to help my parents buy a house in Brooklyn. A house made from bricks.

★　★　★

My mother told me about Felshteen when I was five years old. She sat me down in the kitchen of that brick house in Brooklyn and asked me to imagine a cold, wooden hut. "I remember being happy, there, too," she said. "Our family was close. We trusted our neighbors. I kept baby chicks in the attic."

I loved my mother's stories. I listened to them in awe and I begged her to repeat them. But they always seemed to be about somebody else, a girl named Chaya Manya Siegel, not Ida Fischkin, not my mother. I could not see my mother in Felshteen, or even running from Felshteen. While she spoke, I looked at her hair, which she bleached silver blond, at her polyester slacks, and at the long, red-polished nails on her large hands. I tried to imagine her playing with chickens in an icy hut. Or escaping a burning building or bundled aboard a boat. I couldn't. She showed me a picture that was taken before she sailed for America, and I couldn't believe that little girl with her dark hair sticking out of a ragged kerchief was my mother. My mother didn't even have an accent.

The street on which our brick house stood was tree lined. In those days the neighborhood was more akin to a suburb. *That* was where I saw my mother: in our neighborhood, walking to the beauty parlor in her slacks to get her Miss Clairol hair touched up, her manicure done.

My mother met the Almonte children and their mother, Roselia, during their first year in New York, while I was writing a newspaper series about them. But even before she met them, when she had only heard and read about them, she insisted that they would seem familiar to me because I was her daughter, the daughter of an immigrant. I thought she was being silly and simplistic. We had no common history or culture. All that my mother and the Almontes had in common was their status as immigrants. I was ten years older, and a mother myself, when I turned my newspaper series about the Almontes into this book. Instead of a year, the book covered five decades in their lives. As I wrote, I became overwhelmed, not by the years and certainly not by any great similarities between our families, because I still didn't see them. I don't think I ever will. What amazed me, instead, were the common threads in our disparate backgrounds, the smallest details, gossamer lines. Our families sounded the same when they spoke about the materials that make a house, for example, or when they used a particular appellation for an oppressor. When I hung on to those words, I could see how the Almontes fit into America. I could see Felshteen and my mother in a wooden hut. This is a book about movement, change, motherhood, fatherhood, and, as Cristian says, about love, too. But ultimately it is about the good and bad mix of America and about leaving and never leaving the hut.

PART ONE

DOMINICANOS

1
1993

As he climbed his old hill, Javier Almonte, the abuelo, looked down at the river with its white stones. This is pitiful, he thought. I crossed the river without getting wet. You could never cross the river without getting a little wet, not even in the dry season, and it's autumn and rainy now. The stones never stuck out like that and there used to be more trees, different kinds of trees. I only see one or two kinds now. There used to be more river.

At the top he glanced back and stepped onto an overgrown footpath that led to the spot, now empty, where he had been born a half century earlier. He stared out at the silver-misted peaks of the Cordillera Septentrional, his mountains, turned, saw the mango tree, shrunken but alive, and imagined a palm hut behind a wooden gate. The palm hut, the *casita,* where he had lived with his parents. Mami and Papi. Alemán Almonte and Demetria Mercedes. He opened his imaginary gate, picked a yellow flower, and walked carefully past the spaces where his mother dried her coffee beans and kept her chickens, past the spaces that used to be the front door and their tiny sitting room. He walked into the patch of air that once held the bed he had shared with his parents until he was fourteen. He could see his mother asleep in her beautiful four-poster bed, painted black and varnished, even though it was long gone, burned so that neither her children nor her ghost would ever have to watch it decay. What a relief to be up here in Juan de Nina and remember without shame that he had shared that bed in the most innocent way. In America, where Javier had lived for the past ten years, even the *Espanish* mothers stopped their boys from sleeping with them when they were still babies.

Javier, a fifty-year-old grandfather, the proper age for an abuelo *dominicano,* stood in his parents' imagined bedroom and memorialized his young self. He remembered lying under his mosquito net listening to Mami and Papi fret over a cousin or friend from the city who had disappeared after being taken away by El Jefe's police. He felt the old fright, the exhilaration, too, since horrors were what quelled the monotony of the countryside. How desperately he had wanted to leave the *campo* and live where lights blazed all night. In Juan de Nina, the only nightlife was the roosters crowing for the first time at 2 A.M. to let the farmers and farmhands know they had another hour or two left of sleep. Javier could hear the roosters now. *Quiquiriquí. Quiquiriquí.* Sometimes he believed he could hear them in the din of a New York morning, rumbling off the Flushing line on Roosevelt Avenue.

As a boy he had dreamed of an airplane. Only one flew over their hut, but it came twice a day. He had dreamed of being a pilot, but had only imagined himself in the air over Ciudad Trujillo. Some dreams turned out better than he had hoped, even though he was just a carpenter. He held on to the yellow flower he had picked inside the gate. It came from a cascade that Mami had planted. He was thrilled that it was still there, alongside her mango tree. Mami's purple flowers were gone, but the yellow ones were growing in a strong block, a living tombstone with petals as her epitaph.

Javier was sure that Víctor had sent his workers to prune the mango tree. Víctor, Javier's father-in-law, was a catalyst. Long after their family had dismantled the hut, long after Javier had settled in America, it was still Víctor who had the mango tree trimmed and kept the yellow flowers alive. Víctor didn't own the land where they stood, but he owned most of what had been Papi's land and felt proprietary about the rest. Víctor González liked to take over, but he always did it nicely. Even now, aging and hobbled by a stroke that could make anyone nasty, he was the same. As a young man, Javier might have thought he hated his father-in-law. But he had just wanted to get away from him. Javier was sure that if it had been possible, Víctor would have saved the purple flowers, as well.

Papi had sold his land to Víctor, as if to complete a circle: Parcel by parcel, Papi had bought his small tract, forty-two *tareas'* worth, with the wages he had earned cutting Víctor's sugarcane. Javier looked into his mother's old sitting room and imagined the two negotiators. His father's ears stuck out (a lot of people in Juan de Nina had ears like that), but he looked like a rich man because he had white skin. Víctor, the true land baron and taller than any of the other farmers, was brown like a pauper. "All a dead man does is stink," Papi had said to Víctor. He claimed he was selling his land so that his children would mourn him, not fight over his *tareas*. The truth was that Papi needed cash to get him through his last bit of old age. But Víctor never let on that he knew that.

Hardly anyone lived in Juan de Nina now. Most of its residents had moved to Camú because it was more convenient or because, like Javier, they had been flooded out. But Javier remembered all the houses of his old village. He could draw a map showing each one.

Javier climbed back down the hill. He had a band of silver hair around his half-bald head. But his compact body was lean and muscular. He rarely worked construction anymore, although he renovated enough apartments to keep in shape. His dark brown eyes still danced boyishly, particularly when he was near pretty, large-breasted women. Around his neck he wore a gold chain with a gold medallion in which his name, J-A-V-I-E-R, had been cut along with the outline of a rabbit. He could reminisce without feeling pitiful, and he let his memory of the hut wash him like the water he remembered from the river Camú at its true height. Then he got into the driver's seat of the black 1987 Toyota pickup truck he had shipped from New York for Cristian, his middle child, and her *esposo*. Javier had been heartbroken about the way Cristian had returned to Camú. But she had made him an abuelo, and he wanted to help.

He drove from one end of Camú to the other. As his truck bumped and skidded on the rocky road, he gave thanks to his saint that he had four-wheel drive. The hilly farming village was delineated by two curves in a badly rutted portion of the road. Juan de Nina might be deserted, but one thousand five hundred people still lived in Camú, on grids of palm *casitas,* concrete-block houses, dirt paths, fields, riverbeds, and steeper grazing lands east and west of the road. Camú hadn't shrunk but it hadn't grown much either since he had left for New York a decade earlier. Javier saw a few zinc roofs, half-finished walls made from concrete, and satellite dishes, all signs of upward mobility, usually achieved with money sent from relatives in New York or New Jersey. There were still no telephones and with one exception—La Gallera de Camú, the cockfighting arena he had built before he left—the attractions were the same. There was the river Camú, where women washed clothes while men bathed; the Bar Osiris, on its last legs now; two *bodegas,* one selling a wider variety of food, the other open all the time; and a Catholic church run by a lay minister who also delivered the mail. Javier was proud that the *gallera* had been the last thing he built before leaving for America, proud, too, that people still called him "the best carpenter in Camú."

His truck sputtered and he wondered if he should have left it in Queens, where thieves and crazed gypsy cab drivers were the only dangers. The road, the Carretera Luperón, was at its shabbiest in Camú, despite a recent resurfacing, which, according to a billboard, would not have been possible without the efforts of President Balaguer. Outside of Camú, the road wound more smoothly, north fourteen kilometers or so toward the resorts and south to the city of Santiago in the fertile Cibao valley. The resorts—Puerto Plata, Playa Dorada, and Sosúa—were bastions of beachfront hotels and time-share condominiums, which attracted European tourists by the planeload. Santiago, a rich, sophisticated city, was the country's second capital. Camú spit out workers in either direction, men like Javier. (He had worked construction on the Dorado Naco condominium complex.) But people came to Camú only to see relatives or consult with Fransica, the village's witch and healer, La Bruja de Camú. Fransica had a small but loyal following; it was said she could cure muscle aches, cancer, even broken hearts.

Javier wondered if she could get grown children to behave.

Mauricio would say he was behaving: in college, even if he refused to be a doctor. Elizabeth loved to work, have money, go out with her Greek boyfriend; but finishing her bachelor's degree? Forget about it! And Cristian. *Ay.* Javier smiled at the thought of his disobedient grown children. When he had done exactly as his father wished, it had gotten him nowhere.

He drove to the shell of a concrete-block house Cristian was building with her *esposo* on Javier's land, with Javier's money. He parked his truck, stopped to admire the house, and imagined a circular front porch, a small balcony, a picture window. It would be almost as good as a house on Long Island. It would be the grandest house in Camú. At least his grandson would live in a house made from *bloques* instead of a *casita.*

He walked behind the house to the adjoining palm huts and remembered when he had moved his family to that *casita.* No one lived there now, although Cristian used the kitchen, and someone, her *esposo* probably, had hung up in the bedroom a picture of a nearly naked blond woman. Ordinarily, Javier would linger at a picture like that. But all he could see now was Roselia seven years earlier, getting ready to join him in America.

Abuelo Javier is at his kitchen table in Queens, back from his fiftieth-birthday trip home. He is wearing work clothes but his gold medallion is around his neck.

"*Sí!* I am glad to be in America. We *dominicanos* love America," he says in Spanish. After ten years in New York, Abuelo Javier only knows a few words of English.

"No. No. You don't have to remind me about what America did to my country. I know what America did to my country. America occupied us twice, meddled in our wars and finances, took over our businesses. Did I get that right? And, yes, it is true that after all that America is very particular about which *dominicanos* it lets into its beautiful country. *Ay,* what can I say? Everyone I saw in the *campo* wants to come here. They still want to come here.

Anyone who can is coming here. Read the *Espanish* papers. They say there could be a million of us in America, and I'll bet it's more than that. One out of seven *dominicanos* lives in the United States!"

He drums his fingers on the table. It is dinnertime and Roselia is late coming home from the small clothing factory where she has worked for years. Elizabeth won't be home from the city for an hour, and she always leaves right away, to work out at the gym across the street. Mauricio is at college upstate, and he wouldn't be cooking for his father anyway.

"*Ay,* what do you want me to say? We *dominicanos* are too interested in making *dólares* to care about the past. That is true. It's the *dólares* and it's the airplane. Don't forget it only takes me a few hours and I'm back in the *campo* where they think I'm a VIP. But if you want the whole story, you have to take a good look at my country. Don't misunderstand me. I love my country. I sing '*Quisqueyanos valientes . . .*' even when my own children won't sing it. Mauricio can't even remember the words. But my country is in trouble. It's always been in trouble. Why? Trujillo? You think it is because of Trujillo? That's part of it. He certainly helped to make my country into a place people wanted to leave. But we were in trouble before Trujillo. We were in trouble before there was an America."

He gets up and walks through the living room into the bedroom. A few minutes later he returns holding a newspaper clipping. "I cut this out of the *Espanish* newspaper for you. It's about the history of my country. If you want to know why there are so many *dominicanos* here, read the history of my country. You have to start with Columbus. You know, I've always said that. In the *primaria* they made us read about Columbus from the first day. *Ay yai yai.* Some days it was all Columbus. All Cristóbal Colón. But not the whole story. We got that when we went home to

**our mamis and papis and they wouldn't let us say Colum-
bus's name out loud. They put their hands over our
mouths. 'It's bad luck. Call him El Almirante.' Five hundred years later he could still bring us bad luck.**

2

1986

On a tepid February night, Roselia Almonte, Víctor González's
daughter—his eldest and favorite—sat awake in the darkness of
her palm *casita*. She clutched the first letter Javier had sent her
after he left for America. In it he called her "my life, my love,
my sky, my being." He described the cold weather, the snow,
his sister Marta's apartment in *Nieu Yersey*. He had been home
to visit twice since that letter, most recently a few weeks ago.
But those were just visits. Roselia felt Javier had been gone for
three years and a dozen days, since February 5, 1983, the first
time he left. She remembered how her handsome husband,
with his balding head and new, white teeth had boarded an airplane, promising that someday she and the children would join
him. She had not known whether to believe him. He still
seemed like a young man, like a swaggerer, even though he was
no longer mustachioed, as when they first met. In New York,
Javier Almonte did not need Víctor González's daughter.

Roselia smiled at the memory of Javier's first visit home,
after he was gone almost a year. He unwrapped a turquoise
dress—a *yanqui* dress from a store near Marta's apartment—
and told her to hurry and put it on. "We have to go to Puerto
Plata, *mi amor*. We have to get married." It was then that Roselia
knew that while Javier might not need her in America, he
wanted her there. She knew he could bring her to America only
if they were husband and wife, the way the *yanquis* said it. Not
merely *esposo y esposa*. She had felt so elated but silly at the civil
office in Puerto Plata, marrying the man with whom she had
lived for fifteen years. They had been *juntos* for fifteen years,

since Roselia was seventeen, since the night he took her to sleep with him at his parents' house. In all those years there had never been any reason to get married; and it was inconvenient, too. The priests from Puerto Plata almost never came to the little church in Camú.

Now, their children weren't even children anymore. Mauricio was eleven, Cristian fourteen, and Elizabeth sixteen. And now, three years after Javier first left and two years after their marriage, Roselia and the children had been called for their *cita,* an appointment with an American visa officer. In the morning they would begin a two-day trip to the American consulate in Santo Domingo. They had all been to the capital a week ago for medical examinations, which they had passed. But the *cita* was the important event. What Roselia said to the American officer would determine whether she and the children got visas. Javier assured her there would be no problem. He made a lot of money in New York. "Just tell them the truth, *mi amor."* Roselia didn't know if she wanted to go to America. But she did want to live with her husband.

Gently, Roselia put down Javier's old letter and opened the shutter of her window. She stared out into the blackness and turned her head in the direction of the *cordillera.* She could not see the mountains at night. But she could see them in her memory. She had looked at them since she was a child. She could see every bit of Camú in her head. Her parents' house, the *primaria* where she had gone to school until sixth grade, the dirt paths she took home in her yellow khaki uniform. On those paths she had first felt Javier looking at her. He had scared her. She was eleven. He was nineteen and her father's farmhand. She closed her eyes and could see the places where she'd stopped being afraid of Javier— the small grocery her father used to operate by their house, the Bar Osiris, the hill to Juan de Nina that they climbed together the night they became *esposos.*

Javier told her to remember everything. When Javier spoke, Roselia concentrated. Usually she did not disagree with him. If she did, she would turn and continue cooking her *sancocho.*

Every woman made *sancocho*. But Roselia's stew, held together with her deep yellow yam sauce, overflowed with different meats and vegetables, although a few ingredients sometimes popped out as if they did not belong.

Javier said she would have a better life in America. She would drink milk from cartons. Roselia liked milk from the pails her father brought her. She was happy with her thatched roof, her lime, orange, mango, and breadfruit trees. She was happy with the *yerba buena* leaves in her garden which she made into the tea she drank as she looked out at her soothing morning view of silver mountaintops. Some nights, she and the children stayed with her nieces and nephews in Puerto Plata because that was close to their schools and Elizabeth's English lessons. But after a day or two she yearned for her *casita*, her milk, her roof, her trees, her tea, her mountains.

Javier said the children would get a better education in America. It was the boy who most concerned him. Mauricio, her youngest, the baby, her eleven-year-old with his small head of closely cropped black kinky hair. It was while she was pregnant with Elizabeth that Javier saw an airplane and told her he would go up in one someday. She thought he was joking. He never said it after Cristian was born. But after Mauricio was born he said that all the time. Now she knew the truth. If Elizabeth received a good education in America, it would be a bonus. If Cristian did well in school there, it would be a miracle. Roselia knew that Javier believed, more than he believed anything, that it was a necessity for Mauricio to be educated in America. But how would Mauricio learn anything in an American school if he didn't know English?

She didn't want to leave her parents. Her father, Víctor, was her protector. As a girl she watched him, taller than anyone in Camú, riding home from the fields on his white horse. Now they were friends and confidants. Víctor would tell her about problems with his land, or his workers, or with the *ingenio*, the mill in Montellano where he brought his truckloads of sugarcane. Fian, her mother, was frenetic, and Roselia was the only one who could calm her. As the eldest, Roselia helped to raise her mother's ten younger children, and she and Fian worried about them together.

Roselia heard Mauricio moan and thought she would try to sleep, too. She had not slept in two nights. She shuttered the window and opened the curtain between her sitting room and the bedroom. The excitement tired Mauricio and the girls, and they were asleep under the mosquito nets Roselia had fastened tightly for them hours before. Elizabeth, a solid, awkward girl of sixteen, shared a bed with Cristian, at fourteen prettier and more delicate. The girls slept head to toe, but Roselia could remember how, as children, they huddled together. Mauricio, his white briefs stark against his brown skin, was in the next bed, the one he had shared with his parents and now shared with her.

Roselia tucked Javier's letters under the mattress, unfastened the net, and slipped in next to her son. She put her arms around Mauricio and positioned his head on her breast. She tried to sleep, but she could not.

The U.S. consulate in Santo Domingo was a three-story, fenced, concrete building, but the immigrant visa line that wrapped around it most mornings was dressed for a party. Girls in bright ruffled dresses stood next to boys with bold, striped ties and polyester jackets "just like Papi's." The adults wore sundresses and cheap suits or brand-new T-shirts blazoned with the names of towns, teams, and restaurants in New York, New Jersey, Miami. The faces were as colorful as the clothes. Complexions, even among immediate relatives, ranged from dark brown to Mediterranean white.

Mixed like that, the faces looked festive, but they reflected a small, tired land that had killed off all of its Indians, but not all of their features; a land that had imported African slaves to replace the Indians and had survived conquests by Spanish and Haitian forces, only to be occupied—twice this century—by American marines. Everyone was afraid that they would do or say something wrong and not get a visa. The children clung to their parents as they smoothed their dresses and jackets and looked through the iron gate up at the consulate. The adults tried to hide their anxiety with chatter and laughter; a few intrepid souls read aloud from their Bibles.

Roselia Almonte and her children got on the end of the line. So many people followed them that within minutes they were in the middle of a much longer line. Roselia clutched her pocket-size blue pamphlet of psalms. Her head hurt and she wished she had a cup of *yerba buena* tea. The mint flavor of the leaves in her mouth would calm her worries. Mauricio did not seem worried. Only thrilled. Her daughters thought this was a *fiesta*. They had made up their faces with blue and green eye shadow and tied bows in their hair.

As the line moved, Roselia grabbed Mauricio's hand. She nodded at her two daughters, and they followed behind her. At the gate she read a sign: TO APPLY FOR A VISA YOU NEED TO HAVE: 1. A VALID PASSPORT. 2. A VISA APPLICATION, CAREFULLY FILLED OUT. 3. A PHOTOGRAPH: ONE AND A HALF BY ONE AND A HALF INCHES. 4. DOCUMENTATION OF ECONOMIC SOLVENCY (LETTERS OF EMPLOYMENT, BANK LETTERS, DOCUMENTATION OF SAVINGS OR BUSINESS, CAR REGISTRATIONS, ETC.). "We have everything," she said to Elizabeth. They were led upstairs and then downstairs again, where the four of them wiggled into the last remaining spaces on a wooden bench. Behind them was a painting of Señor Ronald Reagan. He smiled at Roselia. She giggled back and felt lighthearted for a moment.

Mauricio fidgeted on the bench. Roselia put her hand on his leg and opened her Bible.

"Mami, I'm hungry," he said.

She opened her handbag and pulled out a wintergreen mint. "This is the last one," she said.

Mauricio unwrapped it, put the hard candy in his mouth, bit it in half, and handed his sister Cristian one of the pieces.

"*Gracias,* Mauri." Cristian popped the cracked candy in her mouth.

A man came over to their bench. "Everybody raise your hands, please!"

Roselia raised hers; she looked at the girls and Mauricio so that they would do the same. They all promised to tell the truth to the government of the United States of America.

Roselia opened her Bible and began reading out loud:

> He who dwells in the shelter of
>   the Most High,
> who abides in the shadow of the
>   Almighty,
> will say to the Lord, "My refuge and
>   my fortress:
> my God, in whom I trust."

So many people were in the room that their noise made it hard for Roselia to concentrate. These people really did think they were at a *fiesta.* Only the *lechón,* the roast pig, was missing. Roselia tried to pray louder:

> You will not fear the terror of the night,
> nor the arrow that flies by day,
> nor the pestilence that stalks in darkness,
> nor the destruction that wastes at noonday.

More noise came from the loudspeaker. Roselia realized that names were being called and she strained to hear. She wished for *yerba buena* in her mouth and kept reading. For two hours, while she listened for their names, she read all her favorite psalms. Then she began to read them again.

" 'You will not fear the terror of night . . . ,' " Roselia recited.
"Señora Almonte y familia, casilla uno."
Elizabeth poked Mauricio.
"Señora Almonte y familia, casilla uno."

★ ★ ★

They sat in a small office. Roselia gave the visa officer a half smile. Later she would remember him as being tall and wearing glasses and a suit.

"Does your husband have a car?" the visa officer asked.

"No," Roselia replied. She wondered if that was good or bad.

"Who does he live with?"

"With one of his brothers."

There was a pause. The officer looked down at his papers. "Now, which one is Elizabeth?"

Roselia pointed to her eldest daughter.

"What do you do?" the officer asked Elizabeth.

"I am a student."

"Where do you go to school, Elizabeth?"

"Liceo José DuBeau of Puerto Plata."

"What grade?"

"I am in the fourth year of secondary school."

Cristian will be next, Roselia thought. There was air-conditioning, but it was hot anyway. She could smell her daughters' lavender perfume.

"Señora Almonte," the officer said.

Why was the consul speaking to her again?

"Señora Almonte, I can only give the visas to you and your eldest daughter. A wife and three children would be too much for your husband to support."

Roselia was not sure she understood this man's Spanish. This could not be what he was saying.

She looked at her daughters. Elizabeth was shaking her head. Cristian was expressionless.

"In three months you can ask again for your other children," the officer said.

Roselia's head began to pound. She could not find the top or the bottom of her pain. The officer kept talking at her, giving her instructions she would not remember. She tried to focus on the letters of his name. M-u-e-l-l-e-r. She would try to never forget it.

"But with these two it would be too much. You can ask for the others in three months, if your husband's financial situation changes—or if you get a job."

Javier had never said this might happen.

"Is that okay, Señora Almonte?"

Roselia felt tears stinging her cheeks.

"Señora Almonte?"

"*Sí.*" Roselia was crying and could not find anything else to say.

"Mami!" Elizabeth was angry. "Mami. Are you crazy?"

Roselia sent her children to buy lunch from the vendors outside the consulate. She wanted peace when she filled out the forms the visa officer had given her. She wrote her name and Elizabeth's. Roselia knew what Elizabeth had meant. She should not have shown that *yanqui* visa officer—Roselia did not know how to pronounce his name, but she had memorized the letters, M-u-e-l-l-e-r—how bad he made her feel.

She wondered if she was crazy. She hadn't slept for three nights. Maybe she imagined all of this.

She had all the papers they had asked for on the sign outside the building. She knew exactly what Javier, his brothers, and sister had done to get their visas, and she had done the same thing. She had read all the advice Marta had sent in her letters from *Nieu Yersey*. She had answered all the questions. She told the truth. Except for one little lie. She had said they lived in Puerto Plata at her nieces' house instead of in Camú. The mail delivery was better in the city. They had a real mailman there. They weren't going to deny her a visa for that!

She wasn't crazy. The *yanquis* were crazy. You don't separate a mother from her baby, from the boy, the shy, delicate boy who sleeps next to her every night. You don't tell a mother to leave without a pretty fourteen-year-old daughter.

The *yanquis* would say that she and Elizabeth did not have to go at all. Those *yanquis* did not know Javier. He would mull this over and find a way to be cheerful about it. He would want her to be cheerful. And he would expect her to come. He was not nervous the way she was. He had not slept for years with Mauri on his breast. America! Why would she even think of going there if it weren't for Javier? To places whose names she could not pronounce?

"Señora Almonte?"

Roselia raised her head to a blond woman, another officer.

"Señora Almonte, there is an American woman in my office who would like to speak with you."

Roselia nodded. She had no idea what this was about, but she did not want to refuse the visa officer.

She kept thinking about Javier. She could still see Javier a few days after Mauricio was born, standing outside their *casita,* waving again at an airplane and looking like a boy himself.

On his first voyage to the New World, Christopher Columbus stopped on the eastern side of the large island he called Hispaniola and discovered a kingdom he would come to know. It had breathtaking coastlines, confident mountain ranges, fertile valleys, and a centuries-old culture. The Taíno Indians called their land Quisqueya, Mother of All Lands, and celebrated it with *areítos,* musical renditions of their history. They used their lands' resources well, making pots from stone and clay, bread from *yuca,* and medicine from herbs.

On his second voyage, Columbus built the first European colony in the Western Hemisphere in Quisqueya, on a northern coastal site about seventy kilometers west of where the palm huts of Camú stand today. He named his settlement Isabela, after the Queen of Spain, his benefactress, who expected no less. He bragged to the queen that Quisqueya was brimming with gold, that the Taínos wore gold ornaments and mined gold. Certain that the Cibao valley to the south was packed with even more gold, he led an expedition from Isabela.

Columbus never found his gold. In Camú, the *bruja,* a

devout Catholic, would say Columbus brought bad luck to Quisqueya because he was too greedy. Abuelo Javier says Columbus was looking for the wrong treasure. Instead of gold, he should have wanted the land. "*Tierra, tierra, tierra!* Nothing can replace good land. Not even gold."

Columbus tried to save face by moving his colony from Isabela south to the banks of the Ozama River, which had a better harbor. He named that colony Santo Domingo after the patron saint of his father, Domenico, some say. Domenico Columbus was a master weaver but a faltering businessman, and his namesake colony fared no better under his son. In less than a decade, Christopher Columbus turned the Mother of All Lands, still naturally beautiful as is the Dominican Republic today, into a political failure, a would-be plunderer's paradise, and a genocide pit. Columbus was returned to the queen in chains, and, eventually, it was the mineral-rich kingdoms of Mexico and Peru that won Spain's attention, while Quisqueya languished as a haven for European pirates.

Columbus's worst crime, although not one that troubled the Spanish or the Spanish settlers, was the enslavement of the Taínos. The admiral made them get what gold they could from their riverbeds, overworked them so that his men could eat, and set up a system that perpetuated their slavery and extermination. One-third of the Taíno population was killed off between 1494 and 1496, and there are said to be no pure Taínos left in the Dominican Republic.

But the Dominican Republic has always honored Columbus. El Faro is the newest monument to the explorer and governor, an elaborate, cross-shaped, gleaming white lighthouse that cost millions of pesos. Throughout the country, upward mobility is elusive, schools are marginal, roads go unpaved, politicians still have to be watched like thieves. Grandparents, and parents, too, remember times when there were thousands of political prisoners, disappearances, tortures, and brutal murders. And they fear it could happen again. Nowadays, the electricity fails so often that the lack of it has become a bad joke. But Columbus's multimillion-peso lighthouse shines on.

"You want to know what I think about El Faro?" Abuelo Javier asks. "Forget about it. A waste of money. That's what everyone really thinks. You know who it was who had the idea to build a *faro* in the capital, don't you? Rafael Trujillo. El Jefe."

3

1952–1953

Nine-year-old Javier Almonte headed for home as soon as third grade was dismissed. He didn't stop to play baseball alongside the sugarcane fields or pluck oranges and mangoes from branches that stuck out on the roadside. At the river Camú he was tempted by the coolness of the dark water and leafy trees. But he stepped across the river's wet, white stones without stopping to swim. Instead, he ran up the hill to Juan de Nina.

At the top, he shielded his eyes from the sun and examined the sky and the peaks of the *cordillera,* like a young Taíno hunter looking for a dove or parrot. No shadow was on the brown slopes of the mountain range, no flash of silver at the edge, no trace of white smoke. He wiped his dark brow with his hand, pulled his sticky khaki shirt away from his thin chest, and walked confidently down the path to his *casita.* He had not missed his airplane.

Through the fence he could see the branches of his mother's large mango tree and a profusion of *mantequillas* and *moradas,* her delicately formed yellow and purple flowers. Javier opened the gate. He stepped, accidentally, on the collection of coffee beans his mother had left to dry on a sheet of bark, jumped away from it, looked to make sure no baby chicks were underfoot, and walked through the open front door. The door was painted blue and outlined in whitewash. His mother had wanted varnish, too, but Papi said that cost too much and that a varnished bed was enough.

Inside, Javier felt the swept floor against the soles of his leather shoes. Each morning his mother wet the mud and swept it with sand from the river, until it was smooth as cement. Then she dusted the framed dime-store pictures of Jesús and *las vírgenes* Mercedes and Altagracia that stood on the small table in the center of the cramped room. A government photograph of El Jefe was on another table, off to the side as far as it could be. "In this house," the inscription under the bald, white, mustachioed, beady-eyed dictator read, "Trujillo is the chief."

He stopped at the entrance to the kitchen and, sweating even more from the extra heat of the coal stove, watched his mother. With her back to him, she was arranging her yellow flowers in a metal vase. She was a slight, trim woman with dark skin and coarse straight black hair that she pulled back behind her ears. She was middle-aged, but her hands were wrinkled. Javier watched her hands as she delicately moved the buds and stems into place, the hands of an old woman.

"*Bendición,* Mami," he said. At the sound of his voice, she turned and smiled, as he knew she would.

"May God bless you, my son."

Javier was the youngest of his mother's seven surviving children. His older brothers and sisters said he was Mami's favorite, and it was Javier's view, too, that her life revolved around him. He had suckled what he could from her until he was five years old, and he still slept in her black, varnished bed. He could not fall asleep unless his head was on her breast. Still standing, Javier leaned against his wooden slat chair. The back was unsteady. He saw his mother's disappointed face, stood up straight, carefully pulled the chair away from the table, and sat down. Mami dusted some sugar granules from the table into her apron and let them slide into one of her tin cups. She took a pot off the coal stove, brought it to the table, and scooped beans onto the plate in front of him. From another pot she scooped rice. "Look for the chicken in there," she instructed him, pointing to shredded bits of meat in the rice. "I saved it for you." His mother stood while he ate, as she did with his father. Javier ate slowly, to savor his time alone with Mami. His father was working in the *caña* fields of one of the rich farmers of Camú with his brother Ernesto. Ernesto still lived with them as did another brother, Mirito, who was sickly and probably resting in the second bedroom. Mami said that Pedrito, his dead brother, a little boy who had caught pneumonia, was in the *casita,* too. But Javier had never seen him.

After lunch he went to change in the bedroom he shared with his parents. He stopped to look above the doorway and study the photographs of *líderes* Mami hung there for his benefit. Whenever someone brought her a copy of the newspaper, she added to or revised her little gallery. Today Trujillo was above the doorway, alongside Adolf Hitler, who, she explained, was an important man in his day. At the *primaria,* his teacher told him that his mother was well educated for a woman of her age. She had been to school as far as the third grade.

In the bedroom, Javier took off his leather school shoes and put them under his mother's black, varnished bed. He peeled off his short-sleeved shirt and his slacks and heard the roar above him.

"Javielito, your airplane is here," his mother called from the kitchen.

Quickly, he opened his drawer, took out shorts and a cotton shirt, and put them on. He slipped his feet into his other pair of shoes, rubber slippers that Mami cleaned every evening. Then he dug under another shirt, found his metal airplane, and held it between his thumb and forefinger.

"Javielito! You'll miss it!"

He put the airplane in his pocket and ran outside. At the edge of the garden he shielded his eyes and jumped up and down, waving as hard as he could. This was *his* airplane. It flew over his palm hut once in the morning while he ate his eggs and *yuca* and again when he came home from school, if he got home quickly enough. What if one day the pilot saw him waving, landed, and took him aboard?

Javier watched his airplane disappear behind the *cordillera*. He felt in his pocket for his toy airplane, held it up to the sky, and dropped it. *Guauuaw!* A crash on the fence. As he walked outside the gate to retrieve it, he saw the perfect weed, one made from prickly clumps of loose fiber. He lifted it tenderly and placed his toy airplane on top of it.

"Bomb!" he shouted as the clumps of weed cascaded to the floor. "Bomb! Bomb!" He had once killed one of his mother's chicks with a bomb. She believed it had been attacked by a snake. He never told her the truth, although at night when she said the rosary to Radio Santa María, he contemplated confessing.

Two months later, they celebrated Christmas with a roast pig, washed down with *habichuela,* a sweet, thick drink made from pinto beans and milk. Mami stretched the *lechón* she had roasted so carefully by using it in stews and soups. As he drank his *habichuela,* Javier watched Mami's pots because he knew that when every bit of that pig was finished, the two of them would leave for a week's trip to the capital. He had never been to Ciudad Trujillo, but he was excited for another reason. They were going to stay with his Tía Angela—who was really his mother's cousin. Tia Angela had adopted five sons, all grown now, and two of them were pilots, real pilots, in the Air Force. Javier had heard stories about his auntie, whom he had never met, for as long as he could remember. People said she had been a bold young woman who left the *campo* alone, without an *esposo* or anyone. They said she had worked as a maid for important politicians; that she had cleaned house for El Jefe himself. Javier figured Tía Angela must have been one of El Jefe's best maids. How else could she have gotten her sons into the Air Force?

They finished the *lechón* in three days. Before dawn on the twenty-eighth of December, as the roosters crowed around them, Javier followed his mother down the hill from Juan de Nina. At the river he studied the white rocks and planned how they would get across. Mami stepped onto the first rock. He grabbed the worn handle of her brown, metal suitcase so that he could carry some of the weight himself. Once across, and a little damp, they walked to the main road of Camú. From there they took a pickup truck that was the local *guagua*—the bus—to Puerto Plata. As the sun rose, they boarded a real bus for the four-hour ride south. Javier counted cars and trucks on the road and sang the words Ciudad Trujillo in his own made-up *pambiche*. He wanted to try a *merengue*, too. But that would be complicated. The important thing was to make sure he didn't sound like a *campesino* when he said the name of the capital. From Puerto Plata they rode into the green of the Cibao valley, and Javier wondered if the gold Columbus had searched for could still be here, buried under the soft, wet land.

At the outskirts of the capital he pressed his nose against the window. He decided he would count the number of houses made from *bloques,* but as they got closer, he realized that every house was made from *bloque.* Long streets with one concrete-block house after another. Every time the bus stopped to let a passenger off at the home of a relative, he jumped up.

"Sit," his mother ordered him. "Calm yourself. We're near the airport now. Tía Angela's neighborhood is next." She stood and walked to the front of the bus. "The house of Angelica Mercedes, *por favor.* It's on the first street, the eighth house."

The bus stopped short in front of a green concrete-block house. *Bloque,* of course. This was the capital. The driver helped his mother get her suitcase down from the overhead rack, and Javier followed her off the bus. A lot of cats were on the front porch and a few came over and rubbed their legs against Javier. He smelled a strange odor, but it wasn't the cats. It smelled like bus fumes, although it came from the sky. It was airplane fuel! Javier was sure of that. He inhaled deeply so that he could feel the smell inside him.

Javier followed his mother to the back of the house. Sitting on the patio, fanning herself in a rattan chair, another cat in her lap, was an old woman. Tía Angela looked like his mother, except older. She had the same dark skin and the same hair pulled back behind her ears. A lot of people in Juan de Nina, even when they weren't related, looked like one another.

"Meme," the woman called out to his mother, who smiled. Javier knew his mother loved when people used her nickname. The woman stood up slowly and hugged Mami. "And who is this handsome *muchacho?* Not Javielito. Javielito is supposed to be a little boy."

They followed Tía Angela inside to her dining room. While his mother and aunt talked and ignored him, he rubbed his hand up and down the *bloque* wall. It was painted yellow and was even smoother than *Mami*'s floor, nothing like the rough palm walls of their *casita.*

His auntie told them to sit at the large wooden table in the middle of the room, which was set for a meal. She went into her kitchen and brought back a large bowl with flowers painted on it and began spooning chicken and rice onto their plates.

"There's a lot of chicken at the bottom," she said as she put a leg onto Mami's plate. "You have to look for it."

His auntie spoke as quickly as his mother but softer. When his mother wanted him to look for something, the word she said sounded like *buka.* Auntie's word sounded like *boosca.* Javier wondered where the pilots were, but he was too shy to ask.

"How is Marta?" his auntie asked his mother.

"*Ay,* Angela, her baby is beautiful."

Javier waited to hear more. His sister Marta was always in some kind of trouble.

"Marta's still in Moca, Meme?"

"*Sí. Sí.* She's *junta* with a taxi driver. He bought her all new furniture."

"And Alemán?"

"He's fine. The same." That was all his mother said about his father.

When they finished, Tía Angela said she wanted them to meet her family. Javier did not think he could wait any longer to see the pilots. His auntie went back to the kitchen and returned with a wooden tray. On it she had a metal pot with more chicken and rice. She opened a cabinet, took out a stack of plates, two serving spoons, and a small metal dinner bell. "Follow me," she said to Javier and his mother, and opened her eyes wide.

Javier followed his mother and Tía Angela into a hallway. She stopped at a closed door, which Javier thought looked like a bedroom. But when she opened it, a wooden table was inside, just like the one in the dining room, except it was twice as large and with a lot more chairs around it.

Tía Angela set out eight plates.

Javier was sure there were only two pilots.

Then she rang the bell. It sounded more like a bird than a bell.

Miauuuu. A gaggle of cats came in through the open door and surrounded Tía Angela's feet.

Javier couldn't wait to see the pilots. His auntie rang her bell two more times. *Miauu.* Two more cats came in.

Javier went into the hall to look for the pilots. The bell rang again. "*Ay,* Angela!" he heard his mother say. "They are so cute!" Javier walked back in. "Mami!" he giggled. The cats were sitting at the table.

"Wait!" Tía Angela said, smiling. She walked around the table and with her large serving spoon gave each cat a helping of rice and chicken. "*Ay, gatita,*" she said to one of the cats. "There is more chicken at the bottom."

Javier watched as each cat bent over, ate, licked his plate, and then dropped down from the table. Things like this never happened in Juan de Nina.

In the evening two men with uniforms came to the back patio. Javier stood and wondered if he should salute. "And who is this *chiquito?*" one of the pilots said. "I am Mario Wenceslao Almonte Mercedes," Javier said. The pilot picked him up and put him on his shoulders. "I thought you were named Javier."

"Mario's my real name. Javier was the name my godmother picked."

"So why didn't they name you Javier?"

"Mami liked Mario better. But she calls me Javier anyway." He was back on the ground and could not wait any longer. "I want to be a pilot, like you."

"That's not so difficult."

Javier stared up at his cousin and pursed his plum lips.

"You just have to wait until you're older."

"Then what?"

"*Ay,* Javier. You have to finish school. You have to be sixteen. You have to have your identification card."

"Then?"

"Then you first study to be a mechanic."

Javier nodded. Now he knew how to do it.

In the capital, Javier went to markets where the crowds were so thick he clung to Mami, and to the zoo, where the sea lions barked like dogs and seemed to be speaking directly to him. They came home after dark and the street lights were on. Tía Angela said some shops left their lights on all night. He saw a tomb containing Columbus's remains at the cathedral and told Tía Angela that Maestra Quisqueya, his teacher in Camú, thought that El Almirante might really be buried in Spain. His auntie told him that wasn't true and he believed her because she was the one who lived in the capital. Javier had such a good time that he didn't want to leave with Mami. But he had no choice.

After vacation, classes at the Primaria de Camú continued in the usual way.

"*Niños!*" shouted Maestra Quisqueya. "*Niños,* who is the leader of our country?" Javier repeated the familiar chant with his classmates: "Generalissimo Doctor Rafael Leonidas Trujillo Molina, Benefactor of the Fatherland and Father of the New Fatherland."

"Good," said the teacher as she pushed a rickety blackboard to the front of the palm hut.

Javier opened his worn textbook. He squinted and adjusted his eyes to the light that came in through the slats of bark and turned to the history section, his favorite. While his teacher wrote mathematical problems on the blackboard, he reread his favorite page, the one about Máximo Gómez, a famous Dominican soldier who had fought for Cuba. He turned back to the beginning of the book and studied drawings of the Taínos and the *bohíos* where they lived. Those huts were made from vines and palm leaves, but they looked a lot like his *casita* or his school. In the *campo,* nothing ever changed.

"Mario Almonte!" Maestra Quisqueya called out. "To the board!" Javier walked to the front of the room. His teacher picked up a string bean plant from the patch outside and pointed to a number. "Make this into tenths!"

Javier took the chalk from the teacher and held it carefully in his hand. Maestra Quisqueya often told him that he was one of the smartest in the class. He liked to hear that. But she did not tolerate mistakes from him. Once, he had put a decimal point in the wrong place, and she had ordered him outside where she hit him with her string bean plant. He had gotten decimals correct since then.

He marked his dot.

"That is very good, Mario. Someday you will go on to the *secundaria.*"

At home Javier dreamed of nothing but being a pilot. He woke from his dreams in the night and heard his parents speaking to each other. Usually they pondered the few scraggly cows and pigs they owned or the *caña* his father cut for other farmers. Sometimes, though, his parents whispered. A neighbor's cousin from Puerto Plata was missing. A friend who they thought had moved to Sosúa could not be found.

"How did you hear?" his father would ask.

"Radio Bemba," his mother would say. Radio Lips. Word of mouth.

"It's dangerous to say anything bad about El Jefe. Anything

at all," his father would say in his usual calm monotone. "People shouldn't say anything at all."

"Some of the people haven't said anything at all," his mother would argue. "If somebody doesn't like you, they'll make it up to get you in trouble."

"Do you know who I saw?" his father would continue. "Do you know who I saw drive through Camú in a little black car?"

Once, walking through Camú, Javier had seen one of those little black cars and wondered if he should hide. El Jefe's secret police were the only ones who drove those cars, and they tortured people. Everyone knew that. Pilots worked for El Jefe, too. But people never said bad things about pilots. Maybe that was because they could fly above everything. Javier believed they could fly above the boredom, too. He asked his mother when they could go back to the capital, but she kept saying it was too far away. His sister Marta came up from Moca to visit and show off her new baby girl, and he told her that he wanted to live in the capital when he was grown up. "I may go even farther than that," she said.

"Trujillo was already in power for more than twenty years when I was a boy," Abuelo Javier says. "But it was when I was a boy that it started to get really bad. At least that was my impression. What did you tell me American boys say to each other? 'You can't make me. It's free country.' *Sí?* We used to say we would get the secret police after one another.

"It was brutal. But that doesn't mean it wasn't silly, too. Once the secret police came to Camú because some farmhands were gambling over dominoes. Everyone gambled, even the police. But it didn't matter. They made those players carry their domino table all the way to the sugar mill in Montellano.

"So who do we have to thank for Trujillo? America, you say?"

From 1916 until 1924, America occupied the Dominican Republic, ostensibly to reorganize the country's ragged finances and protect the Caribbean from German influence. (What America really wanted was a piece of the Dominican sugar trade.) U.S. Marines trained the country's young men in the military skills they were lacking and created the Dominican National Guard. Among the recruits was a former telegraph operator and sugar company guard from the town of San Cristóbal, the troublesome son of an inconsequential businessman: Rafael Trujillo.

Trujillo took to Marine training, quickly rose to the highest position in National Guard, and decided to "run" for president of the country. He stole the 1930 election, primarily by terrifying his opponents, and settled into a job he expected to hold for life.

As El Jefe, Rafael Trujillo was the most dangerous type of small-town boy. He believed that his light skin gave him a mandate to lead, that it negated his crude manner and lack of education, and entitled him to any young virgin he desired. (When the dictator was around, mothers tried to hide their most voluptuous daughters or, at least, dress them modestly.) Trujillo became rich from government projects, built a string of mansions, made the Catholic church his toy. Eventually he was said to be worth $500 million. For thirty-one years his country was a prison. Emigration was halted, he controlled the nation's newspapers and radio stations, its free speech, in general. Even on their own porches and patios people did not dare to speak the truth.

Trujillo's real prisons were horror chambers filled with political prisoners. Torture and murder were commonplace, mutilation a specialty. Murder did not affect Trujillo in a human way. In 1937 he slaughtered eighteen thousand of the Haitians who lived in his country, claiming that they had illegally crossed the border into the Dominican Republic and that he was retaliating for a Haitian takeover in the nineteenth century. But the massacre didn't make sense. Many of the victims worked as quasi-slaves, cutting Dominican sugarcane. Like the Spanish, Trujillo had killed off his workforce, and many assumed it was because he wanted a white country at any cost.

Trujillo supported the Allies in World War II. But he publicly admired Hitler. He said that he only wished the Führer dressed in a more regal manner, befitting his position. Trujillo himself was quite a dandy.

Even the ghost of Columbus did not frighten Trujillo. His capital had been called Santo Domingo for more than four centuries. Under Trujillo it became Ciudad Trujillo. El Jefe was only frightened, it seemed, by the witches and healers, the *brujos* and *curanderos,* he regularly consulted for psychic predictions. One *bruja* told him to beware of darkening skies. Eighteen days after Trujillo stole the presidency, the Dominican Republic was hit by the worst hurricane ever recorded in the Caribbean. That *bruja* told him that a hurricane would also mark his downfall.

"What are you asking me about witches for?" Abuelo Javier says. "I don't believe in them. I never did. Nobody in our family ever did. My mother-in-law, Fian, only started believing in Fransica in her old age. Forget about it. I don't believe in them. But El Jefe did. Maybe he should have listened to them."

Javier kept asking his mother when they were going back to the capital. Her answer was always the same: "*Ay,* Javielito, it's too far."

4.

1955, 1958

In Moca, a large town in the fertile Cibao valley, Javier's sister Marta knew that her restlessness had returned. The sight of her pretty, light-skinned face in the mirror made her uncomfortable. As she combed her short, dark hair close to her cheeks or lifted her petite, bosomy body from her carved wooden chair, she felt hot and tired. She imagined illnesses and aches and pains and could not concentrate on the ingredients she cooked for the evening's *sancocho*. Worst of all, her furniture brought her no joy. She hoped for a crisis or the creativity to create one.

Purito, her taxi-driver *esposo,* answered with his own disintegration. His temper, often barely in check, exploded. When that happened, Marta scooped up their two-year-old daughter, brought her to Purito's mother's house for safekeeping, and went to the police station.

"He tried to kill me with a knife from the kitchen," Marta reported to the officer at the Moca station. "He said I embarrassed him." She sat across from the officer and crossed her legs. Her voice was high, staccato, and accusatory. Marta was not afraid of the police, as long as they weren't the secret police. Her first *esposo* had been a Puerto Plata policeman, and the first time he stayed away from her all night was also the last. In retaliation, she had thrown all his uniforms down the latrine, given away all his furniture, and left on a bus south to Moca.

"Purito said I embarrassed him," Marta repeated to the officer. "That was his problem. He said his friends told him I was out in the street looking for him. He said that he did not want to hear I had been calling his name in the street."

"How much rum did he have?" the officer asked.

"He's been drunker than that."

"Do you want us to hold him?"

Marta nodded. People whispered about how much they

hated El Jefe's officers, any of his officers because you could never tell who was really in the secret police and who wasn't. But the police were good at keeping order.

"How long?" the officer asked.

She knew exactly what she was going to do. "Until I can get out of town."

Leaving was what Marta did best. She had been with Purito for six years. But life always got better when she left. It didn't matter where she went. Her mother told her that even as a baby she had tried to leave the *casita* by crawling to the door or jumping up toward the window. Marta remembered looking out at the *cordillera* and wondering what else she might be able to see beyond it.

Now she would have to tell Purito's mother to keep the baby, her Cándida. This was new for Marta. She was good at leaving, but she had never left a child. People said that mothers were not supposed to be able to do that. But a lot of women left their children. Everywhere she looked, grandmothers were raising their grandchildren. Some of those abuelitas had children of their own; some of them had a little milk in their weary teats, too. This is hard, Marta thought. But I have to do it. I am going to the capital. I don't have a job and I am going to share a flat with a girlfriend. I can't bring a baby to that. She did not know whether that sounded right or not. She decided to think about her furniture instead.

The furniture Purito had bought for her was much better than the first set from her policeman, whose uniforms went down the latrine. The bed was larger, the table and chairs more intricately carved. Marta scribbled a note to her baby brother, Javier: "Bring Mami," it said. "I want to give her my bed, table, and chairs."

She gave the note to the driver on the Puerto Plata bus. He looked at her admiringly and promised to find a way to get the message to the *campo*.

★ ★ ★

A lot of men in Moca were willing to help Marta. One of them put her furniture in his truck and brought it to the bus depot. Javier and Demetria were waiting for her there. Demetria looked fine. Marta did not understand how her mother was able to survive so many years in the *campo,* with so many children, an illiterate, bossy *esposo,* a dirt floor, and not enough sugar. Whenever Marta thought about her mother, she saw her brushing granules of sugar from the table to sweeten an extra cup of coffee. Marta never wanted to live in the *campo* again. Javier would be out soon, too, she expected. She watched with pride as her baby brother lifted the bed, chair, and tables Purito had given her and tied them to the rack on the top of the bus. He was eleven years old and the muscles on his thin arms were beginning to bulge. Marta saw that he fastened rags around the legs of her chairs so that they would not be scratched. Javier understood furniture, an important sophistication for a man. Marta had little schooling herself, but she admired sophistication in men. Sophisticated men understood furniture, but they did not have to work as carpenters. Every farmhand in the *campo* thought himself a carpenter.

When Javier finished, Marta gave him a hug. "Ooooh. After you finish the *secundaria* you won't be lifting so much," she laughed with a happy screech.

Then she boarded a different bus, which was going in the opposite direction, south to the capital. On the way out of town she passed Moca's most important landmark, the statute of Ramón Cáceres, an assassin and a hero. In this country, a person could be both. Cáceres had killed Ulises Heureaux, a brutal dictator. The murder had occurred in Moca. Marta was glad to be leaving the Cibao and heading toward Ciudad Trujillo and civilization.

On the bus, she tried not think about her little girl, Cándida. She had not told Cándida she was leaving because she did not know how to explain that to a two-year-old. One day she would make this up to her. At least she wasn't sending the child out to be a maid, as her mother had done to her.

★ ★ ★

Marta was only two years old, Cándida's age, when the *doñas,* the rich ladies of Puerto Plata, first began talking about her. She heard the stories from Mami and from the *doñas* themselves who lived in large tropical houses trimmed with *pan de jengibre,* or gingerbread as they called it when they wanted to show off their English. The *doñas* were hostesses. When they weren't having parties in their own houses, they were at their friends' parties. That did not leave a lot of time for housework or children, so the *doñas* hired lots of maids and were always looking for new maids. When they heard that Demetria Almonte of Juan de Nina had two daughters, they breathed sighs of relief. Demetria, they reminded each other, had been a very good maid once. Clean, neat, obedient.

A messenger was sent to the *campo.*

"The *doñas* want to know if your daughters are ready," he asked Demetria. She stood by the window. Sugarcane grew all around, on the fields that her *esposo* worked for other farmers.

Marta was two years old and climbing on a chair to peer out the top half of the wooden door. Mami shook her head. Demetria's flowers had to cascade gracefully from their metal vases. There could be no unexpected bumps or ruts when she swept her mud floor and her daughters would not embarrass her in the big *pan de jengibre* houses of Puerto Plata. Marta's sister, María, was only five, but she sat placidly at the table. "Tell them they can have María," Demetria said softly.

Marta was not sent away until she was ten years old. She remembered feeling so proud because she would be working for Doña Fanny, whose husband was said to be related to the Brugal family, the local rum distillery owner.

"Meme, we'll take good care of your daughter," Doña Fanny had told Mami. "And after she learns her tasks, we'll make sure she finishes the *primaria.*"

Marta saw that her mother was crying and realized that her

schooling was over. She was a little frightened. But, secretly, she was also happy to be away from the *campo*.

It was Marta's job to take care of Doña Fanny's baby: dress him so that his clothes matched, cook his food, and change his diapers, which she ironed herself. In the late afternoon, after the baby napped, she took him for buggy rides in the Parque Central. At night she cleaned Doña Fanny's kitchen and scrubbed its wooden floors.

Marta was lonely at first. But Doña Fanny bought her clothes. Marta was delighted to be paid that way for her work. Doña Fanny also arranged for Marta to have a first communion at the Iglesia San Felipe in the Parque Central, the most important church in Puerto Plata. Her white satin gown, made by Doña Fanny's favorite seamstress, had a wide, rounded collar and cuffed, long sleeves. Marta carried a crocheted pouch and a scepter with a white ribbon, and her net veil dropped below her waist. Fortunately, Marta had *pelo bueno, good,* straight hair, which Doña Fanny set into a pageboy style that rounded below her ears. Marta was pretty, with intelligent eyes and light skin. She was proud of the way she looked. Except for her ears, which stuck out, although not as much as her father's, she believed that she could have been mistaken for Doña Fanny's daughter.

Marta never said, not even to herself, that she was unhappy at Doña Fanny's. But one morning, she decided that she was tired, packed her clothes, and took a *guagua* back to Juan de Nina.

"I am twelve years old," she told Demetria. "I need a rest."

Marta's idea of a rest was to go to parties that exploded from the *casitas* of Juan de Nina and Camú into the roads. Boys offered her sips of beer. They danced with her and asked her to take walks with them. Mami never gave Marta permission to go to the parties. Marta went anyway, and they fought when she came home.

When she was thirteen, Marta went back to Puerto Plata to work for Doña Melín, who also had a baby boy. Doña Melín's house was across from the police barracks, and for a long time

Marta watched Officer Juan Peralta. He was handsome with good hair that was black and skin that was white. People said she was white, but Marta knew she was only light. Peralta was white. And he looked like a man. When Peralta walked up the steps of the barracks, the blue cotton of his uniform was tight against his back and shoulders. Marta kept watching to see if he was watching her.

Marta was fourteen by the time Officer Peralta crossed the street to ask her if she would take a walk with him. They went out walking a few times before he asked her if she wanted to come with him to the Puerto Plata Hotel. She said that she would, knowing what she was doing, more or less. The hotel was near the Brugal distillery and the smell was thick and sweet.

Afterward, Marta stayed in the hotel while Officer Peralta went to tell Doña Melín that she would not be coming back. Within a month Peralta found Marta a house. When he showed it to her, the furniture was already in it—chairs, a wood table, and a brown wooden bed that was almost as nice as Mami's black, varnished one in the *campo*. Marta dusted her furniture every day, which made her feel very grown up.

When Peralta went to work, she washed and ironed his police uniforms. When he came home from the barracks at night, she cooked him rice, chicken, beans, *tostones,* whatever he wanted. After dinner, he took her to the bed that was almost as nice as Mami's. On his days off, they walked together in the Parque Central and on the Malecón, the promenade alongside the sea. Marta watched the expressions on the faces of the city girls they passed, and she could tell they envied her.

Marta and Peralta had been together for six months on the day he came home at dawn, instead of dinnertime. He peeled off his uniform and dropped it on the floor for her, put on a fresh one, and left for work without saying a word. Marta picked up Peralta's pants and his shirt and took them to the sink on the patio. As she smoothed out the shirt, she saw a small mark of red lipstick on the chest.

Marta gathered Officer Peralta's shirt and pants, took them to the latrine, dropped them down the hole, and waited to hear them plop on the bottom. She liked the idea of their mixing with all of Peralta's other droppings, and she went back to their bedroom to collect his four remaining uniforms. Piece by piece she threw them down the hole, listening for each one to hit bottom. She would never iron that thick, blue police cotton again.

She went back inside, but there was still too much of Peralta there. "You can have our bed," Marta called out to the first neighbor who passed that morning. "*Oye,* do you want a chair?" she asked another. When the furniture was gone, she put all of her clothes in a tin trunk and took a bus to the Cibao, to Moca. She never thought about Peralta after that, except when she told people how she threw his clothes down the latrine. Later, she heard he had to stay in the barracks prison because they thought he had sold all his uniforms. Marta loved to tell that story, and when she did, she called him by his last name: Peralta. Officer Peralta. She never thought of him as Juan anymore.

In the capital, Marta got off the bus and vowed that after Purito she would not see any more men. She spent time at Tía Angela's. She admired her auntie's house and her furniture and played with her cats. Then she met another taxi driver, Jesús Antonio Cabrera. He was not handsome, the way Officer Peralta and Purito had been. Both those men had light skin. Jesús Antonio was so dark that his nickname was "Negrito." But he took Marta to movies starring Arturo de Córdova, the Mexican star with flashing eyes. And he drove a lucrative route from San Juan de la Maguana, his hometown, to the capital. Eventually Marta told him that they could be *juntos.* She told herself that she did not think she would stay with him forever.

Jesús Antonio bought Marta a house, a whitewashed house made of *bloques,* not palm trees. House number sixteen on Calle Uno, the first street in the Ensanche Espaillat. It had a zinc roof, two patios, and big windows in the front, which Marta loved to keep open. Jesús Antonio bought her a new set of furniture, her best so far. Better than any of the furniture either of her first two men had bought her. The wood was carved with even more intricate designs; there was enough plastic to make it modern. She had a larger bed and a wooden wardrobe with a glass window so that she could peek in and decide what to wear. Jesús Antonio gave her money for bingo and to pay a girl to cook and clean for her.

"I once was a maid," Marta told Jesús Antonio. "But I never had a maid."

Minerva Mirabal was a smart, strong-willed dreamer, the beautiful daughter of a well-to-do, prominent family from the Cibao. Trujillo noticed her and, in the fall of 1949, invited her to a Columbus Day dance in San Cristóbal.

When she arrived, one of El Jefe's assistants—his procurer, really—took Minerva onto the dance floor and then switched partners with Trujillo. El Jefe tried to flirt with the young woman, but she boldly refused his advances. Trujillo was infuriated.

Years later, Minerva and her sisters, famous albeit unlikely revolutionaries, nicknamed "Las Mariposas"—the Butterflies—helped to precipitate Trujillo's own defeat. It didn't rain on the day that El Jefe fell. But the Mirabal sisters—or the specter of them—created a storm from which he never recovered.

"Eventually, we all heard about Minerva Mirabal." Abuelo Javier recalls wistfully, as though thinking about a former love. **"We felt like we knew her. But by then she was a heroine. You know that she slapped El Jefe across the face?"**

The Mirabal family has claimed that never happened. But in the Dominican Republic, the legend of Minerva has a life of its own.

"It was the Mirabal sisters who really made me hate El Jefe," Abuelo Javier says. **"They made me see there is no way around a dictator. I should have known that myself. I had one in my own house.**

"My father's real name was Antonio, but they called him Alemán. He told me it was because of his white skin; that everyone thought he had German blood in him. When I was older I heard a story that he got his name from a bull. One of the rich farmers had a bull named Alemán, and my father was napping in that farmer's field when the bull got loose. My father woke, saw it, and started running so crazy that he looked like a *loco* bull himself. After that nobody called him Antonio anymore. Not even my mother."

Marta had been with Jesús Antonio for almost three years when she received a terse message from her mother. Demetria explained that she would join her daughter in the capital. She had taken a job as a nanny—Marta knew she would not say "maid"—for one of Tía Angela's sons and his family. Javier was coming with her. Marta was thrilled by the prospect of seeing her favorite brother again, although she did not understand if Mami was leaving the *campo* for good or just taking a short rest from her father; or whether she was tired of sweeping mud and sugar granules and wanted to earn some money.

It made sense to Marta that Mami would have had enough of Papi. Marta had never been close to her father, a distant man even to his own *esposa*.

5

1993, 1955–1958

In Queens, New York, almost four decades later, Javier Almonte, by then a grandfather with a band of kinky, graying hair around his half-bald head, sits at the kitchen table of his family's apartment, waiting, still, for his wife to come home and make him dinner. He takes off his boots and socks and rubs one of his sore feet. Then, barefoot, he stands up, walks into the living room, and straightens the painting of his parents that hangs on the

wall next to his leatherette bar. The painting, copied by a New York City artist from an old photograph, is the focal point of a shrine Javier has erected to Alemán and Demetria. He is from the old school. No matter what, respect your parents.

"I remember my father's exact words," Javier recalls. "He said, 'School is good. But six years is enough.' "

Abuelo Javier is fifty years old and aching from a day of banging a hammer at a renovation job. But he becomes as excited as Javier the boy as he remembers the day Maestra Quisqueya interrupted sixth grade so that she could speak to him outside by the string bean plants.

" 'I want you to go to the *secundaria*, Javier,' " she said.

He had never seen the *secundaria*. But he knew that it was in Montellano, where the sugar mill stood. People said the sugar mill was a large warehouse with a green metal roof; the sweetest place in the *campo*. Inside there was a mountain of newly processed sugar, which grew larger each day.

"My mother wanted me to go to the *secundaria*," Javier Almonte the grandfather, the abuelo, explains as he puts on a pair of slippers. "But she could not disobey my father."

The boy took his cues from his mother. Instead of arguing or running away, he lived the life his father had envisioned for him. Each morning he woke the second or third time the roosters of Juan de Nina crowed. He dressed, put on his rubber slippers, and went outside to milk his father's two cows and feed his mother's elderly chickens. In the kitchen, he helped his father and brothers Ernesto and Mirito make breakfast and fill lunch pails to carry to the fields. Javier fried eggs for breakfast and codfish for lunch. He fried plantains, flattened them, and fried them again to make *tostones*. Alemán insisted that they do the work themselves, instead of waking Mami; this was a kindness Javier noticed in his father.

After breakfast, Javier left for the fields with his father and Ernesto. Mirito, with his heart condition, was too weak to go and stayed behind to draw portraits of people he knew or practice his penmanship. On good days, Mirito ran errands for Víctor González, which amazed his father and brothers. They had known Víctor as a poor farmer who always ran his own errands. But now Víctor was growing so much *caña* people wondered if he had gone up the *cordillera* and found a *bruja* to work magic on his fields.

Javier walked with his father and brother down the hill to the fields of one rich farmer or another. He spent his days cutting sugarcane when the season was right, doing other field chores, watching out for bulls, and trying to distinguish himself from the Haitians who worked alongside him. He made angry swipes with his *machete,* and tried to act superior. While he worked, he wondered about his six classmates who had gone on to Montellano. "Come with us, Javier. You are as smart as us," they had said. He wondered if they went to the mill after class and dug their hands into the sugar mountain. He didn't know why he thought about them. What good would it do him? He sweated while he cut the *caña,* but he was in a lethargy and felt immobile. He could not leave the fields or the *campo,* but he did not know why. Even when he turned fourteen, stopped sleeping alongside his mother, and was astonished by the charms of girls his age, he could not bring himself to walk away. On his days off he played dominoes with his father, his brothers, and their friends, or watched two of his uncles who were master carpenters. He helped his uncles without realizing that he was also good at that kind of work.

When he was fifteen, his mother announced that she had taken a job in the capital and that Javier was, once again, coming with her. Javier did not ask any questions, although he had several. He wondered if his mother was leaving his father and, if she was, why Papi didn't try to stop her. He noticed a change in her face. It was wrinkling to match her hands, and she acted rashly, like someone who had nothing to lose.

For a year he worked in the capital as an apprentice to a furniture maker, just to pass the time until he was old enough to study to be a pilot. Tía Angela promised to help him. He learned to make pretty chairs and sleek tables, which even Marta admired. He forgot all about *caña* and began to dream again. When Mami said that she was ready to go home, he assumed she knew that she would be leaving alone.

In Queens, Abuelo Javier gets up and moves around his kitchen table. Since his wife and daughter aren't home, he can be silly. He is certainly hungry enough to be silly. He decides to reenact his last day in the capital, playing all the roles himself. He is sixteen-year-old Javier, Tía Angela rocking with cats on her lap, his mother with her wrinkled face and hands.

Tía Angela: "Javier, what do you want to do with yourself?"

Young Javier: "Tía, you know what I want to do. I want to be a pilot."

Tía Angela: "Meme, he is sixteen. Now is the time. What are you going to do with this young man?"

Demetria: "Angela, I won't leave him."

Tía Angela: "Meme! What is he going to do back with you in the *campo*?"

Demetria: "What he did before."

Tía Angela: "He'll go back and fight with the cows and the pigs and the chickens. Meme, that isn't a life. That isn't a future!"

Abuelo Javier returns to his own seat at the table and rubs his slippered foot. Sadly, he concedes that he did go back to the *campo* with his mother and languished there for years. Even now he still does not know why he obeyed

his mother. Why didn't he just stay in the capital with Tía Angela? Why didn't he refuse to leave?

He often wonders if he was influenced and stymied by the style of the dictatorship, the potency of the authority under which he had grown up. After almost a decade in New York, he guesses that the politics of his country—and his *casita*—and their histories of defeat had clung hard to him when he was a boy.

"I don't know why those things never affected Víctor," Abuelo Javier says. "He's the one who should have been immobile. Do you know his story? It is a story of our country. Víctor's mother was white, but his father was black. His father never lived with his mother, and Víctor did not stay long either. Even today Víctor'll tell you that his mother sent him away because he looked like his father. He was still a *muchachito* when he became a farmhand, maybe only five or six years old. Now, it's not that strange for a family to send girls away. My mother was neither brutal nor unusual in that respect, not in the world in which she lived. But you had to be really desperate to send a boy away. *Guauuw.* Only, Víctor doesn't think it had anything to do with money. He thinks his mother sent him away because of his color.

"It's amazing. But he didn't let that defeat him. It didn't make him immobile. He worked those fields and imagined himself on a white horse riding an entire day through *tareas* of his own sugarcane. Whenever he could, Víctor set aside a peso or two from his wages. When he was twenty he took all his money—it was only forty-three pesos—and bought a small patch of land on which he planted his own *caña. Guuaw.* He grew a lot of *caña* with those forty-three pesos. He knew how. He had spent his childhood doing it. When the *caña* was high enough, he marched right over to Camú, to the house of a rich farmer named Felipe who lived on the top of a large hill, and asked if he could have his daughter, Fian. Fian was fourteen and a good catch. She had those yellow-green eyes. *Espanish* blood. Pure *Espanish* blood.

"It was Felipe who made Víctor a rich man. When he saw that *caña,* he loaned him money to grow more and said that he wanted half the profits back in return. The two of them operated that way for years."

In 1921, the following memo was issued by the United States Department of State: "It is well to distinguish at once between the Dominicans and the Haitians. The former, while in many ways not advanced far enough for the highest type of self-government, yet have a preponderance of white blood and culture. The Haitians on the other hand are Negro for the most part, and, barring a very few highly educated politicians, are almost in a state of savagery and complete ignorance. The two situations thus demand different treatment. . . . In the Dominican Republic . . . I think that we should endeavor rather to counsel than control."

In 1938, President Roosevelt, searching for a sanctuary for German Jews, called a meeting of thirty-two nations in Évian, France. Only the Dominican Republic, led by Rafael Trujillo, offered to take the refugees. Even Australia, a country built by prisoners, refused, saying, ". . . we have no racial problem, we are not desirous of importing one." El Jefe, however, agreed to accept one hundred thousand Jews.

(The story is told that FDR once said about Trujillo: "He may be a son of a bitch. But he's our son of a bitch.")

In the Caribbean, where they knew El Jefe, there was talk of an ulterior motive. Jews might be the Haitians of Europe. But in the Dominican Republic they would be the whitest citizens. If they married Dominicans, the whole country would be whiter. Nothing, except perhaps a never-ending supply of plump virgins, would please El Jefe more. As it turned out only six hundred Jews came. They settled in Sosúa, began a dairy business, and eventually moved on, leaving the Dominican Republic as brown as they had found it.

The Cold War made life even more comfortable for Trujillo. He was a dictator. But he was not a Communist. In fact, he was considered a bulwark against Communism.

Marta, Javier, and Víctor labored in their own worlds and tried not to think about politics or history. Marta tried to stay still because she wanted another child, even if it was with Jesús Antonio. Javier worked as hard as he could to make nothing of himself, as a mad proof that his lethargy was right-minded. Víctor worked madly, too, but only for his *caña* and his local redemption. As the sixties approached, the three noticed noises in their country, but did not think they would be affected. Those noises belonged to other classes: to the doctors, lawyers, students, intellectuals. Javier would not wake up to the noises until 1960, and he would be a much older man before he did anything about them. Oddly, it would take Marta a few more years than Javier to see, once again, that the only way was out. But once Marta saw, she was ready to go. Víctor would never wake to the noises. He would pretend he did not hear them and turn over in his sleep. But in the process, he shook Javier alive.

In 1958, Fidel Castro crumbled the neat wall Trujillo had erected. America began to worry and contemplate the domino theory that would propel it into Vietnam. If Cuba went, the Dominican Republic could be next. Trujillo was as wicked as Batista, if not more so, and a Dominican Castro, if not Castro himself, could be lurking in one of the *cordilleras.*

An *anti-Trujillista* underground movement had been operating for years, led by members of the upper and middle classes, who just might be a match for a former telegraph operator from San Cristóbal, even one as savvy as El Jefe. The movement had heroes, even heroines, including Minerva Mirabal, the young woman who had slighted Trujillo at his Columbus Day party, and two of her sisters.

Radio Bemba made Minerva's story a legend. People still spoke about the Columbus Day dance, and about the way the dictator later arrested her well-to-do father to pressure her to stop her political activities. Throughout the country, people fretted over the Mariposas, cried when they were put in jail, rejoiced at their release, traded rumors about spotting them, and hoped that El Jefe would be killed before he killed them. "They have children," people said to one another. "Would he kill mothers?"

Trujillo reacted to America's nervousness and his country's anxiety with mass arrests, which accelerated as Castro tried, unsuccessfully, to invade the Dominican Republic. "The imprisonments came in great shuddering waves," Robert D. Crassweller, a Trujillo biographer wrote in 1966. "Professionals of every description, students, society women, engineers, businessmen, seminarians. They were herded into cells like cattle in stockyard pens, jammed together in fearful, sweating masses. . . . Jailings were followed by quiet trials for some of the captives and sentences of up to thirty years at hard labor were handed down. . . . Within four months the total number of persons who had been arrested in this season of vast repression was four thousand."

As the arrests continued, two foreign bishops began to organize, politically, as they never had before. They were led by a new papal nuncio whose last posting had been in Argentina, where he was credited with orchestrating the downfall of Juan Perón. (Perón was in exile in the Dominican Republic, and according to Crassweller, he left as soon as he heard the new papal nuncio had arrived. "Watch yourself carefully," he warned El Jefe.)

By the end of January of 1960, the country's clerical leaders were ready. Through coded announcements on the government-controlled radio stations and clear ones on an ever-growing Radio Bemba network, they urged every citizen to attend Mass the following Sunday, ostensibly to celebrate the Feast of Our Lady of Grace. The tacit message, though, was that politics more than religion was on the agenda. Thousands of Dominicans went to Mass at scores of churches that Sunday and heard a long pastoral letter unlike any other ever read in the Dominican Republic. Although couched in florid, polite, and evasive liturgical language, the letter condemned Trujillo, his arrests and abuses, and stated that the church could not "remain indifferent about the grievous blow that has afflicted a good many Dominican homes . . ." The letter enumerated basic human rights "to life, to form a family, to work, to trade, to immigrate, to one's good repute." And, before concluding with a *bendición*, noted that the church had ". . . directed, in the exercise of our pastoral ministry, an official letter to the highest authority of the country, in order that, by a plan of reciprocal understanding, there can be ended excesses which, in short, only bring harm to those who commit them, a plan to dry those tears, to heal the wounds and restore peace to so many homes."

Over the months that followed, the dictator retaliated against the church with his usual terror spiced with the bizarre. Without informing the papal nuncio, Trujillo fabricated a formal affair at the nunciature and invited more than a thousand dignitaries. A baffled staff sent everyone home after explaining that they had not prepared any food. Trujillo, in black tie, was among the "disappointed" invitees. That was in the spring of 1960. A year later, one of the dictator's radio stations announced a "Repudiation of the Bishops" contest. Five hundred pesos, double the yearly per capita income, would be awarded to the listener who, in twenty-five words or less, wrote the best condemnation of the foreign, rabble-rousing bishops.

As for the pastoral letter, Trujillo replied a month later that he could not interfere with the nation's justice system. He released eight of the hundreds of women he had arrested in January. One of them, a physician, told the *New York Times* that she "was stripped and put in a cell with men and later was placed unclothed in a room with soldiers."

"One thing about Trujillo, though," Abuelo Javier says. "There was no crime. When I go back to the *campo* now, I keep a *pistola* with me. Yes, I have a license for it. It's for the *campo*. I leave it there. No, I don't keep it here in New York. No, no. I never had one before I emigrated. Yes, that's true I couldn't afford to buy one. But I'm talking about Trujillo. With Trujillo we didn't have keys. Some people didn't even have doors.

"You're asking me if I'd rather have crime or Trujillo? *Ay,* I don't know. Once, I don't remember the year, we heard that Trujillo had sent a *merengue* band to a church in Moca. The band was supposed to say El Jefe sent them and that he wanted the priests to stop Mass and let them play *merengues.* Of course, the priests let them play. You didn't disobey El Jefe."

6

1960–1961

With fifty centavos from his farmhand wages, Javier Almonte bought a ride in a *carro de ruta,* a collective taxi. It was a splurge; he would have to forgo something else, but he wanted to arrive in Puerto Plata like a gentleman. At the Parque Central, he got off, stretched, tried to make himself look tall. He was just seventeen and working as a farmhand had made his arms muscular. Lethargy had, at least, been good for his looks. His unawakened teenage face was handsome and leering, his hair cut close. To emphasize his masculinity, he had grown a mustache, a small, trim stripe, neat like a Mexican movie star's, and all that he could manage. When he walked, he moved his hips and bent his legs as though ready to *merengue*.

He stopped to get his shoes shined. Wipe the Juan de Nina dust right off of them. As a boy rubbed polish into the worn leather, he watched the girls, thin, slippery fish making their way through the park as though it were a clear pool, fresh like the weather after the fall rains. In a Taíno myth, woodpeckers nipped holes into the midsections of eel-like creatures until they became women. Now the girls, eels with pelvises, walked clutching crispy pieces of crackling, which they tried to eat delicately. A few of them sat in the gazebo, comparing purchases from the shops and stalls near the park. Those city girls scared him, and he looked instead for girls he knew from Juan de Nina or Camú. He didn't see any, but they would be at a party in the *campo* that night and he would be prepared. He would buy a Bazar-brand nylon shirt with blue and white checks on a wine-colored background. His shoes would be shined. If he didn't have any grand opportunities, at least he had some money in his pocket, thanks to Víctor González, who kept growing *caña* and hiring more hands.

Javier paid the boy and resumed his *merengue*-walk around the park. As he swaggered, he tried to listen to what the groups of city girls were saying. At first, he heard laughter, teasing. Then, suddenly, voices were lowered. The tone changed. Everyone in the park seemed to be whispering the same thing.

"*Oyeeeeeeee!* They killed the Mirabal sisters! *Oyeeee, mataron las Mariposas!*"

Javier sat on a bench. He touched the shirt of an old man who walked by him.

"The Mirabals are dead?" he asked with the frightened wonder of a much younger boy.

"*Sí, m'hijo.* That is what they are saying."

"How?"

The man shook his head.

Javier was ready to cry. This was not politics. This was the first death close to him, not counting Pedrito, his mother's first child. Javier had never seen the Mirabals. But, like his only dead brother, whom he had also never seen, he knew them. He got up and walked to the shoeshine boy.

"*Muchacho,*" Javier said in a whisper. "Did you hear the Mirabals are dead?" The boy nodded.

Years later, Pedro Mir, a Dominican poet who had been exiled in Cuba when the murders occurred, wrote:

> When I learned that the three Mirabal sisters had
>   fallen
> I said to myself:
>   established society is dead. . . ."

The party in the *campo* that night was solemn. Over the following days and weeks, Radio Bemba broadcast at full frequency. Javier knew boys who had turned away from Trujillo because of the bishops. But the bishops had not moved Javier; religion was his mother saying the rosary to Radio Santa María. It was the Mirabals who moved him. He repeated each detail of their deaths to himself, as if it were a prayer. The sisters had been on their way to visit their husbands who were being held in Puerto Plata, in the *fortaleza* built by the Spanish to keep out pirates. The sisters were killed and then put back in their car and pushed one hundred and fifty feet over a cliff. Javier knew the place. La Cumbre. The peak. From Santiago, it was at the third kilometer of the Carretera Luperón, the road that had two curves marking Camú. Camú and Juan de Nina were at the fourteenth kilometer from Puerto Plata. He wept to himself and thought, Jefe, this is too far. You killed the good *doñas* who would have been nice to me if I worked as their driver. You killed the girls I dreamed about marrying, the magic eels in the park. As a rich man, I would have married a Mirabal sister. I would have been a pilot married to Minerva, Patria, María Teresa. El Jefe made me a widower in my dreams. Except for a *machete* and fields of someone else's *caña,* dreams are what I own. You killed the dream mothers of my dream children. You killed my own mother, my own sisters. Mami, Marta, María.

According to Robert Crassweller—Trujillo's biographer— the Mirabal sisters were "enticed by a ruse. They had applied for permission to see their husbands. They were now told that the permission had been granted and that their visits would be facilitated. Instead, they were taken into custody and fresh abominations were practiced upon them, followed soon by the assassinations. Their bodies were placed in their own Jeep, and the vehicle was pushed over a high cliff, a short distance beyond Santiago, on the winding mountain road that crosses the Cordillera Septentrional to Puerto Plata. An automobile accident was thus simulated, but the crime could hardly be called a subtle one."

Two months later, according to the biographer, Trujillo took an evening walk on "the stretch of the same beautiful mountain road to Puerto Plata where the Jeep had been pushed over the cliff with its load of dead passengers. . . . Trujillo paused, gazing silently over the precipice and down the deep slope. Then, to the eerie surprise of his companion, he said, 'This is where the Mirabal women died—a horrible crime that foolish people blame the government for. Such good women and so defenseless!' "

Time magazine published a photograph of the murdered Minerva Mirabal on December 12, 1960. "Tragic coincidences are not uncommon in Dictator Rafael Leonidas Trujillo's Dominican Republic," the magazine stated. It noted that "there was, of course, no hint of foul play in the reports from Trujilloland."

Three decades later, Abuelo Javier can still remember

at which kilometer they found the bodies of the Mirabal sisters.

On a morning the following spring, the last Friday in May, Javier woke with the roosters in Juan de Nina and put on his uniform, which was made of yellow khaki, like the ones he had worn in *primaria*. He looked at himself in the small mirror that hung over his bed and marveled that he could feel such satisfaction and yet be so troubled at the same time. He was wearing the uniform of Trujillo's civilian reserve, marching up Isabel de Torres for the reserve every Friday, Saturday, and Sunday, but still thinking about the Mirabal sisters. He knew exactly why he was doing this. The reserve was his escape from the *campo,* his only escape. He left every weekend, and Papi never said a word to stop him.

He stepped outside, saw that his father and brothers had fed the animals for him, and went back into the kitchen to help them with breakfast. Then he walked outside, down the hill to Camú, and out to the Carretera Luperón. He was tempted to take a taxi to Puerto Plata. But when the bus came, he got on and felt prudent. Now he would have an extra ten pesos to buy a drink and sweets on Sunday night when he walked the Malecón and tried to talk to city girls. Since January, when he'd begun his stint in El Jefe's civilian reserve, he had ended all his weekends on the Malecón. Close to water, city girls seemed more beautiful, easier to reach.

"Mario Almonte!" an officer shouted as Javier and the other teenage recruits lined up at the *fortaleza.* "What is courtesy?"

"Military courtesy is one of the marks of military discipline!" Javier shouted back. "In all spheres of life, sir, well-educated gentlemen are respectful and courteous to others."

When the morning drill was finished, Javier marched with his fellow reservists, well-educated *primaria* graduates like himself. They marched through the streets of Puerto Plata, up onto Isabel de Torres, the city's mountain. On its ridges they camouflaged their uniformed bodies in trees and tested barbed wire for electricity by tapping it with the ends of their rifles. Their officers taught them how to hide from one another and from airplanes they were supposed to imagine overhead. If a real airplane flew by, Javier barely looked up. Even in Juan de Nina, two or three a day now passed over his hut.

Javier tested barbed wire and at the end of the day, as they marched back to the *fortaleza,* he wondered who they were being trained to fight. He recalled Máximo Gómez, the nineteenth-century Dominican military strategist he had read about in the *primaria.* Gómez had gone to Cuba to fight the Spanish. Was Javier now supposed to be preparing to fight the Cubans? Or the Americans? Who hated Trujillo more?

He couldn't stop marching, although he felt as though he had stopped. His thoughts at the mirror came back to him. He hated Trujillo, but he was marching for Trujillo. He wanted Tru-jillo dead. It was Trujillo who did it. Everyone knew that. Until Trujillo killed the Mirabals, Javier had only felt vague dislike mixed with fear and awe. But now he really hated the dictator. For six years in the *primaria* Javier had pledged his allegiance to Trujillo, and all it had gotten him was a place in the reserve. This wasn't even the real army. Trujillo said he loved the *campesinos,* but Javier's father still had only a few *tareas* of land.

He was thinking one thing and doing another because there was no way to get out of reserve duty. Or was there? He kept marching. If he obeyed his officers and marched well, someday he might get into the real army and get a government house, a house made of *bloques.*

Abuelo Javier, three decades later, says that yes, the politics of his country and its history of defeat had clung hard to him. But he should have fought it, the way he should have fought his parents.

On Sunday evening, Javier played baseball with the other reservists on a flat field surrounded by *caña.* They used old pieces of wood for bats and mitts made from a burlap bag they had taken off a mail truck. On the Malecón, Javier ate *dulce de leche* and savored its sweet caramel taste. He talked to some girls, but it amounted to nothing. In the morning he rode the bus back to the *campo* and resumed his other life, which also did not change.

On Tuesday morning, the roosters began their crowing at 2 A.M. The *quiquiriquís* pounded in Javier's ear until he gave up an hour later, woke, crawled out from under his mosquito net, and dressed. He met his father and Ernesto outside. He milked a cow and brought it out to graze while his brothers fed corn to the chickens. Thanks to Víctor's wages, Alemán owned a few more fat pigs now, too, and Javier watched while Ernesto fed them more corn, palm leaves, *yuca,* potato skins, and whatever else was left over from dinner. By the time they came in, Mirito was at the table eating his breakfast. When they finished, Javier left with Ernesto and his father.

They cut Víctor's *caña* until lunch. Then they sat where they had been working, ate from their pails, napped, and woke to Víctor's riding over to them, tall on his white horse, with a message for Javier to bring home to Mirito. If Mirito was feeling well, Víctor would send him to the capital, to buy lottery tickets. Víctor loved to play the lottery, but he had never learned how to be comfortable in cities, so he sent Mirito instead.

Later, back home, Javier helped his father and Ernesto bring the cows in and feed the other animals again. They sat around the table while Demetria said her rosary to the radio, prayed that their animals would get fatter, and ate a small supper. Javier went to bed early. The farm made him more tired than the reserve. By Wednesday morning imaginary guerrilla training sounded a lot better than the roosters at 2, 3, and 4 A.M. Javier crawled out from his net and thought about Friday in Puerto Plata.

His mother was at breakfast. That was the first thing that wasn't right. She looked tired to him. And what was that small lump at her throat? *"Oye,"* Demetria said. She stopped spooning out *yuca* and held the bowl to her chest. Down the path their neighbors had gathered, which was also unusual so early in the morning. Their voices were loud.

Javier shook his head. "What are they saying?" His father stood and walked through the living room to the doorway.

"They are saying it," Alemán said when he came back to the kitchen. "I'm going outside." Alemán's voice was as flat as always. Javier thought he saw his father's hand shake, as he left. He returned a few minutes later. "No one would say anything," he explained.

"They didn't know they were being that loud," Javier said.

"Marta's in the capital," Demetria cried out.

Javier turned on the radio. There was no news. None of the usual raucous *merengue,* either. Not even a simple *pambiche.* Instead, they were playing slow, serious music. Javier tried to remember how long the batteries had been in. He wanted to let the radio play for a while in case a bulletin was broadcast.

Demetria went to the door. Javier followed her, and through his mother's yellow and purple flowers he saw their *alcalde,* the mayor of Juan de Nina riding up the path on a horse. The *alcalde* stopped outside their hut. He was a fat white man who had to struggle to get his body down. Breathing hard and sweating, he opened their gate and stuck his head in the doorway.

Alemán got up from the table and walked into the sitting room. "Alcalde, they're saying someone killed El Jefe."

"Did they?" The *alcalde* always spoke deeply and slowly. "Well, that's still a question." The *alcalde* often identified questions but rarely answered them. "Actually, it's not a question. It's a big secret. All I can tell you is that anyone who is in the Army had better be ready."

On the clear night Rafael Trujillo was assassinated, his chauffeur drove him down a shoreline stretch of a boulevard named after George Washington. El Jefe was riding in his American car, a light blue Chevrolet with twin fender horns.

He was on the outskirts of the capital city he had

renamed for himself when his car was passed by another
Chevy, a black one. The windows of the black car opened
and machine guns fired at Trujillo. Inside his blue Chevrolet, a wounded, bleeding Rafael Trujillo refused to flee. He
ordered his chauffeur to stop. Then, the man who had run
the Dominican Republic for thirty years by terrifying his
people balanced himself on the right front bumper of his
car near the fender horn, and fought off his assassins and
their machine guns with his .38-caliber revolver, until he
fell dead on the ground.

Many Dominicans believed the CIA was behind the
assassination.

In the capital, Marta Almonte was alone in her whitewashed
bloque house in the Ensanche Espaillat when the neighbors
began knocking on her door. One neighbor, then another, a long
chain of whisperers: "Did you hear they killed El Jefe?" Marta
listened for as long as she could stand it. She wished that Jesús
Antonio was home but he was out driving his taxi. She shuttered the windows she loved so much, turned on the radio,
and waited. When she heard the official news, she vowed not to
go outside for days. "If they can kill El Jefe, they can kill me,"
she said to herself. All over the capital, Dominicans were telling
themselves the same thing. Ciudad Trujillo on the day after
the assassination of its ruler and namesake was subdued by
shock, dislocation, and a generalized fear embedded over three
decades. Marta heard on the radio that there were street fights.
But only a few, and not, as far as she could tell, anywhere near
Calle Uno.

In Juan de Nina, Javier and his family sat by the radio, too,
until the news was official. They looked at one another,
breathed a thirty-one-year-old sigh, and held each other tight
with their eyes. Should it be relief or fear they felt?

In Víctor González's large new house, which he had built on
stilts near the river in Juan de Nina, his wife, Fian, and their
ten-year-old daughter, Roselia, their eldest, and her Papi's

favorite, were making *tostones* in the kitchen. They kept their eyes fixed on the younger children and listened to the radio.

"It could be a trick," Fian whispered to Roselia. "Maybe El Jefe is pretending to be dead, to see who is loyal and who isn't."

Roselia kept mashing *plátanos* and did not answer her mother. Suddenly her sister Ramona, two years younger, prettier, chubbier, and more ebullient than Roselia, ran in the house shouting, "Mami! Mami! They killed El Jefe. El Jefe's dead!"

Fian grabbed Ramona by the arm, and clamped her sticky hand over the child's mouth. Her green-yellow eyes were blazing. "Don't you say that out loud," she cried. "Don't say it outside! Don't let anyone hear you say that!" She turned to Roselia and her other children. "Don't let me hear any of you say that!" Some of Fian's children were so small they didn't talk yet. "If someone hears you they'll kill you." It was only after the *alcalde* rode by her house the next day and showed Fian his black ribbon that she would permit any of her children to say that El Jefe was dead.

Thousands cried at El Jefe's funeral, many because they feared what would become of their country. Joaquín Balaguer, who had been Trujillo's figurehead president, was now their leader. On the morning after the assassination, Balaguer called for nine days of mourning and said, "The disappearance of such a great man is an irreparable loss to the republic." The families of those who had "disappeared" during Trujillo's long reign took note of their new jefe's choice of words. Balaguer lasted eight months before he was driven into exile. But he would be back. He would return to power in the 1966 elections and rule the Dominican Republic for twenty-two of the next thirty years.

Javier did not cry over Trujillo's death. He did not return to the reserve, although he would have if an officer or the *alcalde* had ordered him back. But no one even mentioned the reserve to him until months after Trujillo's assassination, when he received a certificate saying he had completed his service to his country. He kept it as a souvenir of the Trujillo years.

A year and a half after the assassination, Javier went to the *primaria* to vote in his first election—he was finally of age. It was the first free election in Javier's lifetime. He thought about his choice carefully and signed a ballot to elect Juan Bosch, a leftist writer who had returned from exile, as president.

Juan Bosch was elected president of the Dominican Republic in 1962 with 64 percent of the vote. But his presidency lasted less than a year and he was ousted by a coup. It was said he had been in exile too long; that he didn't understand his country. He was branded a Communist by Dominican businessmen, and although most of his support had come from poor city dwellers, he could not keep his country's workers from striking, which they did with abandon.

"*Sí*, that's right, I voted for Juan Bosch," Abuelo Javier says proudly from his kitchen table in Queens. Roselia, finally, is home from her factory job and making his supper.

In America, Abuelo Javier, although not an American citizen, favors the Republican party. "Well, in those days Juan Bosch was our hope," he says as he spears a chicken leg from a bowl of rice. "Yes, they thought he was a Communist. But he was our hope. And we really needed a change. Do I like Balaguer, now? Well, he made everything. But he lets you know that. Every road, every improvement has a stamp on it that says Balaguer made this.' *Ay*, Trujillo did the same. But do I like Balaguer? Forget about it. He's an old man."

Javier kept working as a farmhand. Without the reserve, he had more time to help his uncles, the carpenters. He had more time for girls, too. Instead of city girls, he watched the ones in the *campo* with a more serious eye. In particular, Javier noticed Roselia González. She was only eleven years old, but he couldn't stop himself from wondering how her prettiness would look on a woman. He watched Roselia walking home from school and whenever else he could catch her. He always tried to fix his sight a bit beyond her. If Víctor found out that Javier was watching Roselia, he, his father, and brothers would all be out of work.

7
1964–1965

Javier opened the door to his family's *casita* expecting to see Mami cooking the evening meal and to feel the heat from her coal stove. But the house was cool. Neither Ernesto nor Mirito was around, and Papi sat at the table alone and unserved.

"*Bendición,* Papi," he said, tentatively.

"Mami had an accident," his father answered. "She fell. She broke a leg. We had to take her to the hospital."

Javier couldn't believe his father was telling him this in his usual flat tone. He wished he had a father who cried.

"Where is she?" Javier demanded.

"Santiago, *m'hijo.* We took her to Puerto Plata, and they moved her to Santiago."

He was sure his father's voice had gotten higher.

If he wanted to go to the hospital, he would have to take a *guagua* or a taxi to Puerto Plata and a bus to Santiago. But it was too late in the day for that. Too late to see if anyone could give him a ride to Santiago. If he'd had his own car, or even a motorcycle, it would have been different.

"Javielito," his mother said in a flimsy voice when he appeared at her bedside at the María Cabral y Báez Hospital the next morning. She was a tiny woman wrapped in a swirl of bedsheets and a rough blanket. "*Dios te bendiga, m'hijo.*"

"*Bendición,* Mami." He placed his hand on the hard cast that covered her leg.

"I was climbing."

"Mami, that hill is too high." Javier could see the lump growing in his mother's throat.

"I was just climbing for some coffee beans."

Every Wednesday Javier began looking for a weekend ride to Santiago. If he couldn't find one by Saturday, he took the bus. His brother Mirito, equally devoted to Mami, always went with him, despite his weak heart. Some weekends the Almontes were all there, one of several large families hovering over a sweaty bed in a crowded ward: Javier and Mirito, their father, their sister María and her small children, Marta up from the capital, and Lilo, Chichito, and Ernesto, the other brothers. As his siblings rearranged Mami's bed, sang *merengues* to her, and chattered, Javier realized that only he was discontented. María was *junta* and raising her small children in another hut in Gran Parada, one of the larger *campo* towns. Marta was still with her black taxi driver, and they'd had a son, Jesusito, who was now a handsome toddler. She did not speak anymore about leaving, at least not to Javier. Ernesto was still a farmhand, too, but cheerful about it. Chichito, who worked at a cheese factory near Puerto Plata, had reason to be content since he had a good job. Even Lilo, whose wife was always pregnant, was happy with life in his three-room hut, although there was always a child naked, a child crying, a child throwing up.

Mirito, his heart as weak as ever, was content, too. Javier often marveled at Mirito's patience and his skill. He could draw anyone. He copied songs and poems from their old *primaria* textbook; his handwriting was only one or two rough steps away from being a girl's. And Mirito was closer to Víctor González than any of the rest of them, as close as Javier wanted to be. His ailing brother had learned to speak to the sympathetic look in the rich farmer's eyes. Mirito was still the only one Víctor would send to the capital to buy his lottery tickets. Mami only let Mirito go that far because it was for Víctor. Víctor had convinced her that Mirito, as sick as he was, needed the freedom of a man. Javier felt that he needed it, too.

By the end of November, Mami was still in the hospital. "Mirito needs you home, to take care of him," Javier said tenderly.

"Javier needs you more," Mirito teased him back as he drew a picture of his mother's face to show her she was improving. "Javier needs his mami."

That night as they returned to Juan de Nina in the back of a friend's pickup truck, they were caught in a bad autumn storm. Mirito coughed and shivered, and by the time they reached the *campo* he was feverish. In the morning he could not get out of bed. Javier stayed home from the fields and spooned syrupy medicine into his brother's mouth, but by Wednesday morning Mirito's face was sunken. As Javier tried to figure out what to do, he noticed Víctor walking up the path.

Once inside the *casita,* Víctor announced that he was going to take Mirito to see Dr. Brugal, in Puerto Plata. Javier knew that Víctor didn't like to leave the *campo.* But Dr. Brugal would treat Víctor the best of any of them, since the farmer was among the richest of the *campesinos.* Víctor supervised as Javier, Ernesto, and Alemán moved Mirito to the floor and tied thin slabs from a palm trunk onto the legs of his bed. Then the four men lifted Mirito back on his bed and carried him down to Camú, where a Chevrolet that belonged to a friend of Víctor's was waiting for them. Víctor helped the others lift Mirito into the car, got in himself, and told them to wait for him in his fields.

It was almost time to stop working for the day when Javier spotted Víctor on his white horse.

"The doctor gave me more syrup, and antibiotic, too," Víctor called from a distance. When he was closer, he dismounted, walked to Javier, and put his hand on his shoulder. "He told me that what we really need is a miracle. I'll keep Mirito in my house. Fian and Roselia will watch him."

After a week Víctor told Javier they needed to bring his brother back to his own *casita*. His soul would have more luck that way. They brought Mirito home on his bed, and he died on the last day of 1964. His father and brothers buried him near the baby, Pedrito, in the cemetery that looked out over the peaks of the *cordillera*. For nine days the blue and white door of the *casita* remained shut and visitors came through the back entrance by the kitchen. Every evening the *rezador* from Camú, the praying man, led them in the rosary. They said it front of an altar with candles that they had erected in the sitting room alongside the pictures of Mami's *vírgenes*.

Javier took Mirito's dagger and put it in his drawer so that he would always have a memory of his brother. He looked at the chair where his brother used to sit to draw his portraits and felt that he could still see him there.

On the afternoon Demetria was released from the hospital, Marta came up from the capital with Jesús Antonio and Jesusito. Javier was glad to see his sister and her family. He hoped that the baby would distract Mami and keep her from asking questions. He had been lying to her for weeks, saying that Mirito was just tired or that he had a *gripe* from the rain but was well enough to draw and practice his writing.

Jesús Antonio positioned Mami in the backseat of his 1963 red Chevy Impala. Javier sat next to her and gingerly touched her knee. "Now I will see my Mirito," she said to her son.

Two hours later they arrived in Camú. It seemed as if the entire village had come to meet them. His mother smiled weakly, but Javier knew she was suspicious. It wasn't as if Víctor or the *alcalde* was coming home from the hospital. It wasn't as if she'd had a life-threatening illness. She was just an old *campesina* from up the hill who had foolishly slipped while trying to get her coffee beans.

A few of Víctor's other farmhands arrived with Demetria's black, varnished bed. They had attached palm slabs to its legs, as they had done for Mirito. Javier saw that his mother noticed her bed from the window of the car. "And my Mirito?" she asked Javier.

"*Ay,* Mami. It's just his *gripe.*" Javier was feeling weak himself. At the hospital the doctor had warned him not to let his mother get excited and fall.

The farmhands helped Javier carry Demetria on her bed up the hill and to the front door of her *casita.* "And my Mirito?" she asked weakly. "Why isn't he waiting outside for me?" Without speaking, they carried her to her room.

"The only one who should tell her is her husband," whispered Víctor, who was standing outside with Javier, his sister and father. Javier nodded and looked at his father who was nodding, too. Alemán went inside.

Javier listened from outside his mother's window.

"Where is Mirito?"

"Demetria, I am going to speak to you honestly. I am going to tell you the truth. This is difficult but we have to accept it. Mirito caught pneumonia. It was a very bad case."

"*Ay.*"

Outside, Javier felt as if he had heard the shortest, sharpest word ever uttered.

"Víctor took him to Dr. Brugal."

"*Ayyyyyy.*"

Javier ran inside.

"*Ay, Dios, Dios, Dios!*" Demetria was screaming. Javier was afraid she might fall off her bed. "I knew. I knew something happened to him. This is my fault. If I was here, I could have taken care of him. Where is Javier? Javielito!"

Javier couldn't speak at first, but he stayed up all night with his mother trying to convince her that Mirito did not die because she had wanted some more coffee beans.

Often, during the years that followed, Javier would find his mother crying when nothing seemed to be wrong. "No, nothing, nothing," Demetria would agree. It was after Mirito died, too, that her memory began to fail. Javier noticed that the small lump in her throat was slowly becoming even larger.

It never stopped bothering him that on the night of his

mother's accident he could not get out of the *campo* to see her. He was ashamed that he hadn't even tried to find a ride; he could have tried to hitchhike. But he had felt too defeated, as if he had been maimed and could not walk anywhere.

In Juan de Nina there is an amber mine, a forty-foot-high cave that contains layers of yellow rock. The few young boys who still live in the village know that lumps of amber can be found in those layers, and they have heard that a pound of the stones sells for a thousand pesos. Although they would have to give the government a portion of their earnings, they could still make money. But instead of mining themselves, they watch a man from Puerto Plata, who is the only prospector. The boys swear that he once spent three days inside the cave, digging out rocks.

Abuelo Javier, when he hears about these boys, nods his head. When he was a youth, the woman who owned the land where the mine stood invited him to look for amber in it. Javier thanked her and never tried. Perhaps, he felt the same hopelessness as those boys, the same lack of will. "It was dangerous to go in there, too," he says. He did not have good luck in those days and did not want to tempt fate.

The Dominican Republic is known for its amber, precious stones formed by the fossilized resin of locust trees. Typical specimens look like lustrous gold coins that have melted together and then been oddly frozen. Some pieces date back 120 million years, and a few—one in a hundred—contain fossils of their own: lithe insects and plants trapped before the resin hardened. It was from a piece of Dominican amber that the world learned it had been wrong about the age of mushrooms. They are 40, not 20, million years old. The fantastical dinosaurs of *Jurassic Park* were grown from the blood of a mosquito fossilized in Dominican amber.

The ancient Greeks found that amber picks up a

charge when rubbed against silk; they called the stones "electron"; that is how electricity got its name. Amber feels warm to the touch. But it is fragile despite its warmth and its current. Set a piece of amber on fire and it burns like wood.

The Dominican Republic turned out to be too much like its amber. Quisqueya was the same. According to Samuel Eliot Morison, the sea captain and Columbus scholar, ". . . the policy and acts of Columbus for which he alone was responsible began the depopulation of the terrestrial paradise that was Hispaniola in 1492. Of the original natives, estimated by a modern ethnologist at three hundred thousand in number, one-third were killed off between 1494 and 1496. By 1508 an enumeration showed only sixty thousand alive. Four years later that number was reduced by two-thirds, and in 1548 [sixteenth-century Caribbean historian Gonzalo Fernández de] Oviedo doubted whether five hundred Indians remained."

The Taínos were amazed by how much their conquerors ate. The colonial priest Bartolomé de Las Casas, another prominent historian of that era, wrote that "one Spaniard ate more in a day than a whole family of natives would consume in a month."

"You want to know what they taught us about Columbus and the Indians?" Abuelo Javier asks as he finishes an orange section he is eating for dessert. "What do you guess they taught us? In the *primaria* they taught us that Columbus killed the Indians in self-defense. That was what El Jefe wanted us to learn. After El Jefe it seemed we had no defenses and I tried to forget that we had any history. I didn't think about history, politics, or the world for a long time. If you need to know more, call up Marta in *Nieu Yersey*. Go and see her. Marta will have more to tell you about those years after El Jefe because she was caught in the middle of our civil war."

★ ★ ★

Víctor brought Javier in from the fields to do work at his house. Javier was determined to prove he was a good carpenter. He tried to work with graceful hands, flexible fingers, and confident wrists. He was careful about the angle at which he hammered each nail; he would not walk away from a piece of wood until it was completely smooth and without splinters. After that first time, Víctor brought him in more often. Javier would paint a wall or make furniture for Fian. While Javier worked, he watched for Roselia. He wanted to see if there was any sign she was maturing, although he didn't know what good it would do him. Some evenings, after work, he left and went to see a girl who lived down the path from his *casita*. She was quite willing, as were a few of the other women of Juan de Nina and Camú. One of them became pregnant and told Javier he was the father. "Forget it," he said. "The father could be anybody." Another young man from Juan de Nina took responsibility and the child that was born had the same heart defect as his father. Javier felt relieved but lonely. He did not imagine he would ever amount to much, but he kept checking Roselia's bosom to see if it was growing.

8

1965

"Keep those windows closed," Jesús Antonio instructed Marta before he left. He had gone to work every morning since the fighting began. Drivers were needed, he explained. Marta was worried about him. He was Jesusito's father and, for now at least, her *esposo*.

Marta was grateful she didn't have to think about politics. That was the advantage of being *junta* with Jesús Antonio. He continued to supply her with money for maids, bingo, and movies. What more did she need? She loved the house he had bought for her. She loved to open the windows and let the quiet come in and surround her since she, herself, was such a noisy person. So what if today Espaillat was making more noise than she was? If a city went to war, as Santo Domingo had on Sunday, then even the quiet neighborhoods became noisy. You couldn't expect to keep out a war.

Marta's house was close enough to the Duarte Bridge that she could hear machine guns going off in the Old City, where Columbus's remains were kept.

"*Ay, Dios,* Mami," she shouted at Demetria, who was visiting again.

Her mother was in the living room playing with Jesusito and another grandchild she had brought down from the *campo.* The cousins, attracted by the noise, were pulling at the venetian blinds.

"Mami! Keep the children away from the windows."

The windows were closed and the blinds shut, but with machine guns you couldn't be sure. Her mother seemed so tired. What was that small lump in her throat? Marta wished that her maid hadn't gone north to visit her family the week before. What good was having a maid if she always left? That girl must have guessed something was coming. Marta, herself, would never have imagined this. Wasn't it true that maids were always smarter than their doñas? Even when she was a ten-year-old child maid, she had been smarter than Doña Fanny. And now her girl was smarter than her. That was the price you paid for having someone else do your housework. You became stupid.

The noise of those guns slapped against her head. Marta went to make some *yerba buena* tea, but the guns stopped. She sat down on one of her carved chairs. She jumped up. The guns again. Then the planes flying overhead. On and off, for days she had heard them. At first, the radio had called this a rebellion: "The rebels have toppled the provisional government of Señor Presidente Donald Reid Cabral." Then they said it was a full-fledged civil war. Marta didn't doubt that. Why else would the Americans have landed, as they did, on Wednesday, and announced that the rebels were Communists? Everyone knew that Juan Bosch was behind this, and the Americans were afraid of him because of Castro.

She didn't mean to be thinking about politics, but she did wonder how she would ever get her visa to go to America in the midst of this. She already had her passport. She had gotten it under her real, full name: Heriberta Almonte Mercedes. She was going to America as Heriberta. Heriberta Almonte, still not too old, a petite woman with a full bosom, pretty eyes, and most important of all, light skin. No matter how old she got her complexion would always be light.

There was more noise outside.

Jesús Antonio had told her she could get a visa and go to Puerto Rico if that was what she really wanted. Of course it was what she really wanted. She didn't know why she wanted it. She just had to keep moving. Jesusito could stay with Jesús Antonio's mother in San Juan de la Maguana. "Go, Marta," he had said. "Get to know someplace the way you want to." He was generous because he thought she was only going for a year. And only to Puerto Rico.

The shouts were getting louder. Marta peered through the blinds.

A few people ran by her house toward the bridge. Then a few more, a few more. There were soldiers. Police. The uniforms and clothing were mixing in an angry braid of colors.

"Mami, get the children back!" Marta held up her hands and pushed them toward Demetria.

More people came. They had sticks and large rocks in their hands. People came carrying wooden torches and the fire looked as if it was spilling into the street. In the distance she thought she saw a man carrying a baby, and her hand began to shake. What was a man doing carrying a baby through this?

"Get under the bed, Mami!" Marta could hear Jesusito crying first. Then his cousin. She heard her mother's modest gasps, and tears came to her eyes. But she could not stop watching.

The man with the baby was in front of her house now. He looked straight at her, but he would not have known she was there. She was still peeking through the slats. His eyes were darting. He was trying to find a place to hide. He came closer and his hand was holding a spot on the baby's head. Now Marta could see blood dripping from the baby's head. She wanted to get out there and grab the baby, but people with torches were in front of the man. She was afraid she would be trampled. Afraid to move. She heard gunshots.

The baby looked like a child she had held herself. She imagined Jesusito in the man's arms. Jesusito with his ears that stuck out like hers, his puckered face. And a bloody head.

She heard more shots. The man fell. Marta watched the baby. She turned back to look at her Jesusito. She watched the baby outside again. She imagined the baby was Jesusito. That it was Jesusito falling on top of the man.

She couldn't stop herself from peeking through the blinds. A crowd was around the man and the baby.

"I am going out, Mami," Marta said.

"*M'hija!*" Demetria called after her. Then Marta was gone.

Outside, Marta watched as a man took off his shirt and covered the father's head. Another man did the same and covered the boy. It had been a boy. Marta was thirty-one and thought she had enough of a collection of bad pictures in her head. She had a picture of herself as a fourteen-year-old with Peralta, her first man. Peralta coming home with lipstick on his shirt. Peralta not caring whether Marta saw it or not. She had left her job and her family for him.

She had a picture of Purito coming at her with a knife just because she had been out in the street, looking for him and calling his name. She never knew what she might do that would make him kill her. Kill her in front of their daughter, Cándida, maybe.

She had a picture of her daughter Cándida, thirteen years old now and still living with her grandmother, Purito's mother, in Moca. Cándida thinking Marta was an aunt, or a visitor. Cándida not knowing that Marta had not wanted to die in front of her. Cándida knowing that even though she was a mother, Marta couldn't stay in one place.

There was her oldest picture. Her mother dusting the sugar

granules from the table so that she could sweeten more than one cup of coffee.

And the new picture, of her brother Lilo. Three sick children, maybe more by now, in a palm hut. Their thatched roof had holes in it, and when it rained, they all caught the *gripe*. She could not stand going back to the *campo* in her city clothes and seeing all the women in housedresses and Lilo's dirty children.

Marta watched as they carried the bodies away from Calle Uno, and she thought that she did not want to live on Calle Uno anymore.

"Take me away from here," she demanded. Jesús Antonio had come home in a good mood, as though this had been a typical day. "Everyone's gone crazy. Take me somewhere where I can sleep. Where the boy will be safe."

They wrapped the children in blankets, gave one to Demetria, and drove through the night in Jesús Antonio's red Impala.

"Do you want Cándida?" Jesús Antonio asked Marta when they passed the turnoff to Moca.

She shook her head. On the road they were stopped at each checkpoint while the car was searched. They passed La Cumbre, the peaked spot on the highway where the Mirabal sisters' Jeep had been pushed. Then, finally, they were in Camú. They left the Impala there and walked up the hill to Juan de Nina, and to Demetria's yellow and purple flowers, which had survived another of her absences.

In the *campo*, Marta knew the neighbors were talking about her. They said whatever they wanted, even to Mami. "*Ay, Meme, another* man? *Another* child?" Mami explained that Marta was going to America. "Meme, she'll go there and forget about all of you." Marta lasted three weeks. Finally, she'd had enough.

Calle Uno was as quiet as ever when the red Impala parked in front of House 16. "There are soldiers on the patio," Marta said, as if everybody couldn't see that for themselves. Jesús Antonio got out. "Stay here," Marta said to her mother, who had refused to remain behind. Demetria had Jesusito on her lap.

"Don't get out," Marta said to her maid, whom they had picked up on the way. She hoped the girl would listen.

Marta climbed out and followed Jesús Antonio into their house. She walked past the soldiers on the porch, past two more soldiers she found inside as though she was the doña, which she finally was, and they were the help, or just more furniture.

She walked toward her bedroom, hoping Jesús Antonio would not follow her.

Under the covers of her bed, there was another soldier.

Marta saw his stripes.

"*Buenos días,* Lieutenant!" she shouted.

He opened his eyes.

"*Buenos días.* I live here."

The lieutenant didn't speak.

"How are you? This is my house."

"It's okay," the lieutenant said slowly.

Marta could not believe he thought this was okay.

"It's okay, we'll leave." He sounded awake now. "We were only here because no people were living here. We didn't go into the houses that had people in them."

Dominican soldiers were silly. Marta would have bet her bingo and movie money that the American Marines didn't apologize for anything. The lieutenant got out from under the ruffled covers of Marta's bed, and she wondered how he could have imagined that people did not live here.

The floors were dirty. When the soldiers left, Marta and her maid cleaned them together. The lock on the front door had been broken and the glass in the door of Marta's bedroom wardrobe had been smashed.

The Americans left Santo Domingo after six months. The rebels were worn down, a provisional government

was in place, and elections were scheduled for the following June. The elections would bring Balaguer back into power.

The Americans were proud because they had routed Communism from a Latin American country and prevented "another Cuba." Later, it would turn out that American intelligence was faulty. Communist leanings among the rebels and their connection to Castro were not nearly as pervasive as had been thought. While American troops had been in the Dominican Republic, the American presence in Vietnam had escalated from 17,000 to 245,000 troops.

Marta left Santo Domingo four months after the Americans. She had trouble with her visa, at first, but a neighbor knew a couple in Puerto Rico who had two children and wanted a nanny. They would sponsor her. Marta didn't want to be a maid again, but it was her only way out. Arrangements were made quickly and quietly and Marta knew that the people expected her to stay for years. They were as foolish as Jesús Antonio. She would be gone in a few months. She had her visa. Nobody on a domestic flight from San Juan to *Juan Kenadee* Airport would check to see that she was supposed to be working for a family in Río Piedras. She could get on that plane like any other Puerto Rican woman who wanted to see her relatives in Manhattan.

On the plane to San Juan, Marta used these practical thoughts to drive out a new picture that now competed with the others: Jesusito asleep at 7 A.M. in the little bed Jesús Antonio's mother had bought for him. The day before, Marta had taken him there, to his new home and, in effect, to his new mami. Marta had slept there with him on her last night in the Dominican Republic. He was her little boy with ears that stuck out like hers and her father's. She left for the airport before he was awake so that he would not cry and she would not break down. It had been easier to say good-bye to Cándida. She had already left her once. Now she was leaving both her children. Marta had not said anything to Jesusito about her departure. She could not imagine how to explain it to a two-year-old. She tried to keep herself from remembering too many of the details of her silent farewell. She did not want to remember which pair of pajamas he was wearing. She told herself that someday her children would understand that what she was doing was worth it. *Vale la pena* now. *Vale la pena* much more someday. Someday they would see it was worth it, worth all the pain.

9

1966–1969

There was a dress Roselia González wore. It was made from a cloth patterned with small, different-colored checks, like Javier's old, favorite shirt or a child's pinafore. But the dress itself had a short skirt and a tight waist. It had been sewn to show off a woman's body. Javier could not stop thinking about that dress and the way it clung to Roselia's fifteen-year-old shape. He lay in bed in his *casita,* listened to the roosters, and imagined Roselia and her brown eyes, the indented bridge of her nose, her strong arms, and her bosom growing out of the top of her dress.

Javier knew that Roselia read the Bible. He knew that she wasn't a flirt like her sister Ramona. She didn't have a reputation as a party girl, like other young women in the *campo.* She didn't drink beer, *merengue* with too many partners, or take walks with different boys, as his sister Marta had done. But she was already two years out of the *primaria,* and sometimes she gave Javier a half smile that made him think she might let him touch her.

It was easy enough to see her. Víctor had set up a small grocery in a shack in front of his house, and Roselia worked there. Javier thought about Roselia and her stock: rice, beans, herring, codfish, garlic, oil, packets of sugar, boxes of spaghetti, and bars of soap. The trick would be to find her when Ramona wasn't helping, too, and to buy something that made sense.

After he fed his father's animals and ate breakfast, Javier took a clean, white towel from his mother's bedroom, folded it neatly, and put it in his lunch pail. When he finished in Víctor's fields, he took the towel from his pail and hung it around his neck.

At the door to the shack he saw she was alone. "A bar of Palmolive, please, Roselia," Javier said.

She smiled and it was familiar.

"I'm going to bathe in the river," he said, surprised by his boldness.

Roselia did not answer him.

He went to the grocery almost every day after that. But it was more than a week before he found Roselia alone again. Soap in hand, he kept on talking.

"I like you, Roselia."

"I don't want you to say that." She turned her back to him and studied a large barrel of rice.

The next day, she was not in the store, so Javier went up to Víctor's house. "I have to see your father," he said when, as he had hoped, Roselia answered the door. "Business." Javier walked through Víctor's sitting room and passed Ramona, who giggled at him. What kind of business could he have? He cut Víctor's *caña* for a living.

Finally Javier decided he could stand it no longer. He marched into the grocery without his towel and without checking for Ramona. "I want to visit you in your house," he told Roselia.

She smiled a full smile. "You have to ask my father."

"Okay. Can I ask your father?"

"Just don't do it in front of me."

The following Friday Javier lined up with Víctor's other workers to collect his pay. Víctor rode to his men on his white horse, pulled one long leg over the saddle, and dismounted. Fian, who was watching from her front porch, walked over to stand next to her husband.

"*Gracias,* Javier," Víctor said as he handed him twenty-five pesos.

"*Gracias a usted,* Don Víctor," Javier said. Instead of leaving, he stepped back behind the other men. When Víctor finished moving down the line, handing out pesos, he nodded at Javier.

"Can I speak with you, Don Víctor?"

The rich farmer nodded again.

"I am interested in having a conversation with your daughter, Don Víctor."

Víctor nodded.

"Your daughter Roselia."

Víctor kept nodding.

"I am interested in speaking to her at your house because I am in love with her and I can't just see her in the street, in the road, or at the river."

Víctor smiled.

"I can't only talk to her whenever I can find her somewhere." Javier noticed that Fian was also smiling.

"You would like to visit her at my house?" Víctor asked.

"If she agrees," Javier said.

Víctor looked at Fian, and they seemed oddly young to Javier. "It would be our pleasure," Víctor said.

Javier courted Roselia on her front porch, where they sat with her mother. Sometimes, Fian permitted him to take Roselia to the Bar Osiris in Camú. Holding hands, they walked through the entryway with its palm trunks holding up the zinc roof. The trunks were from the same trees that grew all over the *campo,* but Javier thought they looked so romantic holding up the roof of the Bar Osiris. He would go up to the glass window by the counter and order a Presidente beer for himself and a Coca-Cola for Roselia. They would sit in the rattan chairs or get up to play the jukebox and dance to *merengues* or American rock and roll.

The girl who lived down the path from Javier saw them one evening at the Bar Osiris. Later, Javier heard from the other farmhands that she had been to see Roselia, and the two women had had a wrestling match, which Roselia won. Roselia did not mention it and Javier did not ask her about it. But he was delighted.

The other matter Javier and Roselia did not discuss was Víctor. Javier had heard, from the same farmhands, that people were saying he was interested in Roselia because of Víctor's land. Why else would he be courting her? There were plenty of pretty girls in the *campo,* many of whom were much wilder than Roselia. Everyone said that it was the wilder girls who were more agreeable as *esposas.* Javier thought about his sister Marta, wild and long gone to Puerto Rico and now New York, and he laughed to himself. He wondered, too, how people could talk about him wanting Roselia for the money when they knew Víctor's own history. People must have said the same about Víctor and Fian. Javier kept watching to see if Víctor was affected by the gossip, but he saw no change in the rich farmer.

Javier was in the midst of his romance when Marta came home for a visit. She had been gone for two years and he examined his older sister as though she were a new kind of beautiful animal. She had dyed her hair blond. She wore a pearl necklace and a gold watch and her dress came in a color he had never seen. Javier gaped as Marta opened her four suitcases and presented Mami with more presents than she would ever be able to keep in her small hut.

"These are *Nueva Llork*–style dresses," Marta explained to a beaming Mami. "And these chiffon nightgowns come from *Van-eeet-te Fay-re.* There's *mucho* here. For you, for María. I'll bring some to Lilo's house, too."

Javier watched as his sister held the nightgowns up against her chest. He marveled at her new plumpness.

"I am fat. Very fat," Marta agreed in her joyous, heavily accented English. She held her hands out to the sides of her now wider hips, so that Javier would understand what she was saying.

From Puerto Rico, where she had lasted only six months, she had written to Javier and offered to help him get a visa. But he had turned her down, saying that he had to stay with Mami. They took a walk outside, alone, and Marta asked him if now he wanted to come to *Nueva Llork*.

"I have responsibilities here."

"*Ay,* when God takes Mami, Javier. When you don't have Mami to care for anymore, I'm going to bring you all to *Nueva Llork.*"

When Roselia was seventeen years old, Javier took her to spend the night with him at his parents' *casita*. Ernesto had moved out, the second bedroom was all his, and they slept there. It was not their first time together. Roselia was already three months pregnant. But it was the first time they had slept together openly, in a bed, instead of hiding in a patch of woods. They agreed to celebrate that night, January 4, as the day they officially became *juntos*.

In the morning twenty-four-year-old Javier explained to his parents that Roselia would be living with him in their hut. Then he walked down the hill to tell Víctor and Fian. The Almontes and the Gonzálezes had been expecting this, and with happy solemnity they agreed that Roselia and Javier were now *esposos* for life.

Javier was particularly relieved by his mother's good wishes. He knew she was happy because he was not leaving her. But, he told himself, if he had enough money, that's exactly what he would do. *Cuando el hombre se casa o la mujer se casa quiere casa.* That was one of his mother's favorite expressions. Javier believed it was true. When a man or woman marry, they want their own house. His mother used to say it all the time. But she never said it now.

He wanted to feel that he and Roselia were on their own. But Roselia didn't understand that, either. Every day she walked down the Juan de Nina path to her parents' house. Often, she ate with Víctor and Fian.

"You have to travel in my circle," Javier finally told his *esposa.* "You have to go where I go, stay where I stay, eat where I eat," he explained. To himself he admitted that he wasn't really going anywhere except to Víctor's fields. So when Roselia continued to visit her parents every day, he did not protest, as long as she only drank *yerba buena* tea with her mother and came home to eat with him. Javier was satisfied as long as the spice of the mint and of her mother's conversation was enough to send her happily home. For a few weeks he felt like an independent man. Then he noticed that his wife's stomach was growing. Between the Almontes' *casita* and the Gonzálezes' house, the path became rocky and steep, and the walk was becoming too difficult for her.

It was Víctor who suggested that Javier move into the *casita* he owned, opposite his farmhouse. Javier had guessed that would happen, but he had to admit that the rich farmer had a gracious way. Víctor had explained that he needed work done on the *casita,* so much work that Javier would have to move there. Javier knew people would talk again. He wished the gossips knew how much he wanted to distance himself from Víctor and make his own money. But he still had no plan, so he went to work on their new *casita,* which was sturdy with a floor made from *cemento.* While he worked, he watched the planes that flew over Juan de Nina. One afternoon he pulled a wobbly Roselia outside. "Someday I'm going to go up in one of those," he said. He could tell she thought he was crazy.

He built a porch in front of the house and planted a garden with *yuca* and beans. Inside he constructed a kitchen with wooden storage shelves. He made a small table and chairs with woven rope seats. He made a bed. In the tiny bedroom he built a shelf on the wall above the foot of the bed for their alarm clock and kerosene lamp.

"That shelf was our vanity," Abuelo Javier recalls, his eyes twinkling with the memory of a young man's energy.

★ ★ ★

The weather became hot and Javier woke in the middle of the night and felt the old emptiness in his bed. He heard Roselia breathing, turned, and saw that she was lying on the concrete floor. "The bed was too warm," she told him in the morning, as she flipped through a magazine article on American movie stars. "I like *Eh-leez-a-bet*," she said.

Before dawn on June 8, 1969, Javier woke and realized that Roselia had not moved to the floor. "I feel bad," she said. Javier pulled his pants from the shelf on the wall and went across the road to wake Fian. Then he ran a mile to the hut of the mid-wife, Doña Layla. Doña Layla had delivered Javier and was one of his mami's best friends.

Javier banged on Doña Layla's shutter. "Tía! Roselia is ready. She is ready to give light."

Together they ran back to Javier's *casita*. He was surprised by how quickly the elderly midwife could run. Doña Layla went inside, where it sounded as though Fian had already begun the delivery. Outside, listening to his *esposa* cry and moan, Javier stood as close to the front door as he dared. He knew that the women would not welcome his presence or his advice. Inside they had what they needed. Boiled water, rubbing alcohol, tow-els, and magic. Javier hoped they had magic. He waited outside for an hour and a half until he heard the screams of his first child at eight-thirty in the morning. When the screams did not stop, he decided that something had gone wrong and cursed the way he was stuck without a car, once again. He would go down to Camú, borrow the first car he saw, and commandeer the driver to Puerto Plata so that he could find a real doctor.

Doña Layla came out as he was starting down the path. "It's good, Javier! Don't worry."

He stopped and turned to the old woman. *"Viva Dios!"* he called out, exhausted.

"Come, Javier. Come see your fruit."

Javier walked into the *casita* and its bedroom, bent down to the bed and to Roselia, who was holding a beautiful, dark, baby eel. She had good hair, straight Taíno hair. An Indian with *pelo bueno. India morena.* His first daughter. *Hembra!* *"Guuuuaaaaawwww."* His voice was not loud, just full of wonder.

Elizabeth answered with what seemed to Javier like the same sound, except that it was loud.

Javier put his hand in his pocket and handed twenty-five pesos to Doña Layla, still a week's salary for him. She shook her head. "I do not take money for Meme's children or grandchildren," she said.

Elizabeth slept between her parents, and Javier often woke to find her napping happily with her arms wrapped around the muscles of his legs. He was surprised by the strength and the size of his daughter. When she was two days old, they had brought her to see the doctor in Puerto Plata, and she already weighed ten pounds four ounces. As she grew, she came to resemble Demetria. Her coloring and straight, coarse hair and even her hands, already wrinkled, made her look like a tinier but sturdier version of Javier's mother.

Javier watched Elizabeth turn from a baby into a toddler surrounded by relatives. Since Roselia was the eldest of Fian's eleven children, many of Elizabeth's aunts and uncles were close to her in age. Often those aunts and uncles crossed the dirt path between their house and the *casita* so that they could play with Elizabeth. Or Elizabeth wandered, by herself, to Fian's and waited for her grandmother to finish cooking so that she could entertain her with songs about candy treats and small animals. Javier noticed that his daughter favored her Tío Julio. Julio cried all the time, but he was tall for his age—and smart. That Elizabeth liked her Tío Julio made sense to Javier. His daughter was smart like her uncle. Even her mischief was precocious. Elizabeth had barely started to walk when she began to get into trouble. One day Doña Layla's daughter, who lived in the hut behind them, came running to report that Elizabeth had killed her cat.

"She did it with a stone or a stick, I'm not sure," the woman told Javier.

"How could that be?" Roselia asked. "She's a baby."

Roselia had told Javier that the pain of giving birth to Elizabeth had been unlike any she had ever felt, different in character, not just intensity. Fortunately, Elizabeth was the kind of baby who couldn't wait. She came out quickly. She was like that as a daughter, too. Wounds inflicted by Elizabeth healed fast because she was also quick to delight and surprise. She created explosions, found herself in the midst of them. But she survived and so did the people around her.

10
1970–1973

The decade began with the heaviest of autumn rains. Huts and houses flooded and the river Camú almost overflowed. The González house and the Almonte *casita* both stayed dry, although for different reasons. The González house had stilts. The Almontes were dry because of luck. Víctor congratulated himself and Javier but said that even with stilts he was tired of the uncertainty. He built a new farmhouse in Camú, on a dry road on the other side of the river and a distance from its banks, and moved his family there.

For the first time in his life, Javier had privacy. He bought livestock with help from his father and felt rich and independent, even though he owned only half of each of cow and pig and had been left in charge of Víctor's animals, too. Roselia, he knew, found the solitude terrifying. Within months after her parents moved, she was pregnant again. At night, while Elizabeth slept between them, Roselia confided to Javier that she did not know if she had the courage to give birth again. The pain from Elizabeth had been so bad. What if this time the pain was not only bad but long as well? She said that she did not believe, as Doña Layla did, as many people in the *campo* did, that the pain was worth it, the more pain the healthier the baby. "I am not Fian," she told Javier. "I am not my mother. I am not your mother." She asked if she could have her second child in the clinic in Puerto Plata. "*Sí, mi amor,*" Javier said. He hated to refuse her and his own terror was that she might ask for something he could not provide. To pay for the clinic he sold four of the hogs he was raising for his father.

But when Roselia's pains began, they were mild. She told Javier that she could walk down the hill to Camú, herself, to tell her mother she was ready and arrange for Elizabeth to stay with Fian. Javier could get Elizabeth ready and meet her there. In Camú, they would find a ride to Puerto Plata.

In the early morning of September 26, 1971, Javier waited outside the delivery room of the Hospital Ricardo Limardo, a polyclinic that had been built by El Jefe, although there was no longer a sign announcing that. He braced himself for Roselia's screams. But there weren't any. When the doctor brought him in to see his second piece of fruit, another girl, he was told he should be proud of his *esposa*. She hadn't needed any pain medicine. All Javier could think was that Roselia could have done the same in the *casita*. He wondered when he was going to have a son. Then the doctor handed Cristian Almonte González to him, and he saw she was beautiful, fairer and more delicate than her sister. Her hair was curlier than Elizabeth's. *Pelo malo,* definitely. But her hands were smoother. Oddly, she looked so much like Víctor that Javier instantly saw his father-in-law in a different light. Perched on Víctor's tall, strong body was the face of a baby.

Four days later, Javier walked down to Víctor's house to see his wife and children. Roselia and Cristian had come home the day before and stayed there with Elizabeth. But Javier needed to sleep in Juan de Nina so that he could tend to the animals.

It was four in the afternoon, but the sky was already getting dark.

"You'd better not go home tonight," Fian warned him from her porch. "The rain is going to be bad." The sky got darker as she spoke, and she looked up respectfully. "Nothing good will come of this."

"I have to go." Javier was no longer afraid of Fian. "The animals are up there. Everything is up there."

In Juan de Nina, in the darkness, Javier milked the cows, fed the pigs and chickens, and shooed them into a small corral he hoped would last the night. As he finished, it began to rain. He filled a pail of water from the outdoor spigot and brought it inside. He put the chairs on top of the small wooden table, along with a bowl of eggs, a plate of *yuca,* a sack of charcoal, and the pail of water.

In bed, sleeping next to his flashlight, he dreamed that his *casita* had filled to the ceiling with water. But what woke him were screams. He thought he heard a woman.

He sat up, listened, and realized that he was hearing the screams of his animals. The sounds they made were so pained. It was only because he knew the particular tones of their voices that he could identify which animals he heard. The pigs cried *kwwiii, kwwiii, kwwiii.* The cows cried *nooooohhhhh.* The roosters cried *coco techl coco techl coooooocooooooo techl.* Javier grabbed for his flashlight, stood on his bed, and lit the kerosene lamp on the shelf above his head. He stretched, grabbed the window shutter, and pulled it open. All he could see in the darkness was rain, too much rain, and the wind moving tree branches with more motion than he had ever witnessed. He wanted to check his animals, he could almost feel his hands on their wet bodies. But he was sure that by now they had fled in fear and were scattered. He would have to be satisfied that he had his own life. As he turned to sit back down, he saw that the bedroom floor was covered with water.

The wind blew out the lamp. Javier lit it again and watched the water. It seemed to be receding slowly. Or was he imagining that? His bed was dry. He tried to stay awake in case the water rose again.

Muddy Cup

In the wet darkness he found his old scapegoat, the *campo*. He had to leave the *campo*. He had to get his *esposa* and children out of the *campo*. His brother Chichito now worked in a sugar mill in the Cibao. He would ask Chichito to get him a job there. That would be easier than getting a job at the mill in Montellano, where Víctor was his only connection. He wondered about Marta. She had not been back to the *campo* since her first trip four years earlier. But she wrote to him. Javier could still see her, fat, blond, and bejeweled, unpacking all those clothes that Mami would never wear. Javier wondered if he could accept Marta's offer to bring him to *Nueva Llork* now that he had an *esposa* and two children. Forget about it. Marta expected him to stay with Mami. The lump in her throat was still growing, and she became more disoriented each day. Even if Mami was well, Roselia would never agree to let him go to America.

The floor now had a carpet of mud. Maybe the water had receded; maybe it had never been as high as he had thought. It did not seem as though the sun had risen, but Javier guessed it was time to wake up, although there were no roosters. He stood on the bed and looked for the clock on the shelf. It was after seven. He got up, opened the door, and saw emptiness. There were no pigs or cows. He couldn't bear to think where they might be. All he saw were a few chickens sleeping on the high branch of a tree behind the *casita*. But no roosters. His porch was covered in brown silt, and trees, even his strongest palms, had been dismembered.

He turned away and began trying to clean the mud off the floor with a sponge and the pail of water he had filled the night before. From outside, he heard the noise of an engine, a normal noise. Javier stopped, unshuttered a wet, sticky window, and saw Víctor's new John Deere tractor parked in front of his *casita*. One of Víctor's farmhands was driving. Víctor never drove his own tractor. The vehicle stopped and Víctor got out. He was followed by Felipe, Fian's father, Roselia's revered grandfather. Javier was mortified. Felipe had come down from his mountain in this weather to see if he was all right.

Without knocking, they opened the door and stared at Javier until he understood that they had expected him to be dead.

"*Compadre!*" Felipe said to Víctor. "This boy has to get out of here."

From the floor, Javier looked at Víctor, one of the tallest men in the *campo*. And at Felipe, who was, if possible, even taller. People used to say that even when he rode a horse, Felipe's feet touched the ground, and age had not stooped him a bit. They motioned to Javier and he got off his knees and followed them outside.

The horses, cows, and pigs were truly gone. Javier and his father had branded their ears with a knife. If they were still alive, another farmer might bring them back. Javier remembered their screams and expected he would find their drowned carcasses.

"Javier, you come back with us right now," Víctor said.

"Not now. I need to clean the house first. I'll come in the afternoon."

"Now, Javier," Felipe said.

Javier shook his head, surprised at his will. The two tall men looked at each other and walked back to their tractor.

Back inside, Javier took the still dry charcoal from his wooden table, lit a fire in the *fogón,* a smaller metal stove they sometimes used outside, and cooked himself a breakfast of eggs and *yuca.* He knew that might be the last of the *yuca.* Their vegetable patch outside had been destroyed. He tried to finish cleaning the floor, but the one pail of water he had saved was not enough to get the drying mud off the concrete. With a broom made from fine wisps of straw he tried to sweep up the mud. But the mud stuck to the floor and to the walls as well. He would never be able to clean the house well enough to suit Roselia. He wanted to go to sleep, but Víctor and Felipe would be looking for him, and he had already pushed them as far as he dared.

★ ★ ★

He was tired, muddy, and wet from cleaning, the sight of the river, high and rough, only made him feel worse. The water covered all the white stones, and to get across he would have to wade as deep as his waist. He stripped down to his underwear, put his pants and shoes into his shirt, and tied the whole bundle under his chin with his shirtsleeves. When he reached the other side he stopped to put his dry clothes back on his soaked body.

Fian was on her front porch.

"Well, what good did it do you?" she asked. Javier could tell by the way she looked at him that he was a sight. "Did you save any animals?"

She would really laugh if he told her the only animals that survived were the chickens who slept in the tree.

"It didn't do me any good," he said. "But at least I was there."

"Well, you're here for good now."

"But everything's there."

Fian rolled her eyes, as only she could do. "Do you want to eat? I have everything inside. Eggs, cheese, salami, olives." Javier knew there would also be *tostones*. With Fian, there were always *tostones*—plain, substantial, and the best in the *campo*. He began to tell her that he had already cooked his own breakfast and only wanted to see Roselia, when Julio, Roselia's whiny baby brother, opened the door of the house.

"Felipe and Víctor want to see you," the boy said.

Javier walked nervously into Víctor's new farmhouse. It was made from palm, but Javier knew that Víctor wanted to tear down the wooden walls and put up *bloque*. Even with palm walls, Javier found the house daunting. The sitting room was a tiny space, but instead of shutters, its windows were covered with wooden blinds. In the center there was a red upholstered couch, so luxurious compared to the wooden benches most people had. When visitors brought presents, they were displayed on a round wood and aluminum coffee table that had been painted white, but with good paint, not whitewash.

Víctor nodded at Javier and motioned toward the back of his house. "If you want, you can build a house on that empty spot behind us."

Javier couldn't think fast enough. He would have to be honest. He was too tired to lie. "That would be comfortable, Víctor," he said without hesitating. "Very comfortable for us. Thank you. I can't thank you sufficiently. But I can't do it, Víctor. I am grateful but I can't do it." Javier looked toward the breezeway between the front part of the house and its kitchen. The Gonzálezes had only been in their new house a few months, but territories had been staked out. The front porch was Fian's; the patio in the breezeway was where Víctor sat. "When I leave my new house, I'd have to pass your patio. When I come home, I'd have to pass your patio, too."

Víctor nodded and looked at Javier carefully, as though he were a doctor trying to make a diagnosis. "Okay, *compadre*. It's your decision. We have to respect it."

"That's all fine and good, Víctor," Felipe interrupted. "But where is this boy going to live?"

"Look," Javier said. "I'll just bring Roselia back to our house." He thought about the floor he had left streaked with mud. "If there are any problems, any more floods, I'll bring her down here to stay with you." This was, he knew, useless. Roselia belonged as much to her father and grandfather as she did to him. There was another long silence and Javier spent it looking at the floor.

"Look, Javier," Felipe said. "I have that piece of land down the road from Víctor. You can't even see his house from there. You can build on it."

"I couldn't, Abuelo."

"*Sí. Sí.* It's good land."

"I mean I couldn't take it."

"I'm not giving it to you."

"I can't buy it."

"No. No. No. You're going to work for it. I like living on my mountain, but it's too rocky for us. We're too old for those rocks. Borrow Víctor's tractor and smooth out the rocks for me and the land down below is yours."

"But, Abuelo, wouldn't you rather move yourself down to the flatland?" Javier was trying desperately not to take from Roselia's family again. Although this offer was tempting. Dry land, and Roselia would be only a minute's walk from her parents. And he wouldn't have to look at Víctor's house.

"I like my mountain, Javier," Felipe insisted. "I like it up there better."

Javier wanted to move the walls from his *casita* in Juan de Nina to his new plot of land in Camú. The walls were good. There was no reason to make new ones. He measured the foundation of his *casita* and built one the same size on his new plot of land in Camú. Back in Juan de Nina, he sawed his walls apart, put them in the back of Víctor's pickup truck, along with their few pieces of furniture, and brought them to Camú. He brought his roof frame, too, since that was also good. He would have to make a new thatch.

Delicately, as though each section were a child, he nailed his Juan de Nina walls together in Camú. As he worked, Javier admired the trees—lime, orange, mango, and breadfruit—that stood around them. He built a kitchen in a separate *casita,* alongside the house so that the leftover cooking aromas would not bother his family as they slept. He salvaged thirty-five pesos from his wages and bought a gas cooker with three burners so that Roselia would not have to cook on a coal stove or a *fogón,* as she had in Juan de Nina.

When he moved Roselia and the children into their new home, there was no water or electricity. In Juan de Nina they at least had water. Javier told Roselia about his plans. When he had extra pesos, he would buy piping and build an aqueduct from Víctor's. In the same piecemeal way he was going to buy wire and posts so that they could hook up to Víctor's generator. The posts would have to be put by the *casitas* of the other people who lived in between them and Víctor. But Javier told Roselia not to worry. Nobody would object because the project involved Víctor.

As her papi built their new *casita*, Elizabeth watched with interest. Cristian gurgled happily through most of the construction, but Javier didn't have time to register her birth for two months. The papers that would follow her throughout her life said that she was born on November 26. But her papi always reminded her that her real birth date was two months earlier, the week before the floods of the decade drenched the *campo*.

Javier believed that his girls spent hours, if not entire days, chasing baby chicks. Elizabeth was a lean general sounding the battle cry; Cristian the chubby, enthusiastic soldier. Cristian sat to eat. She loved her mami's *sancocho* and ate the thick yellow stew slowly to savor it. Elizabeth grabbed her food and ran with it. She loved to run while chewing a stalk of *caña*. When Cristian saw the *caña*, she wanted some, too.

Two decades later, Abuelo Javier remembers his first two babies and still cannot believe that it was Cristian who, as a teenager, hurt him so much. There wasn't even a hint of such willfulness when she was a child. Except that Cristian did become jovial when her older sister put mischief in front of her little face.

Javier only scolded the girls when they were rough with the chicks. Sometimes, after they caught them and set them down, they tried to step on them. Javier smiled through his stern words as he remembered his mushroom bomb and the secret Demetria never found out. He admired his daughters' spunk. It was almost as good as having sons.

Elizabeth proved to be as smart as she had seemed as a toddler. A friend of Roselia's had started a nursery school, the first ever in Camú. Elizabeth was a year too young to go, but the teacher invited her to attend anyway. Javier saw that even when Elizabeth wasn't in school, she was learning. She stood by the narrow road in front of their *casita* and watched everything: the chickens, her aunts and uncles, the occasional teenage girl whizzing by on the back of a motorcycle, the Haitians who worked for Víctor and danced in their colorful costumes, played drums and tambourines, and sang in their strange language.

Javier was amused that Víctor, tall and lean, seemed to have fallen in love with little Elizabeth. He made sure to take her along whenever he gave his own children rides in his pickup. To the others it seemed that Víctor spoke more to Elizabeth than he did to anyone else. Fian said that he treated Elizabeth the way he had treated Roselia. He even toasted her with his glass of rum and giggled as she pretended to toast back.

But when she was five years old, Víctor almost killed Elizabeth. As the story was told to Javier, his father-in-law's truck flipped over with Elizabeth in the back, sitting among a gaggle of her young aunts and uncles. Víctor and a few of his friends were in the front. Elizabeth was caught half under the truck, its edge resting on her back. In the excitement after the accident the men in the front forgot about Elizabeth, their littlest passenger. She saw them walking away and, with all her frightened strength, screamed for them to stop.

"Ayyy. La muchachita!" one of Víctor's friends reminded him. On the way to the hospital in Puerto Plata, with Elizabeth shaking by one side of him, Roselia on the other, Javier tried to restrain himself from being angry at Víctor. Víctor, he guessed, had probably drunk too much rum.

Elizabeth was checked and released after a few hours. Javier told Roselia that she was a tough little girl who would survive anything. The truck had flipped alongside a large ditch, and Javier did not want to think about what might have happened to Elizabeth if the truck had fallen in.

11

1973–1974

By September Roselia was pregnant again. On a surprisingly dry night in the middle of the month, Javier sent his nauseated and exhausted young wife to bed early. Then he took Elizabeth, who was crying and nervous, into bed with him and Roselia. As he marveled at how much his eldest child looked like his mother, Elizabeth relaxed against his warmth. When she was asleep, Javier carried her to the new "children's" bed he had bought and cuddled her next to her sister, who was already sound asleep.

"I'm not having any more," Roselia whispered to him when he returned to her. Her dark skin and eyes were still beautiful. Her long, black hair was loose, and her breasts, larger now from feeding her children, cascaded slightly but gloriously out of the top of her nightgown.

"You mean no more if it's a boy, *mi amor,*" Javier said confidently. "If it's not a boy, we'll keep on going."

"No," Roselia whispered.

After two children she still surprised him.

"No more," his twenty-two-year-old wife said, straining to make her whisper louder. "No more. It doesn't matter what it is. No more."

A few weeks later, Javier sat with Roselia at a clinic in Sosúa. "I want to have a talk with you," the doctor said as he examined her. Javier put his hand on Roselia's knee. She had found out from her friends that if she wanted to be sterilized after she gave birth, this was the doctor to see.

"You have to do some soul-searching about this," the doctor continued.

Roselia was calm, which surprised Javier. Doctors usually made her nervous.

"You have to think about this all by yourself when you are alone. You could get divorced. That's common, after all. Your husband, if God willed it, might have an accident and die. The same thing could happen to your children. If you get divorced from Javier or he dies, how are you going to be happy with another man if you can't give him a child?"

"*Doctor,* I have thought about this," Roselia said. "If there is an accident and my three children die . . ."

Javier wondered if she could continue.

"If there is an accident, that would be God's will. If Javier dies or divorces me, I'll be happy with my three children. I don't need anything else. No more children, *por favor.*"

Javier knew Roselia was right. He also knew she was unaware of the role her decision played in their lives. He had quietly sent a postcard to Marta:

"My dear Sister . . . the memory is always there. I can't forget what we talked about so many times. The hope that I can emigrate like you did to the United States."

Marta had written back: "Don't worry. I'll get you here. Just don't have too many children, like Lilo."

"It is because of Lilo," Javier had replied to his sister, "that Roselia and I practice family planning."

"We're going to have to sell one of my calves to pay for the operation," Roselia whispered to Javier one night while their girls slept. After the floods, her grandfather Felipe had given her a cow, and now, like her, it had two daughters.

"Don't worry," Javier whispered back. He could hear his daughters breathing in the bed next to him and he felt lucky. "You're not going to have to sell any calves because tomorrow I'm going to win the lottery."

"You're counting on that?" Roselia whispered back.

In the morning Javier turned on the radio. "*Guaauuuu!*" he cried out. He was as surprised as anyone. Zero and eight. The numbers he always played. He saw that Roselia heard it, too. There would be money left over after the operation for new baby clothes. Javier composed himself and nodded at his wife, as though this were something other than a wonderful coincidence. She smiled back at him, her half smile.

A month later Javier was sitting in his *casita,* after a day work-ing on Víctor's land, still Víctor's land. He was getting fed up with his father-in-law, who had given him a raise, but only to thirty pesos a week. Víctor still treated him like a farmhand, not a son-in-law. His thoughts were interrupted by Roselia and the girls rushing into the house. They had spent the afternoon up the *cordillera,* celebrating the feast of San Antonio, who was the patron saint of the city of Sosúa, where Roselia would give birth. Javier could tell from the strain on his wife's face that he would soon know whether his last child would be a son. Roselia went to bed, and as the sun went down behind the *cordillera,* she called to Javier that the pains were hard, much stronger than they had been with Cristian. She said they were like the pains from Elizabeth's birth. Javier took that as a good sign, a strong boy pushing his way out. He hoped that the lot-tery win had not been his last bit of luck and went out to do what he usually did when he needed to leave the *campo* in a hurry. He went looking for Víctor, or anyone who had a car or a truck.

He and Roselia arrived at the clinic at ten-thirty. There were no screams again this time, but Javier was sure they were giving Roselia drugs. He felt sure that her pains were sharp and strong because he felt them, too. They were pains that did more than hurt, pains that brought change.

An hour later the doctor called out into the waiting room, "Javier Almonte, come and see your fruit. Your boy!"

Javier took the infant in his arms and called him by his name: Mauricio Javier Almonte. Roselia had heard the name Mauricio on a radio *novela.* It sounded close enough to Mario, and Javier had liked it.

"Hijo," he said solemnly, and he began to cry.

Javier did not think his boy, his son, his *varón,* his *hijo,* looked like anyone else in the family. His peering, wet eyes, coffee skin, and intricate curly hair, which Javier refused to call *pelo malo,* signaled life taking a new turn. Javier made all the correct cooing sounds and touched his wife gently. His guts, meanwhile, brawled and rumbled, and he felt himself rising, rising, on that airplane he always saw. He wasn't flying it, though. He was a passenger, and when the real pilot announced *Nueva Llork,* Javier got off, his newborn son in his arms.

In preparation, he stopped working in Víctor's fields and began doing carpentry work on his own. It was a rash move to leave Víctor, particularly since the Dominican sugar market was booming. But that boom, Javier reasoned, was not doing him any good. He found work building huts in the *campo* and doing handyman chores for the doñas in Puerto Plata, anything so that he would not have to go back and cut his father-in-law's *caña* with his father-in-law's Haitians.

Javier felt confused. His children were becoming part of his world but his parents were, it seemed, getting ready to die. He was supposed to alternate his joy with deep sadness, and he did not know how to do that. His father was aging unremarkably, the way Alemán had done almost everything else in his life. He worked fewer days. He walked to Víctor's fields more slowly.

As his mother faded, he finally asked her why she had not let him stay with Tía Angela, so many years before. He was over that, or at least he said he was. But he still wanted an answer from her. "I couldn't leave you. It was too hard," was all she would say. That didn't explain it. Javier knew then that no matter how much he loved his mother and how well he realized that he could have disobeyed her, he would never forgive her for not providing an explanation.

But maybe he had waited too long to ask? His mother began to hold her rosary tighter. She would only wear dresses that had black-and-white or navy-and-white checks. She explained that she had promised her saint she would limit her wardrobe that way. She did not say what she had asked for in return or what she was repenting.

She began to forget. She would put a packet of sugar or a trinket Marta had sent from America into her pocket, not remember where it was, and insist it had been stolen. Gradually she spoke less, until she lost the ability to speak altogether. The lump in her throat grew even larger, and the doctors said it was a tumor they could not remove because she was too frail. Javier suspected that it was because she was too poor. His mother's strong will continued to flash unexpectedly, only now it took the form of displaced laughs, cries, and furious shakes of her head.

12
1975–1976

Marta decided to keep her New York romance a secret from her relatives. Murray Gordon was American, Jewish, thirty years her senior, an accountant, and a retired Army colonel. Besides English and Spanish, which he spoke like a rich Puerto Rican, Murray knew Italian, *Judío,* which was what he called the "language of my tribe," and whatever it was that the people who lived around Israel and didn't like the Jews spoke. Murray had told her many times what that *idioma* was called, but all she could remember was that the Spanish and English words for it sounded alike. Words, especially foreign words, were not Marta's strength. After a decade in New York, she hardly spoke any English. Murray didn't care, though. They always had enough to say to one another. Marta asked him how he had learned to speak so many languages, but he never gave her an answer. She asked him about his family, and he said that he was from Michigan and his parents were dead. Marta wondered if Murray had been a spy.

Murray would be difficult to explain, even to Javier, and even if the romance itself weren't strange, too. Marta and Murray ate dinner together almost every night. But except for an occasional shopping trip, most of their romancing took place at public dinner tables. Marta kept her apartment up in Washington Heights and Murray had his in Greenwich Village. Usually, they dined at the Andalucia, a Spanish restaurant on Seventh Avenue and West Twentieth Street where Marta worked the dinner shift as a waitress. She ate with Murray during her break. The Andalucia served wonderful *paellas,* but Murray preferred meat and potatoes or sometimes a lobster. He always had a few drinks. When Marta had her night off, Murray took her out to eat somewhere else or bought her clothes. He never asked for anything in return. The girls at the Andalucia, whom Murray treated like family, knew that about him. He wouldn't necessarily refuse your favors. But he would never demand them as gratitude. Or tell anyone about them. If, in a moment of weakness, friendship, or solidarity, Marta decided to comfort Murray in some way, or even sleep with him, it was their secret. Murray would never tell and Marta vowed that she, too, would take that information to her grave.

Marta was thinking about Murray now because she was on an airplane back to Santo Domingo. She was usually so busy working or keeping up her apartment on West 188th Street that she didn't have time to think about Murray or anything else. But she needed to keep herself busy on the airplane. Since reading didn't interest her and she wouldn't have been able to concentrate on a magazine anyway, she spent the time thinking.

It was her second trip home in eight years, a trip she had vowed she would never take. She was fatter and blonder than she had been the last time. She had more jewelry, her clothes were flashier, and she had checked a lot of suitcases, one more than last time maybe. They were filled the same way, with clothes and *Van-eeet-te Fay-re* nightgowns for the women. She was glad she had brought the presents, although this time she didn't feel such a desperate need to justify her life by giving all those gifts. She was more relaxed, more capable of countering the gossip she always heard in the *campo*. The year before she had brought her daughter, Cándida, now grown, to America. Cándida was working and they lived together happily in Marta's apartment.

Marta thought about her first airplane ride, from Santo Domingo to San Juan, and how she had been so upset about leaving Jesusito. She left Puerto Rico after six months, as she expected she would. She arrived in New York, stayed with a girlfriend from Moca, and went to work as a nanny for a French woman who had a little girl. She loved the little girl but she hated that she was a maid again. It felt too strange to be taking care of someone else's child when she had left her own children behind. A friend told her they were looking for waitresses at the Andalucia. It was easy to find, just a few blocks from "Seventh Avenue and Seventeenth Street," where Barneys, *la mas grande* men's store in the world, was located.

Every evening she took the subway downtown from her one-bedroom apartment on 188th Street and Audubon Avenue. She arrived at the restaurant by seven. At four in the morning, when her shift was over, she took the subway home again. Her days were magnificent; they were her own. She could cook, clean her apartment, or shop, especially when she didn't sleep all afternoon. And she was always happy to return in the evening to the Andalucia. With its white stone front, wooden door with wrought-iron grating, and lobster tank in the window, it was just as she imagined an inn in Spain might look. Inside there was a beautiful, long hardwood bar, with a mirror behind it so that she could check her face and hair when she came up to order drinks for customers. Murray usually sat on one of the bentwood chairs at his table in the restaurant room, opposite the stage, where Spanish musicians played.

She had met him during her first week at work. He was a slight, well-dressed, gray-haired American. Nervously, she approached his table.

"My usual, please," he said.

Marta was surprised by his elegant Spanish. "What is your usual?" she asked, conscious of her Dominican accent.

"Seven and Seven," a voice from behind her said. It was her boss, the man from Spain who owned the restaurant.

Marta rushed to the bar. This, she realized, was an important customer. When she returned, Murray asked if she wanted a drink, too. She looked at her boss and he nodded. She went to the bar again, checked her face and her hair, and came back with a shot of Johnnie Walker Black poured over ice, for herself.

"How do you like it here?" Murray asked her after she sat.

"I missed my country a lot when I got here." She usually did not admit this. "But I got used to it. People have been very nice, here." She said "very nice" in English to impress Murray. "And there is work here."

Murray told her a little about himself that night, as much as he would ever tell her. Marta held back. She had stopped being naive about men when she was fourteen. She did not tell Murray about the granules of sugar, the dead boy with his bloody head, or about Peralta, Purito, or Jesús Antonio. She knew that if she spoke about Cándida or Jesusito, she would cry.

"Don't drink too much," Murray said to her when she got up from his table. "You'll ruin your health." She took him very seriously. Eventually, Marta told Murray everything.

She had gone back to Santo Domingo the last time—in 1967, eight years earlier—because Jesús Antonio asked her to. He came to New York, found her, and told her he had bought a new house for her in Santo Domingo, but away from the street where she'd seen the boy with his bloody head. At least, he had said, come back and look at the house. Marta didn't want to go, but Murray said it was time she saw her children. He was right. He just didn't understand how hard that would be for her. Cándida didn't know her. Neither did Jesusito. She kept a photograph of him, a little boy in a gabardine suit with a white shirt and a bow tie, and it was hard enough to look at that.

In Santo Domingo, Marta saw the house Jesús Antonio bought for her and realized that she could not leave her Manhattan apartment. She talked to Jesús Antonio and knew she could not give up her dinners with Murray. Her children thought of her as their tía, at least that was her impression. It would be better not to interrupt their lives with her return, or even her visits. She would go back and work hard and send for them when they were older.

I shouldn't even be coming back now, Marta said to herself as she began to doze on the plane. I am only coming because Mami is sick. All these years Mami belonged to Javier. But now that she is sick, it is up to María and me.

Her thoughts before she fell asleep, thoughts that made her dreams frightening, were about her last visit to the *campo*. She had gone up to Camú and Juan de Nina after seeing Jesús Antonio, Jesusito, and Cándida. She could not believe how everything had deteriorated. Had it always looked so bad? Had her brother Lilo, with all his children, always lived so poorly? This was as bad as a city slum. *"Nueva Llork! Nueva Llork!"* people kept saying to her, as though they were offering imaginary toasts. Some of the toasts weren't even imaginary. People poured capfuls of rum when they saw her and cried it out: *"Viva Nueva Llork!"* She tried to tell them how hard she worked, all night, in *Nueva Llork,* but they kept smiling and staring at her jewelry.

"Lilo, would you like to go to *Nueva Llork?"* she had foolishly asked her eldest brother. He now had eleven children in a three-room *casita* and still only a coal stove for making their meals.

"Sí," Lilo said in his plodding, unemotional way. He seemed more like her father than ever. "If you'll bring me."

She had made promises to her siblings, especially Javier. But she did not know how she would ever keep those promises. She had to bring Jesusito first. And she'd have to become a citizen to bring all those brothers and sisters. She'd never get visas for them any other way. Chichito was the only one who didn't want to go, because he had another good job, as a welder. But how could she afford to have them all in New York on her wages and tips from the Andalucia? What if they didn't find jobs? María and Javier would be all right. But Ernesto was irresponsible, and all Lilo knew how to do was cut *caña*.

From the airport in Santo Domingo, Marta took a taxi to
Puerto Plata and a *carro de ruta* to María's house in Gran Parada.
It was late when she arrived, but she stayed up with María.
"You have to remember that Mami can't talk anymore," María
told her. Marta went up to Juan de Nina with this on her mind.
But when she saw the mother whose voice used to scold her,
she asked the same questions as before.

"Mami, how do you feel? Are you tired? Do you want to
know about New York? Do you have enough coffee, enough
sugar?"

Marta kept trying to get answers from Mami. Finally she
conceded María was right; a desperate laugh was all that was left.

"We are only two daughters," Marta said when she returned
to Gran Parada. "You have to take her to live with you."

"Yes, my sister." María was religious and belonged to the
Legion of Mary. "But I can't do it here." María had six children,
and although she lived far better than Lilo, she only had a two-
bedroom *casita*.

Marta knew there was no way out of this. "I can rent a house
for you in Puerto Plata," she said, amazed by her confidence.
What if she lost her job at the Andalucia? But this was what
they expected of her. "Puerto Plata will be better because the
doctors are there."

Marta went back to New York with nothing settled. María's
husband had refused to move. He wouldn't even consider letting Marta pay for an addition to their Gran Parada house,
María said. Marta was annoyed that her older sister let her husband tell her what to do. Marta had never let the will of stub-
born men stand in her way. Even Mami had left Papi when she
wanted to spend a year in the capital. Marta guessed that María
was not the same way. They were bonded by blood but they
had grown up working in separate households, and Marta did
not know her sister that well.

She told Murray about her mother. He said that she needed

more financial security than she had as a waitress, particularly if she was going to take care of the entire *campo*. To Marta he seemed to have quickly become an old man. He was an old man, dying from arteriosclerosis, but, as he reminded her, an old man with veteran's benefits and no family.

"Will you marry me, Marta?" he asked over dinner at the Andalucia.

"*Sí.*"

"The benefits won't make you rich. But they might make you feel more confident about bringing all those relatives of yours here."

"*Sí*, Murray." He was right. She needed to feel more secure. She had been a legal resident of the United States long enough to qualify for citizenship. She could do that without Murray. This would just make her worry less.

"Then it won't look like I died alone. All I ask is that you visit my grave once a year."

"*Sí.* I just need to know how to get to the cemetery."

Marta married Murray Gordon at City Hall. "Look at the Spanish girl," she heard someone in the chapel say. "She's marrying that old man so that she can stay in the country."

Murray told her to stop working at the Andalucia. Although it was not part of his original offer, he rented her an apartment in North Bergen, New Jersey. But he remained in Manhattan. "I wouldn't live in New Jersey," he told her. "It's the *campo*." Marta loved New Jersey. She fixed up her apartment with new furniture she bought herself and spent her days arranging it and cooking. She worked part-time cleaning houses and waiting on tables. But only in New Jersey and only when she felt like it. Once a month Murray took a bus from the Port Authority, ate a meal with Marta, and left her enough money until his next visit.

In New Jersey, Marta received a letter from María that she was leaving her husband and wanted help to rent a house in Puerto Plata for herself, her children, and Mami.

Muddy Cup

⋆ ⋆ ⋆

The job of bringing Demetria to María's new house in Puerto Plata was given, naturally, to Víctor. With Alemán watching from his hut, Víctor, Javier, and some farmhands carried Demetria down the hill to Camú in her black, varnished bed. They helped her into the front seat and put the bed in the back of the truck. Then the workers went back to the fields while Víctor drove Demetria to a pretty white cottage on Vista Alegre, a few blocks from the Malecón. Demetria was silent for most of the ride. She laughed a few times and cried once.

For seven days María and her eldest daughter watched over Demetria in her black, varnished bed. They sat and spoke to her, waiting for a sign that she understood. She would not eat any of the food they tried to give her, so they spooned broth, milk, and coffee into her mouth.

On her eighth morning away from the *campo*, November 1, All Saints' Day, Demetria's mouth froze shut. María, who had worked as a hospital aide in Montellano, put a cup of coffee to her mother's lips to see if she could coax them open. But Demetria did not move. María slapped her mother on the back to see if she could bring up phlegm so that Demetria would have to open her mouth to spit. That did not work either.

After midnight on the fifth of November, 1976, Demetria became quieter than she had ever been. It was twelve days since she had left the *campo,* and although it was autumn, there was no rain.

María said good-bye to the fine features of her mother's face, to her coarse black and graying hair, to the large lump in her throat, and to the wrinkled hands that had nurtured yellow and purple flowers. She took off the *campo* housedress Demetria was wearing and dressed her in the prettiest of the Vanity Fair nightgowns from Marta. She washed her mother's face and felt, as she later told Marta, at peace because she had done all she could. When the undertaker came, María gave him one of Demetria's black-and-white-checked dresses and asked that her mother be buried in her nightgown but with the dress alongside her.

Demetria was placed in a coffin and moved into the large sitting area of the house. María sent one of her sons to the *campo* to find Javier. She sent her daughter to a neighbor's to call Chichito in the Cibao and Marta in New York. Her daughter returned and said she could not get through to New York. A priest came and performed last rites, and at 6 A.M., fifty members of María's chapter of the Legion of Mary arrived to say the rosary.

When Javier was told the news, he cried through his sleepiness and gently woke Roselia. "We'll be back to bury Mami later," he said. "You should rest." He went to wake Ernesto and Lilo, and together they walked to their parents' *casita.*

"Papi, we have to tell you," Javier said.

"I knew," Alemán replied slowly. "I knew that she would not last long."

"It affects us all, Papi." Javier had begun to cry again. "It is something that happens in life."

At dawn, the four men waited by the Bar Osiris for a *carro de ruta* to Puerto Plata. In María's sitting room, Javier stopped short at the sight of his mother's body. He saw himself as a boy, climbing the hill home from school to Juan de Nina, and for what he believed was the first time, he watched his father cry. Then he went to send a telegram to Marta.

In the afternoon the sky darkened in preparation for rain. Víctor arrived and sat with the Almontes as they waited for Marta, as though she would, at any moment, parachute onto the front porch.

Finally, Víctor stood and opened the shuttered window. "It's going to rain a lot," he said.

"I will stay here with Papi," María said.

Demetria's coffin was put in an ambulance, which drove past the nearest church and then as far as the road into Camú, the edge of her *campo.* The coffin was moved to the back of Víctor's pickup. As they passed the *primaria,* a small crowd of friends from Camú and Juan de Nina joined them, walking alongside the truck. Víctor braked the truck at the edge of the steep hill leading up to the cemetery. Javier, Ernesto, Lilo, and Chichito lifted their mother's coffin from the back. They walked a few steps up the hill so that another set of pallbearers could carry Demetria. After a few more steps, that set of pallbearers handed the coffin to another group, until all the men had had a chance to carry Demetria. As they walked, each woman took a turn touching her coffin. At the top of the hill Demetria was buried in the shadow of her *cordillera,* in a grave next to Mirito's and near Pedrito's.

It was almost midnight when Marta arrived in Puerto Plata. "*Ay!* If I knew I was not going to be able to say good-bye to Mami, I would not have come," she shouted as she marched into the sitting room of the house on Vista Alegre.

Marta drank a cup of *yerba buena* tea and told María not to worry. She would continue to pay for the house. Then she counted out a thousand dollars for the burial and the mourning. For nine days they kept the front door closed and mourned. Marta left three days later, after promising to bring them all to New York. This time, though, she knew she could do it. She had an American husband with veteran's benefits. It wouldn't happen quickly and her siblings would not come first. She would bring Jesusito first. And she would have to become a citizen. Murray would help her study for the test.

"Marta paid for the funeral," Abuelo Javier recalls as he watches Spanish television after dinner. "That's when we knew that someday she really would bring us to New York."

A year and a half later, Murray Gordon, age seventy-two, died in his sleep in his apartment at 268 East Tenth Street in Manhattan. He left everything he had to Marta Gordon, his waitress, his friend, and his wife.

After Murray died, Marta went into Manhattan less frequently. But when she did, she made sure to peek into the

Andalucia so that she could see Murray at his table by the stage, drinking a Seven and Seven.

13

1981–1982

At seven, Mauricio, Javier's only son, was a solitary child but not unhappy. As he walked with his mami to the river, he searched for bushes blossoming with white gardenias and bent down to smell the buds. He never picked any since their perfume stayed with him. At the river, his cousins swam but Mauricio did not know how. He would lie on the bank, hang over the water, and try to scoop up small fish in his hands while his mother washed clothes. One cousin had a rusty bicycle, and if he was lucky, Mauricio would get a turn riding it on a pebbled road that ran by the river. It was the smoothest surface in Camú. Although he clung to his mami he didn't mind leaving her to go to school at the *primaria,* to tend to the animals with his father, or to see his grandmother. He didn't have a best friend, or any friends at all. But he was content watching his cousins and his younger aunts and uncles play. When they all gathered by the river or at Víctor and Fian's, he had something to do.

His grandparents' house was fun, even more so after Víctor bought a small black-and-white television set. Mauricio loved to go there on Saturdays, especially if the electricity was working. Then he could watch *Lucha Libre,* a program with staged wrestling matches. He liked the wrestler called Gallina, who, as his name suggested, was more a hen than a man. Gallina could not stand to be hit. He would cover his eyes, duck, and throw salt in his opponent's face. Mauricio, whose sisters teased him relentlessly, covered his eyes along with Gallina. For as long as he could remember, his sisters had teased him. He could remember being two or three years old and running for his mother's teat as she sat on the porch in her white rocker. How many times had Elizabeth or Cristian, giggling and much too big, pushed him away? Then they climbed together into Mami's lap to pretend that they sucked from her, too. "Mami, Mami! *Mi teta! Mi leche!*" If he cried over this, which he usually did, Elizabeth, still laughing, would scold him, "*Ay,* Mauri, you are so greedy." She would keep at it until Mami shooed her away.

On Saturdays, Mauricio ate a small lunch at home before going to his grandparents' house for *Lucha Libre.* Abuelita Fian always made him *tostones,* and while he wanted to eat them, he hated to feel too full. (Mauricio was endlessly amazed by how much his sisters could eat.) As long as the electricity didn't go out and his sisters didn't tattle on him for eating at his grandparents' house—Papi wanted them to take all their meals at home—Mauricio was happy.

Each night he fell asleep in the middle of his parents' bed with his head on his mami's breast, his arms around her. He knew that his papi always moved him to the other side of his mami. But Mauricio slept so soundly that he didn't wake. Even the roosters of Camú when they crowed for the first time at 2 A.M. did not disturb him. He didn't wake when his parents made love, when the roosters crowed again and again to wake Papi, or when his father left for work, still before dawn.

"What happened to you last night?" Javier would ask him at dinner. "You went to bed in one place and woke up facing the wall."

Mauricio always smiled back when Papi said that and tried, without success, to conjure up a sweet memory of travel the night before. After he ate, his father would take him outside to check on the pigs and cows. Mauricio loved that time alone with his father. Papi showed him his carpentry tools and his *machete* and it gave Mauricio a break from his sisters.

One momentous day, Mauricio taught himself to swim. He and his mother were walking away from the river when Roselia remembered she had forgotten her box of powdered soap. Alone, Mauricio went back to get it and was so distracted by the cool prettiness of the water that he jumped into the middle of the river. He felt himself sinking and looked up for the ropes his uncles strung from trees on opposite banks so that his cousins had something to hang on to. But the ropes were not up. He tried to dog-paddle, the way he had seen the other boys do, and was amazed to discover that he could.

Quietly, he began to distinguish himself at the *primaria*. It was the same palm-hut school his parents had attended, except its thatch roof had been replaced by zinc. They had books for each subject now, too. But the students still had to buy or borrow their own copies. Mauricio used the ones his sisters, who were in higher grades, had completed, and sometimes he shared them with his cousins who were his age. All the cousins recognized that although Mauricio was shy, he was also smart, particularly in reading. He did have trouble with mathematics, though. Fortunately, Maestra Quisqueya and her string bean plants were long gone from the *primaria*. Mauricio loved the stories his papi told him about those days, but he was glad that his teachers did not hit him. Instead, if he did not know his schoolwork, he had to stay late or finish it at home.

He began to need his mother less. One afternoon, when Roselia and Cristian went to see Fian, Mauricio stayed behind because he wanted to sit outside by himself. He sat for a long time, studied his mother's mango tree in front of the *casita* and the yard around them. When he was smaller, he had helped his Abuelo Alemán pull out weeds that were threatening the tree and earned a peso for his efforts. Abuelo Alemán had left him so suddenly, dying when Mauricio was five, three years after Abuelita Meme. Mauricio barely remembered his father's mother.

He turned to watch his mother's breadfruit tree behind the hut and thought about what he might need. His mother had left coconuts under the tree, and when Mauricio saw them, he decided he was thirsty. He wondered if he could peel one by himself. Elizabeth was in the *casita* and could help him. But she was sleeping. Mauricio went into the kitchen and found his father's *machete*.

Outside he made one deep cut into the thick, brown, stringy shell. He made another and peeled off a section of the shell. That was how he had seen his father, his uncles, and his cousins do it. With great confidence he thrust the *machete* deep into the meat of the coconut and then jumped as it slipped into his thumb.

He was too surprised to cry. He stared at his thumb, bleeding and split. A rooster came by, pecked at a little piece of food, and took the morsel in its beak. Mauricio looked again and realized that the rooster was carrying a piece of the skin of his thumb. He ran inside.

"Elizabeth," he yelled into his sister's ear as he tried to keep from bleeding onto her bed. He was holding his thumb with his good hand and, by now, was crying. "Elizabeth, please wake up." He tried to shake her with his arm and elbow, but she rolled onto her other side.

He ran to the kitchen and put his hand into the metal barrel where Mami kept an emergency water supply. He watched the water turn red, looked up, and saw his mother, sister, and father walking up the path to the *casita*.

It was after he cut himself that Mauricio became aware of his parents' conversations. They would sit outside the kitchen, fidget and creak on the chairs his father repaired all the time, some of them woven in rope, others replaced with leather strips. Mauricio, who was supposed to be asleep in the bedroom in the next hut, heard his father talk about *inmigración* and a place he called *Nueva Llork*. He loved to listen but did not imagine himself in *Nueva Llork*. Mauricio preferred the *campo*. He liked the river and the little television at his grandparents' house. He had heard other people talk about emigrating. That was unavoidable, everyone talked about it. His parents said the same things everybody else did. Phrases like "While I am gone . . ." Or questions like "How do you know you'll get a visa?" or "How will you send money? . . . How will you find a job?" Or answers like *"Me lo busco."* I will look for one. He heard his father tell his mother, "Mauricio will go to school in America someday." His father's voice was low and serious. But it was as if he were speaking about someone else.

14

1982–1983

Javier, followed by his sister María, and two of his three surviving brothers—Lilo and Ernesto—made their way past the flashing clothes and shaded faces of scores of nervous visa applicants. Javier had been in crowds like this on the Malecón in Puerto Plata. But he couldn't remember ever seeing so many people in one building. All these *dominicanos* want to go to America? Well, why not? The four of them wanted to go. Only their brother Chichito, who still had a good job in the Cibao, had decided not to go. Javier could not believe that they had made it past the wrought-iron grating, the guards, and the concrete walls to the inside of the U.S. consulate. He might as well be flying one of El Jefe's majestic old silver airplanes over the capital.

They walked past the portrait of Ronald Reagan, who looked like a nice enough man, and upstairs, where there seemed to be no seats. Javier looked into the eyes of the people in one row that did not seem too packed, and they shifted over until four small places appeared for the Almontes.

Javier chuckled at Ernesto's silly jokes, calmed María, and admired Lilo's stoicism in the face of all this turmoil. Lilo out of the *campo* was hard to fathom. Javier also tried to pay attention to the loudspeaker so that they would not miss hearing their name. *Familia* Almonte. In America, they would be without their spouses and children. The four of them and Marta would be *familia* Almonte in *Nieu Yersey*. It was, Marta had said, so close to *Nueva Llork* they wouldn't know the difference.

If all went well at this *cita* and they got their visas, Javier would be able to say that the last thing he built in the Dominican Republic was a resort. He had been hired as part of the construction crew that was building the Dorado Naco condominiums in Playa Dorada. More European tourists were coming to Playa Dorada every day, and it was said the service would one day be good enough for Americans. That sounded like exciting news to Javier. But not exciting enough to keep him from leaving. Some of his neighbors in the *campo* believed that Playa Dorada would make them rich. Javier had already seen how rich it was going to make him. On the Dorado Naco crew he had earned four hundred pesos a month. Sure, it was a lot more than the thirty pesos a week Víctor had finally paid him in the end. But Marta told him that in America he could make twice as much money cleaning office buildings. Imagine what he could make as a carpenter.

"Familia Almonte!" Javier strained to make sure they were the ones being called. *"Familia Almonte. Favor de presentarse a la casilla número seis."* "Hurry up!" scolded María. Javier tried to calm her with his eyes. He wanted to remember this moment. It was 12:30 P.M. on the twenty-eighth of November, 1982. It had been four hours since they had arrived at the consulate, nine hours since they'd left Camú, three weeks since the notice had come calling them for their *citas*. It had been three years since Marta, now an American citizen, had sent out the papers that said she would find them all jobs if the U.S. government would only grant them *residencia*.

"Familia Almonte, por favor!"

"Let's go!" ordered María.

From window six, they were sent to an office where an American man sitting at a desk, a black man, told them, in Spanish, to sit on the seats in front of them. They sat, a reflection of their own country's experience with history and color. Lilo was the darkest, Javier was brown skinned but lighter than Lilo. Ernesto was lighter than Javier, and María was almost white. She could be Spanish or American, Javier thought. Then he looked up at the visa officer.

"This *hombre*, this visa officer? All I can tell you is that he was a nice black man," Abuelo Javier says a decade later, from the plastic-covered couch in his Queens living room. The story of his *cita* has reenergized him; he was tired of reminiscing about the *campo*. "That's how we refer to him

still. *Un negrito muy amable.* **That's how you want to remember them. Not by name. With Roselia we learned that the hard way. Roselia's visa officer was named Mueller. Jonathan Mueller. We'll never forget that name. You don't want to remember your visa officer's name."**

The officer began with Lilo. When he called him Antonio—Lilo's real name, Papi's real name—Javier felt a shiver. He had never heard anyone, even Mami, call his father Antonio. He had only seen it written, most recently on Papi's death certificate.

"So, Antonio, how many children do you have?"

Javier studied his brother.

Lilo did not say a word.

"Antonio?"

"I . . . don't . . . have . . . any."

María opened her mouth and looked at Javier. Javier looked sharply at Ernesto to keep him from giggling. Marta would kill Lilo if she were here. She would take his neck in her hands and wring it. "Tell the truth," she had said in her letters. "The most important thing is to tell the truth." Lilo's eleven children were now between thirty-three and fifteen years old. Javier could remember the scenes of all of them inside those three rooms. With Lilo's grandchildren, it could look that way now. Did he mean he didn't have babies anymore?

The visa officer looked down at his papers. He peered up at Lilo. "Antonio, you don't have children? Antonio, tell me the truth."

The black *yanqui* spoke that last sentence softly, drawing out the words, as though he were talking to a child. As though he were Roselia when Javier made one of his grandiose claims. Javier was relieved.

María didn't see it. *"Compadre!"* she scolded. "Tell him the truth. You better tell him what you have."

"Well," Lilo said. "I have eleven. But no more than eleven."

The officer nodded. "How can we do this? Eleven children without a father? Are they all in your house?"

"Yes!" Lilo said brightly. Javier knew that his brother meant he'd had all his children with one woman. Lilo had neither time nor money for infidelity.

"Oh." The officer turned to Javier. "Mario, do you have children?"

Javier stiffened. *"Sí, señor."*

"How many?"

"Three."

"Yes. What are their names?"

"Elizabeth, Cristian, Mauricio."

"Nice."

"Ernesto?"

"I don't have any."

Javier couldn't believe this. Ernesto had four children he recognized and possibly a few more. But the officer just nodded. So maybe he was getting away with it.

In her best religious-society voice, María reported that she had four girls and two boys and asked if she could get visas as soon as possible for her two youngest daughters.

"If you ask for your husband, first," the officer said, "it might be easier to get the children."

María did not say a word.

Late that night, the siblings returned to Camú, jubilant. When Roselia asked Javier if they had all gotten visas, he thought it was a silly question. Of course they had all gotten visas, he told his sleepy *esposa*. That was the way it worked when you had a *cita* together. That's why he had been so nervous that Lilo or Ernesto would ruin all of their chances. He went to the closet in the bedroom and touched Mirito's dagger. It was all he had left of his brother and he would have to leave it in Camú. Javier hoped there would be no discussion with Roselia about whether or not he meant to go. He had told her that he was going. "Mauricio will go to school in America someday," he reminded her before he fell asleep.

★   ★   ★

The next morning, eight-year-old Mauricio found himself in the middle of a small circle made up of his two older sisters, jumping and singing at him, *"Papi se va. Papi se va."* Elizabeth, he knew, had talked Cristian into teasing him. She now went to the school in Montellano, and she thought a lot of herself.

Later, his father took him aside.

"I have something very sad to tell you, Mauri. I am going to be separated from you for a while."

Mauricio raised his dark eyes to his father but did not speak.

"It is better," Javier continued. "I'm doing it for your education and our finances. One day you will all come to America and live with me."

Mauricio did not really understand. They seemed to have all they needed. He liked the *primaria.* He wandered back outside and Elizabeth curled her arm around him. He was glad to see she was out of her teasing mood. "Mauri, he once told me that I might go on an airplane to America. I thought it was a joke."

His father came over to him. "When I go, you will be the man of the house." His father smiled. "Keep an eye on the women. Make sure Elizabeth and Cristian behave!"

"Papi!" Elizabeth complained.

Mauricio did not know what to make of this.

"Can you buy me a bicycle in America, Papi?" he asked.

Now his parents talked about the trip during the day, when they knew he was listening. Mauricio liked it best when they made jokes, which were usually about Tío Ernesto. As far as Mauricio could tell, Ernesto was showing off his visa at the Bar Osiris and using it to try to make women fall in love with him. It took months for Papi, his aunt, and uncles to leave. They couldn't even set a date until Jesusito, Tía Marta's son, was settled. Jesusito, who had grown up with his father, Jesús Antonio, in the capital, had gotten his visa at the same time. Marta wanted to enroll him in a school in *Nieu Yersey.*

After Jesusito left for America, Mauricio's father, aunt, and uncles seemed to be rushing and worrying whenever he saw them. Tía María burned Abuelita Demetria's black, varnished bed behind the Vista Alegre house. It had been splintering and breaking, and Tía María said she did not want to come back from America and see it sitting in the trash in pieces. His father needed to finish the *gallera* he had started in Camú. That, Mauricio thought, would be the last thing his father would build in the Dominican Republic. He was proud of the *gallera*'s height. He told himself that he would never forget that his papi had built the highest structure in Camú, higher even than the roof of the church.

Papi sold some pigs to pay for the plane ticket. Then Papi needed new teeth for America. He came home from Puerto Plata one day with his mouth gleaming and white and began to pack.

His father left for America on February 5, 1983. Mauricio was eight and a half by then and he went to the Puerto Plata airport to say good-bye. The boy, still slight and a bit short for his age, did not think life without his father would be too bad. It was not as if Mami were leaving, too. As long as Mami stayed, he was fine.

At the airport there were too many people, too many sights. He was not used to crowds. He had only been in crowds like this on the Malecón. He couldn't ever remember seeing so many people in one building. In the midst of the airport crowd there was a smaller but even more terrifying group. People Mauricio was supposed to know, friends and relatives of his father's and of his aunts' and uncles'. Mauricio had never imagined that he was connected to so many people. He had seen many of them before, individually. But never all together like this. His delicate head bounced back and forth as he watched all those people he was supposed to know and tried to keep track of all of them. They hovered around the baggage lines and the kiosks that sold bottles of Coke and Country Club soda. The ones with cameras went to the window and took pictures of the Capitol Airlines jet that would take Papi to

America. Then they took pictures of Mauricio and his sisters and pointed them out to other people. *Mauri, el varón de Javier. Elizabeth y Cristian, las hembras.* Some of those people cried. Mauricio didn't cry. Cristian did. He knew she would. Elizabeth didn't. He knew that, too.

"What are you all crying for?" thirteen-year-old Elizabeth shouted to no one in particular. She sounded even more angry than usual. "They're not dead. They're not dying. You people are acting like they're going to die."

Through the crowd Mauricio searched for his parents and saw them sitting next to each other on hard plastic chairs by the window. His mother's head was on his father's shoulder. His uncles Ernesto and Lilo were standing nearby.

Mauricio walked over and sat next to his mother. Tío Ernesto bent over toward his father and asked to borrow money for the departure tax.

"You had the money last week," his father said to his uncle. "That's why Marta sent it. We need *dólares* to leave. It was your responsibility not to spend it."

"Ernesto." Lilo sighed. Mauricio thought his elderly uncle sounded even more tired than usual. "I barely have enough money for myself."

Mauricio watched the group around Ernesto grow. How could his uncle have spent so many American *dólares* in Camú? One of María's sons joined them and offered to give Ernesto pesos to exchange, if he agreed to pay him back with interest.

"*Nueva Llork.*" Mauricio heard them call his father's flight. People began moving all around him, away from him. He felt himself being grabbed. He turned and saw his father's new white teeth gleaming down at him. His father's smile had changed with those teeth.

"I'm taking off!" He picked up Mauricio and kissed him on the lips and on both of his cheeks. "You will be the man of the house!"

Mauricio followed his father with his eyes. He saw him on line. He saw him showing his ticket, walking through a door.

That night, Mauricio fell asleep in his mother's arms, as he usually did. At dinner the next evening he expected to see Papi and felt uncomfortable when his father did not arrive. He remembered things he had done not just with Papi but with Abuelo Alemán, who also seemed to have left him suddenly.

"You are the man of the house," Mami told him during the days that followed. He became tired of hearing it. He still slept with her every night but would wake up in the same spot where he had fallen asleep. He tried to imagine *Nueva Llork*. But all he could see was a boy waking up in a familiar bed with his face against the wall. He didn't want to go to *Nueva Llork*. He wanted Papi to come home, instead.

One night Mami put her feet on top of his and said she was cold.

He felt the chill and remembered that he did not want to be the man of the house. He wanted to be alone. He loved his mother. But now she was bothering him.

Mauricio kicked her away and jumped out of the bed. "Why don't you get a torch or something?" he asked.

He began to wait for Abuelo Víctor to return from his fields in the late afternoon. But when Víctor arrived on his white horse, Mauricio had to set his sights as high as the *cordillera* to look his grandfather in the eye. Víctor would get off his horse and hug him. But Mauricio still felt Víctor was too tall to reach.

Mauricio spent a lot of time at his grandparents' house, anyway. Two of his older uncles had motorcycles and they gave him rides. He ate meals made by Fian, whenever he could. Mami did not get angry. With Papi gone, she had changed the rule.

Mauricio noticed that his sisters seemed interested in boys. Since the Montellano school now stopped at eighth grade, Elizabeth had enrolled at the Liceo José DuBeau, the *secundaria* in Puerto Plata. Often she stayed with their cousins at María's Puerto Plata house so that she could take English lessons in the evening. Elizabeth had a boyfriend who came over after school. The boyfriend always gave Mauricio twenty-five centavos and sent him to the grocery to buy himself wintergreen mints. They were two for five centavos. One afternoon Mauricio returned from the store and found Mami screaming at Elizabeth. When Elizabeth wasn't with her boyfriend or studying, she was watching *telenovelas* with Fian. Mauricio tried to stay away from the television when the two of them were watching.

An old fat man, whose name he did not know, seemed to be watching his other sister, Cristian.

15
1983–1986

Javier Almonte was in the backseat of a blue Chevrolet Caprice, riding west from Long Island on the Northern State Parkway. His brothers sat on either side of him but they were falling asleep, so Javier studied the road. Even in the dark he could make out the green mounds and northern trees he remembered from the ride out. These *yanquis* had built a park and its only function was to surround the road. They had the wherewithal to do this here, and, it seemed, no need to congratulate anyone. At home a project on the scale of this Northern State Parkway, if it was ever finished, would have a sign enumerating its virtues in the same breath as the name of the *presidente:* EL SEÑOR PRESIDENTE MADE THIS ROAD WITH ITS SMOOTH ASPHALT AND SCENIC BOUNDARIES FOR THE PEOPLE OF THE DOMINICAN REPUBLIC. Even if they never finished it, somebody would be thanked.

Javier couldn't imagine there wasn't somebody who needed to be thanked for the Northern State Parkway. But there was so much to do in a new country. You couldn't stop and search for an explanation each time. Forget about it. Some of your curiosities had to remain suspended, nagging reminders that you no longer lived in the place where you were born. He wondered if he should be suspending his disappointments, too. The small ones, at least. He was disappointed, for example, that this Chevy was not his. Just like every other car he had ever been in, in his entire life. Just like Víctor's pickup, Víctor's tractor, the cars he had commandeered the two times his wife had babies in clinics, the *carros de ruta* and *guaguas* he took to reserve duty in Puerto Plata, the big buses that took him to the capital three times in his life, hopeful as he began each trip.

He had only been in America for three months and he hadn't expected to have a car of his own so soon. But at the least, he had expected a full-time job, with a reasonable salary. Instead he had just spent three hours mopping floors, cleaning toilets, and learning to use *el vacuum cleaner* in an office building in one of the wealthiest places he had ever seen, although they paid him the minimum wage.

It was spring. At home it was time to cut the *caña*. He had been better off in Víctor's fields, with Víctor's Haitians. He had been better off not knowing how to work a vacuum cleaner. He had certainly been better off building Dorado Naco, which at least afforded him the honor of a job in construction, a man's field.

How could he explain this to Roselia? It had been so much better when he and his brothers and sister first arrived, even with the snow and cold. The four of them were living in Marta's apartment in *Nieu Yersey* and she had helped María find a job taking care of an elderly widow in Manhattan. She found a job for Javier renovating the bathroom of an apartment owned by a friend of hers. The woman had paid Javier a hundred dollars a day because Marta had said that was what Javier was worth. As long as he was renovating that bathroom, Javier had believed everything he'd heard about America. He sent money home to Roselia, told her to buy new pigs to replace the ones they had sold for his ticket.

Now he would have to tell her that here, like home, one good job did not always follow another. He was lucky to have this job cleaning an office building. That was because of Marta, too.

How to explain this to Roselia? Finally Marta had called Feli Colon, the husband of her daughter, Cándida. Feli, who owned the Caprice and was driving it now, was a foreman for a cleaning company. He had work for all three brothers. It was on Long Island, far from *Nieu Yersey*. But he had told Marta not to worry. He had a friend in Queens with an apartment to rent. There would be enough room for María when she came home from her widow on weekends. What would Roselia think? Javier wondered. Would she think that Marta was trying to get rid of them?

His brothers were snoring. Javier craned his neck over one of their shoulders and then the other. They were almost back to Queens. Javier was hungry. After work Feli had offered to make them coffee, right there in the office. He had prepared American coffee with nothing but powder and hot water from a pot he plugged into the wall. Javier had been amazed that it was ready so quickly. "So modern," he said as he lifted the cup to his mouth. But it had been such a disappointment. He still couldn't get the terrible weak taste of it out of his mouth. He wanted to ask Feli why the *yanquis* made such good roads and such rotten coffee.

He leaned forward to the driver's side. "Feli, what did you call that place?"

"What place?"

"Where we worked?"

"Merrill Lynch?"

"No, the *residencial.*"

"Long Island?"

"There was another name."

"Garden City?"

"Excuse me?"

"Jardín Ceetee."

"Ay. Sí."

Feli had said it was a village. Hmm. Some village. Wide streets, all of them newly paved, perfectly clean, and filled with houses good enough for a *presidente*. Javier had always said that *tierra* was the most important thing. But he liked to think of himself as a builder, too. And he couldn't get over those houses. *Guaaauw!* Houses with three stories, wide front doors, large windows or lots of small ones with shutters painted purple, blue, or black. That kind of paint was expensive. And the houses had land, too. Land behind them and, in front, green gardens blooming with so many buds Javier could feel his mother caressing and arranging her *mantequillas* and *moradas*.

"Why don't you live there, Feli?" Javier asked.

"What are you talking about?"

Javier was only half kidding. He had seen apartment buildings in *Jardín Ceetee*, like ones in Queens, only not as tall. If someone like Feli, who was a foreman for the Gotham Building Maintenance Company in Manhattan, could live there, Javier wanted to know about it.

"Whew, Javier," Feli said. "I couldn't live there. Forget about it. It's very expensive in this country. People live where they can."

As they traveled west toward the city, the road became bumpy and there was more traffic. Javier smelled gasoline instead of grass. They turned from one highway, briefly onto another, and then drove away from the highways altogether. Feli took a right turn onto a wide street crowded with apartment buildings. Junction Boulevard, the sign said. *Yunshun,* Javier repeated. On the way out to Long Island that afternoon, those apartment buildings on *Yunshun* had seemed stately and elegant. They had reminded Javier of Marta's apartment building in *Nieu Yersey*. He had seen white, rectangular signs that said DOCTOR in some of the apartment windows, luxurious draperies hanging in others. But after Garden City, he was not as impressed. He wondered how so many lives could be crammed into one building. The house in which he and his brothers had rented their apartment had only three floors, but each had a different tone. The three of them, and María on weekends, lived upstairs. The landlord lived downstairs with his family. In the basement, a few small rooms were rented out to single men, immigrants mostly, who had come without any family.

The people on this part of *Yunshun* looked Chinese. As they traveled north on the boulevard, the faces became more familiar, more *Espanish*. The houses were smaller. They rode underneath an elevated subway platform and passed rows of attached houses made from a red brick Javier had never seen at home. The windows were barred with pieces of wrought iron shaped into curlicues. Then the houses were replaced with shops, the heart of the boulevard. They passed garbage-strewn streets filled with *bodegas,* Argentine, Colombian, and Peruvian restaurants, and travel agencies advertising trips to every Spanish-speaking country, except Cuba. Feli competed with each gypsy-cab driver who tried to cut him off. One of the taxis belonged to a Quisqueya Car Service, and Javier was comforted. The big Dominican neighborhood was in Manhattan. But there were enough *dominicanos* here. Their landlord was from Santiago.

Feli made a left turn onto Fortieth Road, and stopped in front of a wood house covered with yellow aluminum siding. Javier and his brothers got out of the car and opened the chain-link fence. Javier walked up the uneven brick steps, followed by Lilo and Ernesto. He took out his key, opened the door. Inside the foyer, painted a mossy green, Javier checked the mail the landlord had left on top of the radiator and took his letter. Then he walked with his brothers up the wooden staircase. Inside their plain, furnished apartment Javier sat down on the couch, put his feet up, and looked out the window at the side alley, at another house that was like this one but without yellow siding. He opened a letter from Roselia, read it, and thought about making himself a slow cup of coffee.

Abuelo Javier gets up from the plastic-covered couch. He says he has to be at work early. He is making a friend's basement into an apartment. There are so many immigrants coming to Queens, it would be a pity if his friend couldn't make money from that space.

"There were plenty of *dominicanos* when I first moved here ten years ago," he says. "By the time Roselia arrived, there were even more. Unemployment in my country was at twenty-five percent by then. You say it was history and politics that created the Dominican community in

America? You say it was the immigration law? It's okay if you think that. Do you want to know what I think? I think it was Marta." He stops to laugh. "The Dominican community in America was created by Marta. That's why Marta is La Cabeza."

The Dominican community in America was created by a lot of Martas. Many of them came after Trujillo's assassination when, for the first time in decades, restrictions on immigration were relaxed. More came after the civil war in 1965, convinced that even without Trujillo, their country would not improve politically or economically. Often, the immigrants were people like Marta, who had moved from the *campo* to the cities and were now taking the next step.

In 1965, a few months after Marta left Puerto Rico for New York, President Johnson signed a new immigration law. One of its provisions limited the number of immigrants who could come from the Western Hemisphere—until then immigration to the United States from any other nation in the Western Hemisphere had been more or less a free-for-all. But despite the way it seemed, the new law did anything but limit immigration from the Caribbean. That was because another provision made family ties the all-important requirement for prospective immigrants. The Martas of the world began studying the law—there was a hierarchy under which some relatives received preference—and preparing to bring their families to America.

"Count how many of our relatives wouldn't be here if it wasn't for Marta starting it," Abuelo Javier says as he heads toward his bedroom. "It's over twenty now. It's our family, María and her children, her ex-husband, his new wife and her children. Some of Lilo's children. Some of his grandchildren. When we went to Juan de Nina on my fiftieth birthday, remember we saw one of Lilo's daughters at the river? Didn't she say she had been called for her *cita*? Every time I count, another one comes."

Abuelo Javier claims that he will never tire of talking. "But you should speak to Mauricio now," he says. "He's the one in college. He's the young immigrant."

Alone and with time to think, it was the airplane that came back to Roselia. She was pregnant with Elizabeth and Javier had called her outside.

"I'm going to go up in that plane," he said, pointing to the sky. She did not pay attention. She thought he was teasing.

But now she knew it had all been planned. He had planned to go to America, leave her alone with the children, leave *her*. She was not afraid of raising her children alone. They were older now, and she had taken care of her sister and brothers before them. She knew how to be a mother; she had her own mother down the road to tell her if she was doing a good job. But there was nothing she could do to keep Javier from leaving her. For good. Her friends talked about men who went to America, found new *esposas*, and never came home to keep their promises. They said things like that right in front of Roselia. But that was how it was in the *campo*. If you got fat you could be sure that your friends would tease you and call you *gordita*. Being fat used to be a good thing. Even El Jefe liked his women fat. But in America, Roselia had heard, women were supposed to be very thin. She was afraid that Javier would leave her because she did not compare well to women in America, women like his sister Marta. Marta wasn't so thin, but she was an American citizen.

It would be easy for Javier to find someone else. They weren't even married. Javier could disappear into America without any proof that he had ever lived with her. Even in the *campo* Ernesto had gotten away with leaving the mother of his children. Javier could certainly get away with it in America. She had wanted Javier to marry her before he left. But he had told her that Marta could not bring him to America if he was married.

Married siblings could not come. It had to be unmarried siblings. Roselia wondered if that was true. Javier had promised he would come home and marry her eventually.

At night, to calm her fears, Roselia read over the letters Javier had sent her from America. He had written the first one after he had been in New York for five days:

> Sra. Roselia González.
> Carretera Luperón. Kilómetro 14 (Camú) Puerto Plata.
> Dom. Rep.
> Roselia my love, You don't want to know how much I miss you all in this country so far from all of you. It is beautiful and marvelous. But there is a lot of snow now and it's not my favorite. I hope that God blesses you and that you send me a letter for each one that I write you. I am hoping that you take care of yourself and hoping that God with all his power will make sure that we will live together someday in this country. It is completely different from our country. But I like everything that is different. . . . Here in relation to water, everything is hot and cold.

Often he sent her instructions: "Elizabeth should take care and study a lot and pay a lot of attention to English because that is what is worth something here. If I don't have a brilliant job, it is because I do not speak the language."

Those letters, although not romantic, comforted Roselia, too, because Javier sounded as though he was continuing their life together.

At first Javier's letters came from "Kennedy Boulevard, North Bergen, New Jersey." Roselia knew that was Marta's apartment. Then the tone changed and so did the return address: "Fortieth Road, Elmhurst, New York." Roselia could not imagine how any of those places looked. She was sure she wasn't saying their names properly. She liked to think about what was right in front of her anyway, and when she did that she had a sense, for the first time since she had begun living with Javier, the first time ever in her life, that she should earn some money. The work in America was not going to be as steady as Javier had told her it would be. He never promised that he would become rich in America. But she had expected it to be better than this.

When she was finished with his letters, she always put them under her mattress, not to hide or protect them but because she felt that if they were there, it would feel as though her *esposo* were closer to her while she slept. And she would remember to do something about the practical matters he brought up.

After Javier had been gone from the *campo* for a few months, Roselia began to do laundry for the grandmother of one of Elizabeth's friends. The grandmother of the boy who came to visit Elizabeth. (Roselia hoped that he was not Elizabeth's boyfriend.) The work was hard but Roselia was relieved to do it. It didn't take up all of her time so she began to collect money for lottery tickets, which was another relief and also more fun. People needed to see her to buy their tickets.

In the summer of 1983 Javier wrote that he was happier. He had made friends with his landlord, a man named Frank Corona, who was from Santiago but had an interesting job as a longshoreman in Manhattan.

In September he wrote that he did not have to clean offices anymore. Marta had found him a construction job with a builder in New Jersey. The only problem was that he had to get up at five in the morning to get there. He said that he wished he had the roosters of Camú to get him out of bed. But he sounded well.

Roselia wrote back to say that Cristian was now going to José DuBeau, the *secundaria,* with Elizabeth, although she was not as eager a student. In October Javier wrote that things were even better. One of Frank Corona's daughters worked as a secretary for an Italian builder in Woodside, which, he explained, was also in Queens. The daughter had asked her boss for a job for Javier. And he had given him one—for eight dollars an hour! Full-time. *Guauuuw!*

In November Javier wrote that Lilo had found a factory job

in *Nieu Yersey* and had taken a room there. Ernesto was working for a company that cleaned La Guardia Airport in Queens.

Roselia was dazed. So many new names, of places and people. As soon as she memorized one name, another came along. Javier began to send her more money. It seemed like a lot of money to Roselia. She kept doing laundry and collecting lottery tickets anyway and used what she earned to pay for Elizabeth's English lessons. She wanted Elizabeth to be able to speak English when her father came home for a visit, as Roselia hoped he would.

In December Roselia had to write to tell Javier that his brother Chichito, the only one of the siblings not in America, had been killed in a car accident in the Cibao. Chichito, she reminded Javier, had been fifty-four. Javier wrote back to say that he would be coming home for a visit in January. He wrote that while he was home, he and Roselia would go to Puerto Plata to get married. That way he could apply for visas for her and the children.

When Papi arrived home, after being away for almost a year, Mauricio did not know what to make of the man he saw who wore sunglasses. Papi had never worn sunglasses before. Mauricio had never heard his father even complain about the sun. His father wore a new shirt. This American shirt came in a shade of blue Mauricio was sure he had never seen before.

One afternoon his father put on another strange blue shirt. His mother put on a blue dress. They told him they were going to Puerto Plata to get married in the civil building. Mauricio thought that his mother looked peaceful when they returned that evening.

"This means I can bring all of you to America," Papi said.

"Will you buy me a bicycle in America?" Mauricio asked.

His father left again. Mauricio went to the airport to say good-bye.

As before, more news came from America. Frank Corona

had been in a terrible accident at the pier where he worked. He had lost his right arm and his right leg. Papi had visited him in the hospital and had assured his friend he would take care of the house on Fortieth Road.

Papi wrote to say that he and Ernesto had to move again because his landlord Frank Corona, now home and convalescing, needed their apartment for one of his daughters. But they had found another nice place to live in a *bloque* house only a few blocks away, although the address would now be Corona, as in Frank's name, not Elmhurst. He would, he said, always be friends with Frank Corona.

Mauricio finished the *primaria,* and in September 1985 he joined his sisters at the *secundaria.* He was as quiet as before, but still not unhappy, although he made no friends and did not tell his teachers that his papi was in America.

His father kept sending money and his mother bought another pig.

His mother went into the hospital in Santiago to have a kidney stone removed. She convalesced for a few days at the home of Frank Corona's sister-in-law.

In the beginning of February of 1986 Papi came home for the second time in three years. There was no bicycle but he brought blue jeans for Mauricio, boots for Elizabeth, a dress for Cristian, and another one, in that American blue, for Mami. While his father was visiting, Mauricio's cousins came out from the house in Puerto Plata with a notice from the American consulate in Santo Domingo. Mauricio, his sisters, and his mother had been called for their *cita* on February 19. Mauricio heard his mother ask his father to stay and go with them. He heard his father tell his mother that he couldn't because his Italian boss in New York needed him back at work. "With all of us in America, we're going to need a lot of money," Papi said, laughing.

"I'll see you in *Nueva Llork,*" he said to Mauricio. Then he left for his airplane again.

16

February 1986

Mauricio kicked the pebbles on the road that ran down the middle of Camú. The pebbles were nothing. The real problem was the large rocks that popped out of what always seemed like a clear, easy stretch. He could walk around those rocks and Abuelo Víctor's pickup and tractor could ride over them. But with a bicycle he would have to prepare himself before each bump to avoid popping a tire or falling over. That was why he and his sisters rode their cousins' bicycles on the path by the river Camú. It only had pebbles. Mauricio wondered what it would be like to ride his own new bicycle on the smooth side-walks Papi had described. He heard Abuelo Víctor start the engine. Mauricio ran up the hill to his grandparents' house and jumped into the back of the truck.

An hour later Mauricio, his mother, and his two sisters were in a bus traveling south on the two-lane Carretera Duarte, the country's highway. Cars that wanted to pass the bus had to wait until there was no oncoming traffic in the northbound lane. Mauricio held his breath each time a car passed the bus. They drove through the Cibao and he wondered, for the second time in two weeks, what would have happened if Columbus had found gold there.

Before last week he had never been to the capital. Now he was making his second trip. Last week they had all been to the Clinic Abreu for medical examinations. That was where the papers that had come with the notice of their *cita* had told them to go. The Clinic Abreu had been dark and noisy, and it didn't seem that much better than a Puerto Plata clinic. But on this trip he would get to see the consulate.

They stopped in Santiago and spent the night with people who were related to Papi's friend Frank Corona.

At seven-thirty the next morning, February 19, 1986, they arrived at the U.S. consulate in Santo Domingo. Mauricio could not stop smiling when he saw the building. It was made from *bloques,* of course. But these were not the dull gray *bloques* of José DuBeau, the *secundaria* in Puerto Plata. These were white and they shimmered in the sun.

Mauricio skipped so that he could keep up with his mother and sisters. He did not know why his mother was so nervous and complained of so many headaches that morning when she drank her *yerba buena* tea. Papi had said they had everything they needed. The guards at the gate sent them inside and more guards sent them upstairs, but there was no place to sit. Mauricio was surrounded by other children. A lot of the girls were in frilly dresses. The boys were wearing new shirts and jeans, as he was, or sports jackets. Some of the jackets looked too small for the boys. The arms were too short. Mauricio was glad that he didn't have a jacket.

They were calling names over the loudspeaker. But everyone was talking and laughing so much that Mauricio could not hear clearly. Only his mother was quiet. She leaned against the wall and read her Bible.

A man went around to the people who were standing and told them to go back downstairs. Mauricio followed his mother and sisters and took a seat between them on a wooden bench. They had benches just like that in Camú, but it hurt to sit on this one. The wood rubbed against his bottom. It was as though his bottom were all bones. He wanted to get up but he didn't dare. Other people came and filled the other seats and more stood around them. Mauricio squirmed so that he would feel more comfortable and noticed that on the wall behind him there was a painting of Señor Ronald Reagan. Mauricio thought that the president of the United States was smiling at him the way grown-ups do when they are making up their minds.

Roselia opened her Bible again.

"Mami, I'm hungry," Mauricio said.

His mother opened her handbag and pulled out a wintergreen mint. "This is the last one."

Mauricio unwrapped it, put the hard candy it his mouth, bit it in half, and gave his sister Cristian one of the pieces.

Another man came over to their bench. "Everybody raise your hands, please!"

Mauricio raised his and, along with the grown-ups, swore to tell the truth. There was nothing else to do after that except listen to his mother read the Bible and listen for their name. For two hours Mauricio strained to hear their name. His mother was in the middle of the second reading of her first psalm when he thought he heard it.

"Señora Almonte y familia, casilla uno."

"You will not fear the terror of night . . ." his mother whispered.

Mauricio felt Elizabeth nudge him.

"Señora Almonte y familia, casilla uno."

They were sent into a small office where they sat in front of a tall man who wore glasses and a suit. At least, that would be the way Mauricio remembered him years later. He examined the man's white skin. He wanted to see what an American looked like.

"Does your husband have a car?" the visa officer asked his mother.

Mauricio wondered what that had to do with anything.

"No," his mother replied.

"Who does he live with?"

"With one of his brothers."

There was a pause. The officer glanced at his papers.

"Now, which one is Elizabeth?"

His mother pointed to his eldest sister.

"What do you do?" the officer asked Elizabeth.

"I am a student."

Mauricio practiced to himself what he would say when it was his turn.

"Where do you go to school, Elizabeth?"

"Liceo José DuBeau of Puerto Plata."

"What grade?"

"I am in the fourth year of secondary school."

Cristian will be next, Mauricio thought. There was air-conditioning on. But he still felt hot; he could smell his sisters' perfume. He kept practicing: Speak clearly and say, "I am in the seventh grade at José DuBeau."

He waited for the officer to ask Cristian a question. She would probably say something silly.

"Señora Almonte," the officer said. The consul was talking to his mother again.

"Señora Almonte, I can only give the visas to you and your eldest daughter. A wife and three children would be too much for your husband to support."

Mauricio was not sure he understood this man's Spanish.

He looked at his sisters. Elizabeth was shaking her head. When he met her eyes, she put her finger over her lip.

"In three months you can ask again for your other children," the officer said. "But with these two it would be too much. You can ask for the others in three months, if your husband's financial situation changes—or if you get a job."

Papi had never said this!

He might have said that if they didn't get visas this time, they would get them next time. But he never said that some of them would get visas and some of them wouldn't. The consul was wrong. He was dead wrong. Mauricio decided it didn't matter. Mami would never go without him. He didn't think she would.

"Is that okay, Señora Almonte?"

"Sí," his mother whispered. Mauricio barely heard her. He stared at his mother. She was crying. When she told him and his sisters to go outside and buy lunch, he didn't dare refuse.

"Señora Almonte?"

Roselia raised her head to a blond woman, another officer.

"Señora Almonte, there is an American woman in my office who would like to speak with you."

PART TWO

AMERICA

17

January–February 1986

"Immigrants," Don Forst barked as I followed him into his glass-enclosed office. He turned and his eyes were wild.

Some immigrants, I guessed, must have committed a big crime.

"I want you to find a family of immigrants. People who are coming to America, right now. I want you to emigrate with them, move in with them. Follow them for a year, write once a month. I don't care where they come from, but the publisher would like them to speak Spanish. You speak Spanish, right?"

"A little."

"Good! Take some classes."

I nodded and tried not to stare at his tie, which, like all of Don Forst's ties, belonged in the Museum of Modern Art.

He leaned over his desk. "A lot of these people are coming here now and we don't know anything about them."

In 1986, I worked for *New York Newsday,* and Don Forst, the editor, had handed me a gift, a small book to be written in the newspaper. But not on a newspaper schedule. After eleven years as a reporter, I had come to loathe daily journalism with its quick murders, cute features, and press conferences—particularly the press conferences. I had escaped for a year in Ireland, where my new husband, a *Newsday* correspondent and a rabid Irish-American, was on a fellowship to study the "troubles" in the North. (I had told my husband that even a honeymoon on the Falls Road with the IRA would be preferable to what I was doing at *Newsday.*) We had that honeymoon and I wrote pieces about Irish politics for American magazines, but eventually we had to return to our "real jobs" in New York. Almost immediately I began plotting a way to leave again.

Now I wouldn't have to do that. I didn't care about immigrants or immigration. But for an assignment like this, I told myself, I would learn to care. In giddy delight over my new-found freedom, I envisioned high drama—a family of Central

Americans who had escaped right-wing death squads or Colombians fleeing the Medellín drug cartel.

My teacher at the InLingua language school had a better idea. "Why don't you write about Dominicans?" she asked. "There are a lot of Dominicans in New York."

All I knew about the Dominican Republic was the name Trujillo and that it was Haiti's neighbor. Haiti's boring neighbor. Trujillo, I was sure, had been dead for years. "There can't be that many," I replied in Spanish, which was all I was permitted to speak to her. "You never hear anything about them."

Later, I called the Immigration and Naturalization Service and asked which country was sending the most immigrants to New York. "That's easy," the officer replied. "The Dominican Republic." Haiti's boring neighbor, I said to myself.

The INS officer put me on hold, then returned to the phone with a sheet of statistics. During the 1985 fiscal year Dominicans had received more immigrant visas than any other group of foreigners moving to the New York area. Of the 100,071 immigrant visas granted to individuals who went to live in and around New York during that year, 15,858, or 16 percent, were issued to Dominicans. Even Jamaicans weren't getting as many visas. I had thought New York was overrun with Jamaicans. Maybe there were more illegal Jamaicans than illegal Dominicans.

"What about illegal Dominicans?" I asked. I wondered if the INS would answer that question.

"Every reason to believe there are as many, if not more," the officer said.

"Why?"

"They started coming after Trujillo. They just kept coming."

I checked the newspaper's morgue, to see if I had been missing something. *New York Newsday* was a relatively new publication. But *Newsday,* the mother paper on Long Island, had covered the city for years. From old *Newsday* clips, I found out that Oscar de la Renta was Dominican and that Dominicans were good baseball players. But most of the stories were "shorts" about drug busts in Washington Heights, which was identified as *the* Dominican community. Or about Dominicans whose fishing boats had sunk as they crossed the Mona Strait heading for Puerto Rico and illegal immigration. There was nothing that described the fabric of Dominican lives in New York, the fabric of so many lives. We were missing a good story.

I was interrupted by a phone call from my brother, a corporate lawyer who likes to give advice. "You should talk to José," my brother said. Typically, I viewed my brother's suggestions with sisterly disdain. But this time I had to admit he was right. José Duarte da Silveira was a telecommunications executive who knew the Dominican Republic. He and his wife had lived in Santo Domingo during the Trujillo years and, I now remembered, had once spent an evening telling me stories about that haywire country. One of those stories took place in the spring of 1961, when José's wife took their infant daughter to the pediatrician, only to find out later that Trujillo's assassins were hiding in the next examining room.

"A Dominican family would be a great idea," José said when I located him at his office in Puerto Rico. He had grown up in the Azores and spoke with the rarefied air of a European nobleman. "All the Dominicans are coming to America. And, Bárbara, even more are going to come."

The next day, I rode the subway up to Washington Heights. I saw Dominican names everywhere. *Bodegas,* car services, restaurants, and repair shops called Santo Domingo, Santiago, Cibao, Puerto Plata, and of course, Quisqueya. Everyone in Washington Heights, I guessed, was Dominican. I visited community centers, sat in on English classes, and started to talk to people to see if I could find a family.

"I would like to help you but I am Puerto Rican," the first man I approached said. He had a frightened look in his eye. I had heard that a lot of illegal Dominicans tried to pass as Puerto Ricans. Don Forst wanted me to write only about legal immigrants, but I had argued that he was wrong, that there were more illegals in New York. "We don't want anyone who will run away in the middle of the series," he said. I had been annoyed by his caution, but now I could see he had a point.

Eventually, I found about ten people who admitted to being Dominican, had visas, and told me that I could write about their relatives who would be arriving any day. Many were surprised that an English-language newspaper would want to do this. "We're only in your papers when we get busted," one young man told me. But after three weeks, nobody had come through with a family. It was my first lesson in Dominican courtesy. Refusals are impolite. It is better to lie or to avoid answering. I couldn't blame anyone, though. I wouldn't have advised my relatives to do this either. Like many reporters, I often wondered why anyone spoke to me at all. I returned to the newsroom and told an impatient Don Forst that if I wanted to find a Dominican family that was getting ready to emigrate, I would have to go to the Dominican Republic.

"You better come back with a good one," he said.

As I prepared to leave, I began to worry. What was I doing with this assignment? Only weeks earlier, all I had known about the Dominican Republic was basic geography and the name Trujillo. I had no idea whether I would have any better luck finding a family in the Dominican Republic than in Washington Heights. I wasn't even sure I would be able to speak to anyone. My résumé said that I had minored in Spanish literature in college. What it didn't say was that I had read all the assigned works in English translation. Even after a month at InLingua, I felt I could only manage the most rudimentary interviews, particularly with Dominicans who spoke so quickly. I wasn't sure I knew anything about Latinos, period. My editors certainly didn't. In 1986, *New York Newsday* knew it was too white for the city it covered. But it was also too Anglo, as was the rest of the country's media. The impact of the Latino community in America, particularly in the Northeast, was barely discussed. Latinos were not recognized as a cultural, economic, or political force, as they are today. Years later, I realized that by assigning such a series, Don Forst had taken a small but prescient first step.

* * *

I landed in Santo Domingo, rented a car, and drove into the city. Even the airport road, lush with palm trees, was beautiful, although remote. I passed burros carrying packed loads, men pushing carts filled with oranges, and a young couple building a lone house from concrete blocks. The city and its large buildings came upon me suddenly. At each intersection, insistent men washed my windows and begged for money. Others tried to sell me bunches of bananas and plastic bags filled with peppers, pieces of gum, candy, and cookies. I checked into a hotel, the Dominican Concorde, went to the restaurant, and ordered a rice casserole for dinner. I was enjoying my quiet meal when the restaurant manager and his assistant sat down with me. They said they could not bear to see a woman eat alone.

I went to the consulate the next morning. On the phone from New York, a public relations officer at the embassy had said that the staff there would find a family for me. It was a gracious offer but not one I had solicited or wanted to accept. These were American diplomats and career foreign service people. They would, I was sure, find me a family of "well-behaved" Dominicans who would one day become perfect U.S. citizens, people who were being treated well by our government and who would not generate any controversy. My plan was to humor them and then look for a family on my own. Dominicans had not cornered the market on genteel duplicity.

I met with Dudley Sipprelle, the consul general, who was about to leave his post for another in Rome. He was very impressed with the size of his consular section, which was where the visas were handed out. "Fourth largest that the United States has anywhere," he said. "That is in terms of employees and workload. The only ones that are larger than the Dominican Republic are London, Mexico City, and Manila." He stopped and gave me an incredulous look. "Now those are three large countries! The Dominican Republic only has 6.2 million people."

He spoke, unemotionally, about the desperation of Dominicans who went to came to United States. To prove this he took me to see "the wall," which was filled with pictures of those who had tried to get their visas using false documentation. He explained these were not merely people who obtained tourist visas and overstayed their visits. These were *real* criminals. There was a picture of a wedding cake made from paper and another of a woman who, in 1980, tried to emigrate by saying she was married to her brother in America—under the preference system, enacted in 1965, her chances of getting a visa were much better as a wife. She tried to do that again in 1984 and was caught, Sipprelle said, by an officer who had seen her picture on the wall. "The first thing I do with all new officers is take them to see the wall," he said.

Sipprelle introduced me to Barbara Tobias. She headed the visa section and had been put in charge of finding "my family." Tobias was a no-nonsense bureaucrat who spoke crisply and wore sensible, tailored clothes. She came up with a few possibilities that day. But nobody compelling enough for a yearlong series.

On our second morning together Barbara Tobias announced that she had "a Señora Almonte from Puerto Plata" for me to meet. "Puerto Plata's on the northern coast." She stopped to look at her papers. "Señora Almonte has a husband who has been in New York for three years. He lives in Queens. Is Queens okay?"

I nodded, a bit surprised. Everybody else lived in Washington Heights.

"Her husband is a construction worker and she was told this morning that she and her daughter, who is sixteen, can join him."

The Almontes sounded as dull as Tobias's other prospects. I wondered if I could get away with standing outside the consulate and interviewing people as they left after their *citas*. The lines outside were so long, I was sure that even in that random way, I could find a more interesting family.

"I see that Señora Almonte has two younger children," Tobias continued. "But their visa applications were rejected."

I was hardly listening to her.

"The girl is fourteen. The boy is eleven."

That caught my attention. It caught my attention dead cold. "The boy is eleven?"

"Yes, eleven," she said, betraying no emotion.

"Why can't the children go?"

"Her husband doesn't make enough to support them all. We can't send people if it looks like they might wind up on welfare." Barbara Tobias did not exude warmth. But there was a photograph in her office of a child—hers, I guessed. I was not yet a mother myself, and I didn't spend a lot of time thinking about children. But even to me it seemed that she could show some concern. Even if splitting up families was so routine it happened every day, she could at least pretend to feel badly about it.

"I'd like to meet Señora Almonte," I said.

Barbara Tobias brought me to an alcove near her office and introduced me to a petite, slightly chubby woman about my age. Señora Almonte wore a turquoise dress and her dark skin was beautiful against the bright color. Her hair was long, black, coarse, and straight and she had pulled it back from her face with a scarf that matched her dress.

"I am sorry about your children," I said in the most careful Spanish.

She nodded tentatively and wiped her eyes with a shredded tissue.

"Can I talk to you about it?" I didn't know exactly what Barbara Tobias had told her about me. Señora Almonte, I was sure, suspected that I was really another visa officer. "What will you do?"

There was a long pause. Either it was a stupid question or my Spanish was so bad that she hadn't understood. She wiped her eyes again. "I think the girl will be okay. Her grandmother could take care of her. She will be okay if she doesn't fall in love."

I smiled. As I had feared, she spoke a fleeting, clipped Spanish. But I had grasped her words, as well as her tone. She was speaking to me conspiratorially, as one mother to another. I was thirty-one years old. Señora Almonte probably didn't know any women my age who weren't mothers.

"And your son?"

She closed her eyes. "I don't know what to do about Mauricio." She opened her eyes and wiped them again. "He sleeps with his arms around me."

"I'd like to write about your family."

She gave me a half smile. "It would be better if we talk at my home." I handed her my notebook and she wrote: *Ensanche Luperón, Vista Alegre, 14, Puerto Plata.*

That, as I later learned, was not Roselia's home at all but the house in Puerto Plata that her sister-in-law Marta had rented for her sister María's family since 1976. It was the house where Demetria Almonte had died.

By the time Mauricio is asked to reflect on immigration, he has finished college and is a graduate student, on full scholarship, at Bowling Green University in Ohio. He is not only a professional student but a liberal, if not a radical, in the sixties sense of the word. He deeply regrets that he missed the heyday of Bob Dylan, not to mention the heyday of Allen Ginsberg. Still, he cherishes his Master-Card.

Mauricio the graduate student has no intention of leaving America. Two years earlier, in 1994, he officially became an American citizen, although he had long been an American in spirit, a state he describes as "complicated." Every few years he returns to Camú, visits his grandparents and his sister Cristian. He dates a *campo* girl and realizes he cannot live in the Dominican Republic. It was Mauricio who, on his last visit to the *campo*, found the amber mine, the same one his father had known. He did not understand why the boys who were left in Juan de Nina did not try to better themselves by mining it.

I am closer to Mauricio than anyone else in the Almonte

family. Elizabeth, Cristian, and I are girlfriends. But the three of us are so different and we do not see each other much anymore. Roselia, after more than a decade, is still uncomfortable with my role as a de facto member of her family. I love Marta, but she changes her stories and makes me pin her down; we are wrestling partners. Next to Mauricio, Javier is the one I speak to the most. But he is a Dominican male from the old school. Our meetings never involve conquest, and that confuses him.

In addition to being a graduate student, Mauricio is a writer and a poet. He and I share books. At times I am a surrogate mother to him, but not one with the baggage that a real mother must bear. So it is easy. He tells his friends I am his "Jewish mother." I think he means that in the nicest way: that I listen to him and nudge him a little too much. Although he periodically spends days at a time at my house, we speak best during late-night and midafternoon phone calls. Mauricio last visited after a trip to Camú and helped me to remember the time I spent there. But mostly, he slept. He was sleeping off his dreams of Camú. He was under so long that I thought he must be sleeping off dreams of Columbus, as well. The phone is better. Mauricio doesn't mumble as much. He doesn't go to sleep in the middle of an interview. He reaches deep to find his answers. And when I present him with a grand picture, he is able to locate a smaller one within himself.

Why was he so uninterested in America when he was a boy? He loved the *campo,* as his father never had. Even now, he says he is a city boy but is unable to forgo rural life. That is why he loved Fredonia, New York, where he went to college, and why Ohio has grown on him. ("It's the clear skies.") But there was another reason he didn't care about leaving. When he was a boy in Camú, there was no information to jump-start his imagination, at least nothing that appealed to him. The American program *Dinastía—Dynasty—*was on Dominican television. But he didn't

watch it. It was a girl's show, something for his grandmother and Elizabeth. Alexis Carrington, as beautiful as
she was, would not have convinced Mauricio, the boy,
that he wanted to come to America. Marta did not convince him, either. Part of that was timing. She visited
before he was born, when he was a baby and again when
he was grief stricken by his mother's imminent departure
without him. But even if Marta had come more often,
Mauricio would not have translated the jewelry she wore
into something valuable for him. His father did, though.

"Bingo," Mauricio the graduate student says. "I
became an immigrant because Aunt Marta convinced
my father."

Immigration, mass immigration at least, is in the convincing.

The convincing can be unintentional. Thousands
arrived at Ellis Island clutching letters from relatives
who bragged about their good fortune in America. Often
those relatives did not know they should be expecting
company.

The convincing can be blatantly false, too, constructed
of hackneyed lies about mansions, bank accounts, and
gold-paved streets: the maid sends a picture of the house
where she works and says it is her own home. Or it can be
as manipulative as a gold watch flashed in a brother's
face or a suitcase full of frilly nightgowns. All that matters is that it convinces. And sometimes, as in Mauricio's
case, as in his mother's case, the unconvinced are brought
along.

In 1960, only 17,000 Dominicans lived in the United
States. During the sixties more than 90,000 came, and
more than 140,000 arrived during the seventies. By the
1980s the estimates ranged from half a million to 800,000
Dominicans in the United States. Now, it is said, there
could be a million.

In 1965, when President Johnson signed the new immigration bill, he said that it was "not a revolutionary bill. It does not affect the lives of millions. It will not reshape the structure of our daily lives, or really add importantly to our wealth or power." What Johnson didn't realize was that that bill gave people the muscle they needed to bring over the relatives they had already convinced.

In the 1990 book *Coming to America,* Roger Daniels, a historian and immigration expert, quotes Johnson and then writes: "The bill, in fact, changed the whole course of American immigration history, although it did so along lines that were already apparent for the few who had eyes to see. In addition it facilitated a great increase in the volume of immigration. In no year since the bill passed have fewer than a third of a million legal immigrants entered the United States, and since 1978 half a million or more have entered in most years. The most striking effect of the new law has been further to increase the share of immigration slots going to Asia and Latin America. . . . Since the 1965 act went into effect, the preponderance of all nonrefugee migration has been the chain migration of relatives. . . ."

Two days after I met Roselia Almonte, I flew up to Puerto Plata in a two-seater, with a handsome young man at the controls. "Don't worry," one of the public relations officers at the embassy had told me, "Dominicans are good pilots."

18

February–March 1986

In Puerto Plata, I went from the airport straight to the Vista Alegre house, which I assumed was Roselia's. She was sitting on the porch waiting for me. Her children were there, too. Elizabeth had her mother's beautiful deep skin, but at sixteen was taller, more solidly built. Cristian, fourteen, with long brown hair, dimples, a delicate, round, build and light creamy skin was poised to be the beauty of the family. I took a seat next to Roselia, and Elizabeth began explaining herself.

"I have to let you know this," Elizabeth said. "I am in love with computers."

Cristian giggled.

Mauricio, eleven, all eyes and curly lashes, did not laugh or say a word. As I talked with Roselia, he flashed his smile at me, white and endearing like his mother's and sisters', as if I had come to fix what had gone wrong. I hoped he realized that I hadn't and couldn't. Roselia brought me inside to a simple living room with a linoleum floor. A few young women were busy in the kitchen behind it. "My nieces," Roselia explained. I figured she lived with a lot of relatives.

Later, at Roselia's request, I called Javier from my hotel room to find out if I could write about his family. I reached him at his Corona apartment—he knew who I was. He had already been tipped off by Roselia about our encounter at the consulate. He made no commitment, saying only that he wanted to meet me first. It was Javier, though, who told me the truth about Vista Alegre.

"Have you seen my house in the *campo?*" he asked eagerly. When I said I thought he lived in Puerto Plata, he laughed and told me to talk to Elizabeth. She told me the whole story. "The *campo* is where we really live. My Tía Marta rents the house in Puerto Plata for Tía María's children. But we're all from the *campo*."

The first time I saw Camú, I drove there in a rental car with Elizabeth chatting away in the front seat. Roselia and Cristian sat quietly in the back. Mauricio was already waiting for us there. From the house on Vista Alegre, we rode east on the Malecón and up a wide, sloping street called the Avenida Hermanas Mirabal. I did not know the significance of the name, and Elizabeth did not mention it. (As a guide she veered toward the personal, the cheerful, and the obvious.) Just outside the city she pointed out a large white building, the Brugal Distillery, and for a quick moment the air smelled like sweet, rotting flowers.

We passed Playa Dorada where I was staying, pretending to be a tourist and swimming in the ocean between interviews. Outside the pristine hotel complex, there was a sign advertising its Robert Trent Jones golf course. Beyond that was a billboard touting steaks from Omaha, Nebraska. After Playa Dorada the traffic thinned, but the road became busier with the trappings of rural life. We passed sweaty children playing in fields, tractors and trucks bringing thick, brown sticks of sugarcane to the mill. After each stretch, I caught up with another motorcycle and each one sprayed my car with specks from the road, which, although paved, was dusty.

"Turn here," Elizabeth said. "You need to get off the main road." On either side of us was a village, scattered with concrete-block houses and palm huts. The road was narrower, but not too bad. A sign announced that we were in Gran Parada. "Tía María once lived here, also," Elizabeth said. Roselia looked at her, as though she were giving away too many family secrets, but Elizabeth kept talking. I had the impression that Roselia would have been happier if I had never been told Camú existed.

As we drove farther into the *campo*, the air, though still hot, turned fresher. We sweated but it was comforting, like a blanket.

"Turn off to the right here," Elizabeth said when we came to a curve. We now bumped along on a dirt road. On my right there was another shack, with two tables outside where a few old men sat having drinks. The road was studded with sharp rocks that jabbed up from its ruts. My car hit a rock and the jolt propelled us sideways. I rode a foot or two, hit another rock, and went sideways again. We proceeded up the rest of the road, zigzagging like an amusement park ride. Roselia nodded as if to confirm the obvious, that the road was indeed bad. But she laughed wholeheartedly at my gasps.

"Turn left here," Elizabeth said, pointing to a large hill, which appeared to be even rockier than the road. "We'll stop at my grandparents' first."

We zigzagged up to a whitewashed, concrete-block house with a green zinc roof, wooden doors and shutters finished with a light brown varnish. A slight woman with a dark, graying ponytail was walking, carefully, down from the porch.

"Mami," Roselia explained.

Although the old woman was steps away from us, I could see the yellow-green color of her eyes, so odd against her dark skin. Fian González gave me a hug as though we were old *campo* friends. She called me by name and I wondered how she knew. Elizabeth had told me there were no phones in Camú. Then, I remembered Mauricio had arrived ahead of us. Fian kept her arm around me as we walked up to the porch. "Sit in my chair, please," she said, pointing to a wooden rocker. Roselia stood. Elizabeth and Cristian went inside. Fian disappeared into the house as well, and came back with clear-colored drinks she had made. I tasted fresh limes and a lot of sugar. It was the coolest liquid I'd had since landing in Santo Domingo.

Roselia's mother sat down in the hard wooden chair next to me and patted her cheeks with a white, cloth handkerchief. She wore a faded floral-print housedress; one of its spaghetti straps had fallen off her shoulder. Her eyes were like those of a mischievous child. They darted to whatever was new. But her complexion was wrinkled and her face looked tired. She was, she told me, almost fifty.

In front of the house three young boys ran, shouting, after two squawking turkeys. One of the boys grabbed on to a turkey and hugged it.

"They are lonely," Fian said, sighing.

"Handsome boys," I said, carefully trying to make my adjectives the same gender as my nouns. "Your grandsons?"

Fian nodded. "My other daughter, Ramona. Her boys. She is already in America." Elizabeth, who had been in the house, came out and interrupted us. "Doña, did you see the *telenovela*?"

"*Ay, no, mi amor,*" Fian replied. "The electricity went out." Their power came from the sugar mill in Montellano and was, Elizabeth had explained, elusive at best.

A tall, balding man with a child's head and sweet face was next out of the house. Like a little boy, he inspected me.

"Papi," Roselia said. She was glowing.

Víctor González shook my hand. He was more reticent than his wife, more ancient and confused. He didn't seem to know what I was doing there. I asked him if he'd thought about going to New York, too.

"No," he replied. "It is bad luck for old people to travel."

Roselia looked as if she might cry. "I'll show you my *casita*," she said.

Before we left Fian and Víctor's house, I went inside to use their bathroom. Mauricio was in the living room, sitting on a worn, red couch, intently watching a small black-and-white television. He waved and flashed an embarrassed smile as I walked toward the bathroom. The bathroom was fine. Small but tiled. It had a toilet, sink, and shower. I opened the shower curtain and sitting on the drain, directly under the showerhead, was a full-size, plastic, outdoor trash can.

"How many times did you take a shower there?" Mauricio the graduate student asks, incredulous. "Only once when you went back in 1993? Still, once should have been enough. You didn't see that the garbage can was there to save water? You thought the drainage was bad? It might have been, but that's not why the garbage can was there.

"Look, I know I'm only supposed to be talking about America. But that shower was an important immigration issue. You can't write about immigration if you don't understand that shower. Forget everything I said about Aunt Marta. That shower could make people emigrate all by itself. When you took a shower, you were supposed to let a lot of the water drip into the can. Yes, even the dirty water. That way when the pumps broke, there was still water for a bath. Those pumps were very temperamental. There wasn't enough water for everyone. But somebody got a bath out of it. And that was the good shower. My grandmother had the best shower in the *campo*. Remember what we had at our *casita*? A hose behind the bedroom."

Roselia, Elizabeth, Cristian, and I walked up a path behind Fian and Víctor's house. We opened a gate and walked through an empty field. Two palm huts stood on its perimeter, but neither was as nice as Roselia's parents' house. Just past the huts stood a neat row of four bushes, which Roselia told me would bloom into gardenias, Mauricio's favorite flower.

Roselia's home was a "complex," composed of two palm huts. One contained a kitchen, the other was larger and had a bedroom and sitting room. As Roselia and her daughters scattered to perform small tasks, I looked around. The larger hut was spruced up with turquoise blue paint and whitewash. It had wooden chairs, also painted blue, and a pretty blue-and-white bench. Beyond a doorway with an open cloth curtain was the bedroom, which was the size of a monk's cell in an old mission, just wide enough to hold its two beds. A wooden closet had been placed perpendicular to the beds, to save space. Alongside the closet was the back door, which opened onto a shed made from a bent piece of tin. There was a hose there and a hand basin that held a bar of soap and four toothbrushes. About seven feet behind it was another, sturdier shed, made from wood—the outhouse.

The kitchen hut was unpainted and more decrepit on the outside. Inside, it had one room, about twice the size of the bedroom, with a wooden table and chairs and tin pots, pitchers, and cups that hung from nails on the wall. Hens and roosters milled outside and hopped onto the kitchen floor. There was a gas cooker with two burners and, in lieu of a sink, a hose attached to a spigot outside curled into a basin on a shelf.

Roselia was in the kitchen. From a giant brown bag, she scooped rice into a tin bowl. She picked up the bowl, carried it to the sitting room in the other hut, and sat on the blue bench. Her long fingers moved quickly through the grains, locating pebbles and twigs, which she picked out and threw on the floor. As she searched, she hummed a quick *merengue*.

She told me that she had decided she would go to America

because her husband had convinced her that would benefit all her children, even if they didn't all have visas. Javier had assured her the younger children would come eventually. Roselia did not seemed convinced. I wondered if she ever would be. Although now, surrounded by her trees and the view of her *cordillera,* she was tranquil. In the three days since we'd met, I had not seen her so relaxed.

Cristian and Elizabeth came out of the bedroom. Elizabeth was carrying a boom box, a Sanyo with four speakers. "Papi bought this for us in *Nueva Llork."* She put it on the floor, and searched until she found a station without too much static. Then she grabbed her sister's hand, and they began to dance. Elizabeth was in blue jeans and a pair of black leather boots that looked more suitable for snow than the tropics. Her father had bought her those as well. Cristian wore a white chiffon dress with blue polka dots. Both girls had pulled their hair back with scarves. *"Tú vivirás siempre en mi,"* the radio blasted, as if it wanted to wake up the entire *campo.* Cristian and Elizabeth held on to each other and danced as their scarves fluttered in the air. They look liked contestants on *American Bandstand,* circa 1960.

A pig trotted down the road in front of their hut. His sow followed. "First a husband came and then a wife," Roselia called out over the music as she swept outside the pebbles and twigs from the rice. "First Javier, then me." A few minutes later, a group of about ten people appeared. A busy afternoon in Camú. It seemed as if they had descended suddenly from nowhere. "They were up the mountain visiting Fransica," Roselia told me. "The *bruja."*

"What does she do?" I asked eagerly. This story would be even better if a witch was involved.

Roselia looked embarrassed. "I don't go to her," she said adamantly.

From another direction, the fields behind the *casita,* I saw Mauricio coming home for dinner. "Are your television shows over?" I asked. The boy nodded with a shy grin. Then he sat next to his mother on the blue bench. Behind them was a window with its shutters open. There was a view of the *cordillera* in the distance. Mauricio put his head on his mother's chest so that his kinky hair rubbed against her cheek. He wrapped his long, thin arm around his mother's comfortable waist. Roselia clasped her arms around her son's back.

The next afternoon I was given a tour. We crossed the River Camú and went up to Juan de Nina to see Demetria's yellow flowers and the nearby parcels of what was now Víctor's land. As we crossed back over the stones of the river, we saw Víctor, too, riding through his fields on his white horse. He waved but did not stop. Later, Elizabeth brought me to the *primaria*. It had a zinc roof, and red paint was peeling from its door. The light that slanted through the palm slats hit a calendar on the wall which was from a Puerto Plata bank and had a picture of a blue-eyed, blond little girl on it. A beige rotary phone sat below it on a desk. "It's not real," Elizabeth said, reminding me again that there were no phones in Camú. "It's for a game. To teach students how to dial."

"We have one more thing to see here," she told me as we left the school. "Papi's *gallera*."

The cockfighting ring was just a tall, rough set of bleachers built in a circle. Elizabeth greeted a man who was working there and told him who I was. "Javier was a good worker!" he said to me. "Very serious. The best carpenter around here. Look at what he built!"

I had assumed when Don Forst said that I should find a family and "move in with them," he meant it figuratively. Still, I was tempted to ask Roselia if I could stay overnight in the *casita*. I didn't ask her because I didn't know where she would put me. They already had four people in two beds, and I was afraid she would be insulted if I suggested a sleeping bag on the floor. Instead, I went back each night to my hotel room and unrepentantly turned the air-conditioning on full blast. The Dominican Republic was hot.

One morning I arrived in Camú early so I could ride with the children to the Liceo José DuBeau, their secondary school, back in Puerto Plata. From their *casita* we walked out to the Carretera Luperón, listening to the roosters still crowing, and climbed into the back of a *guagua,* a green pickup truck. It was already half full with students in uniforms, and by the time we left Camú, Cristian was sitting on my lap in order to make room for the others.

José DuBeau was a sprawling, two-story, concrete-block building with classes in grades seven through twelve. Each class opened onto an outdoor passageway, but the rooms themselves were hot, stuffy, dark, and noisy. Students paid little attention; their uninspired lessons revolved around memorization. The teachers all looked too sweaty to care. Elizabeth, a senior, acted as though she were the only one in her classroom. She had to. When her teacher asked a question she raised her hand and answered, while boys fought around her and a couple of other classmates napped. In a room of sophomores, Cristian doodled. She could have been anywhere. Mauricio, a seventh-grader, tried to work around the din that was supposed to be a mathematics lesson. He wrote quietly at his desk and didn't say a word. I introduced myself to his teacher, a kindly woman named Mercedes Robles who was persevering along with Mauricio. She was surprised when I told her that his mother would soon be leaving for America. She hadn't even known that his father was there. "But I will watch out for him now," she said. "There are others like him."

A few days later was February 27, Dominican Independence Day. When Mauricio was sure no one was listening, he quietly informed me that this was the day in 1844 when Juan Pablo Duarte—*"el papi de mi país"*—the father of the Dominican Republic, drove out the Haitians and created a republic. "You could really have a lot of independence days," I said. I had quickly read some Dominican history, enough to know that the country could also celebrate being freed from the Spanish, the Americans, Heureaux, Trujillo, and the Americans again. *"Sí,"* the boy said quietly. Mauricio and his sisters took me with them to Puerto Plata to celebrate on the Malecón.

The week before I had seen Santo Domingo's *malecón,* a wide avenue along the sea filled with luxury hotels, including one decorated by Oscar de la Renta, one of the country's favorite sons. At the end of that *malecón,* there was a colonial district with museums and monuments to Columbus and Cortés. The Puerto Plata *malecón* was smaller, less serious, campier. At the beginning there was a reproduction of Michelangelo's *David;* a statue of Neptune beckoned from a perch offshore. At the end, General Gregorio Luperón, a nineteenth-century Dominican patriot who defeated the Spanish, stood staring into Isabel de Torres as his horse fluttered on hind legs. To the left of Luperón was the Fortaleza San Felipe, the only somber note. Originally built to keep out English and French pirates, it had been used by Trujillo to house some of his legions of political prisoners.

Merengue blared while hundreds of families paraded up and down the promenade. Boys dressed as devils hit each other with pigskin bags while little girls, their cheeks painted with red circles and freckles, darted out of the way.

"Where's your costume?" I asked Mauricio.

"Mauricio used to wear a costume when Papi was here," Elizabeth shouted at me through the music and noise.

A few days later, in Corona, Queens, I rang the bottom bell of a brick, two-story house. A short, balding, well-proportioned man with coffee-colored skin and shining eyes opened the door. He had a mouth full of false teeth, which were beginning to yellow.

"*Ay,* Bárbara," Javier Almonte said, giving me a bear hug, as his mother-in-law, Fian, had the first time I'd met her.

Another short man with a mustache jumped up from a couch. "My brother Ernesto," Javier explained. Ernesto hugged me, also. I handed Javier a roll of *dulce de leche* that Roselia had sent. Javier patted the thick, soft roll of caramel as though it were a woman's behind. Then he asked me to have a seat on the couch. Javier sat in a chair opposite me. Ernesto sat by my other side. It was Javier who was going to do the talking.

"What do you need?" Javier asked.

Of course, I wanted to know if he would let me write about his family. On the phone he had said he wanted to meet me first. That had me worried. Like the people I had met in Washington Heights, like people anywhere, he could be saying maybe and meaning no. But if he was saying yes, I was also worried. Why would he hand over his family to a stranger—and a strange newspaper—unless he expected a favor in return, something I couldn't or wouldn't deliver, such as money—or visas. He probably thought I could just call someone and get his children visas. In the Dominican Republic, reporters and politicians probably did each other favors like that all the time.

"Tell me about when you first came here," I said, searching for a neutral topic. "What do you remember?"

"Oh, the snow, the cold, hot water. We never had hot water in the *campo.*"

"Anything else?"

"*Sí,* Garden City."

"Garden City, Long Island?"

"*Sí,* Bárbara," he said, smiling wide with his false teeth.

My husband and I lived on Long Island, but in Long Beach, an irreverent, multi-ethnic beach town. Garden City was another matter. My husband had grown up there and it was the whitest community I knew, a place that dripped with the assurance of wealth and exclusivity. And with houses: Georgian mansions, Tudor cottages, real Victorians with real gingerbread, ranch spreads straight out of American television.

"Bárbara," Javier said, "if I ever make any money, Garden City is where I would live."

"How do you know Garden City?"

"*Meereel Leench.*"

"Merrill Lynch?"

"*Sí.* I used to clean their offices."

"How was that?"

"It was better than being back in the *campo.* Do you know

what I dreamed about in the *campo?* I dreamed about being a pilot so that I could fly away from the *campo.*"

"Why didn't you?"

Javier ignored the question. "You know that work in the country is hard. We always thought about going to the city to better our lives. To live differently, much closer to the theater, a different life. Young people in small towns always dream of the city. There is something about the country. When you finish at night, everything is dark. In the city all the lights are lit."

"But Garden City is very quiet."

"Yes, but, you see, Garden City is where I would go to retire. After I had seen enough lights."

I smiled.

"Are you laughing at me?"

"No. No. Not at you," I said, which was the truth. I was laughing at a vision of Fian and Víctor at the Cherry Valley Country Club in Izod shirts and plaid shorts. But maybe that wasn't so far-fetched. Garden City had its share of Víctors and Fians, people who would never live anywhere except in the midst of their own village. Garden City, I knew, also bred boys like Javier, whom it could never satisfy. This Javier Almonte likes to weave stories, I thought. I'll bet he's never been to the theater, but he doesn't need to. He creates his own. And he's a flier. No wonder he wanted to be a pilot.

Javier got up from the couch and went into one of the apartment's two bedrooms. I peeked in after him and saw two twin beds with Humpty-Dumpty spreads. He came out with a folder stuffed with papers he had sent with his family's visa application. He took out his 1985 tax return. It showed that his net salary was about $14,600. At the consulate, Barbara Tobias had told me that a family of five would need an income of $12,450 for all of its members to qualify for visas. But Javier made even more than that—and it was far from all he hoped to make.

After Roselia and the children had been called for their *cita,* Javier had asked his boss, an Italian-American who ran a construction company in Woodside, for a raise. He was not nervous about the request; he knew he was on firm ground. Construction was booming in New York; he worked long hours six days a week, and was a good carpenter. Besides, Peter Paolo of Woodside was not Víctor González. Javier was not afraid to ask Paolo for anything. His boss, Javier said, had agreed to raise his wages from $8 to $12 an hour. Javier showed me a copy of a letter written by Paolo, which said that with his higher wages, Javier could be expected to make about $24,500 in 1986. Javier had sent that letter to the consulate. I told Javier that a lot of people in New York supported families on money like that. In New York City in 1986, a rookie cop made about as much as Javier Almonte claimed he would. So did a schoolteacher with a master's degree and five years' experience.

"Is it okay to write about your family?" I asked.

"Sí," he said. "And why not?"

I called Barbara Tobias. Even if Javier was making up the story about his raise, even if the letter from his boss was a phony, he still earned more than enough to qualify. Tobias, who had made a point of reciting the income guidelines for me when I was at the consulate, now told me that consular officers do not necessarily have to adhere to them. Ultimately, they make their own decisions about whether a family will be able to manage without welfare. Her officers' decisions, she said, were primarily based on paperwork: on pay stubs, income tax forms, and birth certificates. Often, she said, the veracity of such documents was questioned. As she spoke, I thought about Dudley Sipprelle and his wall. She added that the questions asked during the *cita* are perfunctory. According to Barbara Tobias, most of what Roselia Almonte said to the visa officer hadn't mattered at all.

I asked Barbara Tobias if I could speak to Jonathan Mueller about his decision. She refused to let me do that, citing the Almontes' confidentiality. I thought that was ridiculous. Tobias had with Roselia's permission breached confidentiality more than any visa officer ever could. As a result of that breach, I had been to Roselia's home. I had seen where she cooked and slept. I had seen where she bathed, where her mother bathed. Still, Tobias would not budge. Clearly, it was Mueller she wanted to protect. All she would say about the visa officer was that "he refused them for the time being pending verification of economic documents given to us."

When I was at the consulate, Tobias had described the Almontes as "people who are starting out at the lower end of the spectrum and are not likely to advance quickly. They are handicapped by language and they are handicapped by a limited education." Such families, she had added, are often split up by U.S. visa officers for financial reasons.

They were also handicapped, it seemed to me, by the slow bureaucracy of immigration. While the consulate tried to figure out whether Javier's boss was legitimate—a task that a $24,000-a-year New York City cop could probably have accomplished in an hour or two—Cristian and Mauricio were relegated to the bottom of the barrel.

Tobias told me that while the case was investigated, the children had to go, in effect, to the end of the line. It could take from three months to over a year before they were called for another *cita*. That was going to depend on how many visas were available for Dominicans in general—because so many apply from that country the process is staggered—and how many applicants the short-staffed consulate could accommodate.

"It's a mill," Tobias conceded. "It may be cruel to make it so impersonal. But one of the saving graces of the system is that it is operating that way and there is equity for all of the people around the world. . . . That is cruel and it can be very heartrending. But it is cruel for every single applicant in the world."

I did not know what to make of Barbara Tobias. She recited rules like the bureaucrat she was. On the surface, she seemed to view the split family as an official necessity. Was that why she had suggested I write about the Almontes? Was it that she saw nothing wrong with what the visa officer had done? Or did she have a hidden agenda when she selected them—to show how many families were divided under the American immigration system? (Years later, Dudley Sipprelle told me: "I told her to be honest. I told her to give you an honest case.")

I had seen Barbara Tobias once again before leaving the Dominican Republic and, while we chatted in her office, she told me that she had noticed a boy the same age as Roselia's son, crying in the waiting room. She said that she knew the kind of cry it was without checking her files. She was sure that the boy, like Mauricio, had been denied a visa.

In the late nineteenth century it was estimated that new immigrants added $400 million a year to American coffers. Oddly, Americans began, at the same time, to worry about newcomers as "public charges." A statute was enacted prohibiting such individuals from entering the country, although it had more to do with keeping out the sick, the disabled, and the criminal. It barred "all idiots, insane persons, paupers or persons likely to become a public charge, persons suffering from a loathsome or contagious disease, persons who have been convicted of a felony or other infamous crime or misdemeanor involving moral turpitude . . ."

According to historian Roger Daniels: ". . . despite the growing number of excluded classes, relatively few immigrants were either excluded or deported. In 1905, for example, the first single year in which a million immigrants arrived, deportations and exclusions combined also reached a new high—12,724 persons—which represented barely more than 1 percent of the total."

"There are some things about that *cita* I will never forget," Mauricio the graduate student says. "What I remember most is the hardness of the bench. We had to wait on that bench by the Reagan portrait for hours. Even now if I concentrate, I can remember the way it felt. It was the hardest bench I have ever sat on in my life.

"I can't remember if I read the notice my mother got about Cristian and me when I was a child or an adult.

Whether it was in English or Spanish. But it was as hard as the bench."

"February 19, 1986. Act of Immigration and Naturalization. 212 (a) (15) prohibits giving an immigrant visa to a person that might become a public charge. However, your application for a visa could be considered again if you obtain and present the following to this office: Evidence that your mother is working in the United States."

I went back to Corona and spent a day at work with Javier. I arrived at his apartment, just before seven. Javier was dressed for New York winter in work boots, blue jeans, ski jacket, wool stocking cap, and vinyl gloves. We walked to the subway, at the intersection of Junction Boulevard and Roosevelt Avenue, which was noisy, but cold and dark. Here the subway wasn't a subway at all but an elevated portion of the Flushing line, which kept out what little sun there was in March. With the tracks looming above it, this street could never be light.

On the train, Javier took a seat next to a young woman who was reading her Spanish-language Bible. A homeless man with dreadlocks walked by carrying a milk crate, his seat. He asked for change but Javier turned away and shook his head in disgust.

At the fifth stop, Sixty-first Street in Woodside, we got off and walked a few blocks to a warehouse. Peter Paolo, Javier's boss, was calling out directions in Italian spiced by a few words of English and Spanish. Javier put his hand over his mouth and leaned in my direction: "They all came here twenty years ago from Italy. On this job I have a better chance of learning Italian."

Later I watched him and the other men renovate a storefront in Jamaica. Javier was the shortest. But he was strong, and when he lifted a piece of Sheetrock or a wooden plank and his hips swiveled, it was as though he were trying to *merengue*. The construction site was in the middle of a dilapidated neighborhood, and as Javier and the rest of his crew worked, men sauntered by—shaking, heckling men—some with bottles in their hands.

Javier, working so hard he sweated in the cold, shrugged his shoulders. *"Adictos,"* he said. Then, as if to provide balm, a woman and a little girl appeared on the street of broken-down and abandoned buildings. Javier's eyes followed the child until she turned the corner. When the lunch wagon came, he lined up with the other men and bought coffee and a hero sandwich. I asked if he was tired. "Physically I feel fine," he said. "But the loneliness. This is not a home, but soon it will be."

That evening we returned to Javier's apartment and found a pudgy, aging woman with red, dyed hair waiting for Javier. They embraced. "My sister Marta," Javier said. Marta spoke frenetically, even more so than most Dominicans. When she was excited, she shrieked.

"Marta es La Cabeza," Javier said to me. "It is because of her that I am here, that any of us are here."

I wondered why nobody had mentioned this woman to me before.

Marta examined me. She put on the glasses that hung on a chain around her neck and tilted her head up and down.

"Forget about it," she said.

"What?"

"You think you can write about this family for only one year? Forget about it. You are going to be writing about the Almontes for years."

19

March–April 1986

In between my visits with Javier, I went to see my parents who still lived in the redbrick house my grandfather had helped them to buy.

"It sounds like a big project," my mother said. "These people sure have a lot of relatives, a regular Cousins Club."

We were sitting on the back porch and my mother was rocking on a rusty metal chair, which she had bought when she, my father, my grandparents, an aunt, and an uncle had moved into the house almost fifty years earlier.

"It's a great assignment," I said.

"Do you know why?" my mother asked.

"Yeah. It's dramatic. And you should see where these people live. Palm huts and everything."

My parents' porch looked out over a small yard, a driveway, and a garage, which they shared with their next-door neighbor. The yard was mostly concrete, but the green perennials my grandfather had planted, his "never-dies," still grew in a patch of soil. My father and grandfather had split a $400 down payment to buy this house in 1939.

"It is a good assignment," my mother said, "because you know all their stories."

"What do you mean?" I asked, although I was afraid I did know what she meant.

"You know them because I told them to you."

"Mother," I said. "You were separated from your parents by a pogrom. Being separated by an immigration officer is not the same thing."

"We were separated by an officer, some kind of officer."

"You mean a soldier."

"No, no. Petlyura's soldiers only separated us for one day. I'm talking about Scotland. Don't you remember? When we got to Scotland, they made my father stay behind because he had lice in his hair. I told you that."

She had told me. I had forgotten.

"Your grandmother went on that boat with three small children, alone. Without her husband." Her voice rose, as though this had just occurred. "We didn't see him for weeks, maybe months. I see they still do things like this. You tell that woman not to worry. Her kids will get here."

"It's still not the same thing. These people are coming for money. You came because you would have been killed if you stayed."

"It is the same thing." My mother had that dreamy look in her eye. "They are coming here for their children."

I went back to Camú twice that spring.

On Good Friday, I drove to the *campo,* where I found Roselia standing outside her parents' house, tending to a pit of burning coals. She had wrapped a scarf around her head, and when she saw me she wiped her brow with part of it and gave me a sweaty hug. As we stood together in the sticky heat that seemed to follow every spring rain, I marveled at her effusiveness. She was not the person I had met at the consulate, nor was she the subdued woman I had visited in the *casita.* You have to taste my *habichuela,*" she said, pointing to a large pot behind her. I helped her lift the heavy pot onto the coals and watched her stir the thick brown syrup. "It's easy to make," she said. She explained that the pinto beans had to simmer in water overnight, and then they were crushed, blended, and strained. I watched as she added the festive finishing touches: milk from Víctor's cows, raisins, little round cookies, and, of course, sugar. "Papi brought the coal for the fire down from the *cordillera,*" she said proudly.

As Roselia stirred the mixture with a large wooden spoon, she spoke about her upcoming move, and I realized that in another life she might have been an accountant. A balance sheet was in her head, the poor versus the prosperous, the familiar versus the unknown, taking care of her children now versus working so that she could provide for them later, the calculations—the emotional calculations—of an emigrant. Perhaps now that she had quantified what could happen—and what would happen—she felt confident.

She seemed confident. But then she began to talk about her children. She explained that before her *cita,* she had weighed the advantages and disadvantages of emigration. But she didn't know that she wouldn't be able to take Mauricio and Cristian. That was an extra calculation. It squished all the numbers and gave her headaches. Fian had said that Cristian would sleep with her, in her bed. But what if Fian fell asleep before Cristian? What if Mauricio had nightmares when Roselia wasn't there with her arms around him? She wished she could be like Elizabeth. Elizabeth was like Javier. Elizabeth told everyone that her brother and sister would be in New York soon. Javier had said they would have a better life in America. Now she lived in two small huts: three rooms made from the trunks and leaves of palm trees. Hens and roosters popped into the kitchen at will, four people shared two beds, the toilet was an outhouse, the bath a hand basin in a tin shed. There was a time when none of that had bothered her. She had been happy with her fruit trees, her thatched roof, her soothing view of green mountains. She could walk to her mother's house in five minutes, ten when the rains made the road muddy. Lately, though, she had been imagining the kinds of houses where Americans lived and wondered if she should be ashamed of her *casita*.

"You will have to taste my *sancocho*, too," she said to me. "I think I can find the ingredients to make that in *Quins*. But I don't know about *habichuela*. Roselia took a metal ladle and spooned some *habichuela* into a tin cup for me to try. I told her it was good. But it was too sweet for me and too thick, like the mud on the roads of Camú after a rain. She must have guessed that my *yanqui* tastebuds had taken over because she laughed as I haltingly finished the whole cup. "Javier says that clothes are very cheap in *Quins*," she continued. "Much cheaper than here. I told Mami I would send her money for a refrigerator."

Roselia said that Cristian was doing the things she usually did. She fixed her hair, tried on the American clothes Javier had sent her, and copied down the words to songs she heard on the radio. Mauricio had told her that he wanted a bicycle and seemed pleased when Roselia said she would send him money for one. But her departure was still weeks away.

Before dinner at Fian's, we went back to Roselia's *casita* to talk more. She showed me the letters Javier had written to her and pictures of him as a young man with a mustache in Trujillo's civilian reserve. She spoke for a long time, as if what she said didn't matter anymore. She was about to do the rashest thing she had ever done. Rasher, even, than going home to Juan de Nina with Javier. She told me that when she had first wanted to be *junta* with Javier, her parents had their doubts. But they had kept most of it to themselves. Now, she said, although they were sad about her departure, they were quite impressed with Javier, quite impressed with what she had known when she was a girl.

Roselia talked to me more on that visit than she had before, than she ever would again.

Elizabeth interrupted us to ask if she could go dancing at the Disco Vivaldi in Puerto Plata.

"Not tonight," Roselia said, a stern look on her face.

"I know, Mami. This is for tomorrow."

Roselia told me she hoped that in America, Elizabeth would remember that people who dance on Good Friday wind up with legs like chickens.

Later that weekend, I went with Elizabeth to visit her cousins at the house on Vista Alegre. Marta had flown to Puerto Plata, her first trip back to the Dominican Republic since her mother, Demetria, died. I wondered if Javier had sent her to make sure Roselia was not changing her mind.

Marta was in the Dominican Republic for a week, but I never saw her in the *campo*. I know she was there because people talked about her. But I spent more time in Camú on that visit than Marta did. She stayed with her nieces at the house on Vista Alegre and went to see Playa Dorada, which had not been built the last time she was home. On her last day I watched her walking down Vista Alegre, wearing an elegant print dress with a string of red wooden beads around her neck. Elizabeth and one of María's daughters walked on either side of her, two giggling maids-in-waiting in American blue jeans. They were going to buy some yellow cheese and other Dominican provisions for Marta to take back to *Nieu Yersey*. Marta took a compact out of her purse and handed the bag to her niece. The niece held it while Marta looked at her hair and rearranged some red strands. Then she nodded so that they could walk on.

I also went back to America, to write my first article about the Almontes. It was published on Sunday, April 27, five days before Roselia and Elizabeth were to leave for New York. A photograph of Roselia and her children standing in front of their *casita* ran on the front page of *Newsday,* which, counting its Long Island and New York City editions, had a circulation of about eight hundred thousand. On Long Island, the Almontes received better play than David Stockman, the former economic aide to Ronald Reagan, whose book was excerpted inside. Stockman's picture was underneath the one of the Almontes. The city paper didn't even put Stockman's picture on its front page. It had Javier, instead. A baseball cap on his head, he was hanging on to a subway strap alongside the headline "A Chronicle of Hope: The Odyssey of the Almonte Family." "Good job," Don Forst said when he called me at home Sunday morning.

"Guuuaauuuw!" Javier crowed when I called his apartment that afternoon. I was about to get on a plane back to Puerto Plata so that I could accompany Roselia and Elizabeth when they flew to New York. Since he didn't speak English, it had never made any sense for Javier to buy *Newsday.* But now, he told me, he had several copies and was going to show them to his friends—Dominican men he had met during his three years here—when they arrived for their weekly game of dominoes. I had seen one of those games and could imagine the black tiles clinking as the men matched them and made intricate patterns of intersecting lines while they ate orange sections and listened to Javier.

"Bring back my wife and daughter," he said to me, laughing joyously. He still had not asked me about his children's visas, although I was convinced he would as soon as Roselia and Elizabeth arrived.

"You're going to get that kid a visa, aren't you?" my husband said when he dropped me off at the airport.

My husband liked to portray himself as a hard-bitten reporter. He was now a foreign correspondent and had recently covered the fall of Ferdinand Marcos in the Philippines. But true to cliché, he melted over children. He had been with me on my last trip to the Dominican Republic, and Mauricio, in particular, was breaking his heart.

"And just how am I supposed to do that?" I asked.

"Call their congressman."

"They're not citizens. They don't have a congressman."

"Call any congressman. Look, if you don't send that kid's picture to every congressman in New York, I will."

"I am trying to write a story about typical immigrants. Typical immigrants get their visa applications rejected. Typical immigrants have their families split up."

"I'm still going to send the picture."

"That will ruin the story," I said as I got my suitcase out of the car. "Why don't you go ruin one of your own stories?"

"What made you think about 'Muddy Cup'?" Mauricio the graduate student asks. He is speaking of a poem by the Irish writer John Montague. It describes a mother's distaste for the America her husband has found and that her New York–born son embraces. "Was it my mother's hesitation?

"The split family made you think about it first? That makes sense, but you know you have to be careful when you write about this part of my life. I wasn't like that kid in the poem. I wasn't born in America. I really didn't think I craved America. All I wanted was to be with my mother. That's what scared me the most, that my mother was leaving. If she had stayed, I wouldn't have cared."

20

April–May 1986

Roselia still needed six one-liter bottles of Macorís rum for Javier, who was off Brugal, although she didn't know why. She needed a package of caramels for him and yellow cheese. She needed to take Elizabeth for another fitting. Roselia had hired two seamstresses to make their travel outfits: pleated, floral-printed cotton suits, identical, except for their color. Blue for Roselia. Pink for Elizabeth. But Elizabeth's needed a hem. They had to arrive in New York looking good, as good as the *Americanas,* as good as any woman who might think that in America Javier Almonte did not need Víctor González's daughter. Elizabeth, Roselia remembered, wanted her hair cut in a style she had seen in a magazine. It was a Puerto Rican magazine, so it was probably an American style. Javier had instructed her to send Elizabeth to the dentist. "You would not believe how expensive dentists are in *Nueva Llork, mi amor,*" he had written. Elizabeth needed an eyetooth capped and a bridge put into the space where her decayed molar used to be. They were lucky that was all she needed. She had, after all, grown up chewing on sugarcane.

"All Roselia is doing is buying, buying, buying," Fian said.

"Doña, she's having fun," Elizabeth scolded her grandmother.

Roselia held her head with her hands. Elizabeth played with a strand of her own coarse, black hair. "My friends told me that my hair will get nicer in New York," Elizabeth reported to her mother. "They say the cold air is better for it."

"I am happy about your going. Very happy," Fian said. "I will come to visit you. I want to see all those big buildings. You will feel better once your husband has you in his arms."

Roselia hoped so. She felt awful now. But the arrangements had been made. Fian had promised to watch Cristian. Fian had said she would never stop watching Cristian, even in her sleep. Mauricio would eat with Fian. But he would sleep in the *casita* with his Tío Julio. Roselia's brother, the first in the family to go to college, was home on a work-study assignment. Roselia could remember when Julio was a whiny little boy. Now he was the tallest man in Camú, taller than Víctor, taller than even Felipe had been and thought he knew everything. He was studying agricultural engineering at the university in San Pedro de Macorís and had told his father, Víctor, that one day he would revolutionize the way *camuseros* farm. Roselia hoped Julio would be a good influence on Mauricio.

Roselia wished that Mauricio said more to her. She wished that he ate more. She knew he was smart, particularly in reading. But he was too serious. Elizabeth said that one of his classmates had hidden a book of his, as a joke. "I don't like this type of joke," Mauricio had told him. "If my notebook was really lost, how would I study?" Roselia didn't think an eleven-year-old boy should be that serious. Or that attached to his mother. He was following her around as if he were a toddler again. She half expected him to jump into her lap and ask for his *teta*. At least he didn't cry in front of her. But he did cry. The week before, Elizabeth had found him at the kitchen table, his head buried in an English picture dictionary. When he looked up, his cheeks were wet. "*Ay*, Eliza," he had said. "I feel so terribly sad." Elizabeth, unfortunately, told Roselia everything.

One of Roselia's chickens had hatched some babies, brown fluff balls that hopped into her kitchen, following their mother. They will be Mauricio's brothers and sisters, Roselia told herself. Until he gets his visa. When would that be? Javier's sister María had just gotten visas for her three eldest daughters. But they were all old enough to work.

On the night before she and Elizabeth were supposed to leave for America, Roselia went to a beauty parlor in Puerto Plata. She picked the one that charged three pesos for a wash and set. Mauricio sat on the floor and watched as her hair was set on orange, blue, green, and brown plastic rollers. He watched as the hairdresser's daughter held a cigarette up to her mother's mouth so that she could take puffs without putting her hands down. He watched while Roselia sat under the only dryer in the shop. When her hair was done, Roselia took Mauricio to the house on Vista Alegre. He watched while three of her nieces painted her toes and nails red. Roselia watched Mauricio, too. She saw that he listened while the girls teased her about Javier. "I guess Javier won't be looking at my nails," she agreed, and tried to giggle.

Mauricio began to say something. Roselia couldn't hear what it was. He sounded as if he was crying.

"Mauri, no tears!" one of the nieces scolded gently. "You will go!"

"You will go, soon," another niece said.

Mauricio blinked and shrugged his shoulders. He kept watching Roselia. When her nails were dry, she took him back with her to Camú, for the last time.

In the sitting room of the *casita,* Roselia packed until after midnight. As she worked, Cristian and Elizabeth went into the bedroom to go to sleep. Roselia peered through the curtain and watched as they got ready for bed. They lay down next to each other, head to toe, as they had since they had grown too big to sleep in each other's arms. Mauricio stayed in the sitting room and watched as Roselia wrapped a shirt around the last bottle of Macorís, watched as she made sure that the wrapper on the yellow cheese was secure. "I am ready for bed, Mauri," she said finally.

The boy went into the bedroom and took off everything except his white briefs. He lifted up the mosquito net and climbed into her bed. Roselia took a blue nightgown from her suitcase, put it on in the sitting room, pulled the chain on the lightbulb, and went to join her son. She got into bed next to Mauri. He put his head on her breast. She put her arms around him. Mauricio sniffled twice.

"No, Mauri. No," Roselia said sharply. She was afraid his tears would break her.

He wiped his eyes with his long fingers.

An hour later the roosters of Camú began to crow for the first time. They crowed again at 3 A.M. and at 4 A.M. Roselia heard them as Mauricio nudged her awake. "I am sick, Mami. My throat hurts." Roselia noticed a drop of blood in her son's ear.

Later, the four of them walked down the path to Víctor and Fian's house. Instead of going inside, they walked around the back to the breezeway, where they knew Víctor would be sitting, waiting for them. He was wearing a red cap that said NEW YORK on it, a present from Javier. When he saw his daughter and her children, he stood. "She is my confidante, this one," he said as he hugged Roselia. He held her at arm's length; he might already have had some rum. "I don't want you to leave. But what can I do?" Without letting go, he turned to Elizabeth and hugged her with his free arm. *"Vaya con Dios!"*

Roselia could feel herself crying.

"Roselia!" Elizabeth scolded her mother. "Let's go!"

One of Fian's granddaughters, a three-year-old, began to cry.

"Be happy!" Fian ordered. She put her hand on Roselia's blue floral suit and smoothed it.

Roselia stared at her mother.

"Happiness, daughter! Don't be sad."

"Doña, are you coming to the airport?" Elizabeth asked.

"No, *mi amor,*" Fian said apologetically. "My dress is dirty."

Roselia stared incredulously at her mother.

Elizabeth hugged Fian. "Don't forget to watch my *novelas* for me."

To Roselia it seemed as if Fian and Víctor were the only ones in Camú who weren't riding to the airport. In the midst of the caravan of cars and pickup trucks, she lost Mauricio. Then she saw him waving to her from one of the cars. She ran to another, although their plane wasn't scheduled to leave for hours. When they got to the airport, she did not take her eyes off him. She stood by the baggage counter and watched him. He drank orange Country Club soda, played with a gold medallion Javier had sent to him, and looked outside the window at the airplanes that had landed. But not with the same interest as his father.

Then Roselia lost him, again. She began to panic, quietly, until she saw his eleven-year-old head of frizzy hair at the top of the staircase. He walked toward her, shaking. Roselia ran to him. She pulled a tissue out of her pocket, but when she tried to wipe his wet face, the tissue fell apart. She held him, but he stood with his head twisted away from her. She wouldn't have minded if he had cried in her face. She would have gotten on the airplane with the smell of Mauri's salt in her nose, the feel of it in her eyes and mouth. She held him tighter and he molded his body so that he was as close to her as he could be. His head was on her shoulder. Her hand was on the top of his head. Instead of speaking to her, he played with the white plastic bracelet she wore.

Elizabeth and Cristian were hugging each other, but they stopped to look at her and Mauricio.

"I want to go home," Mauricio whispered to her. "It is better for me to go."

Roselia stayed at the baggage counter, watching as Mauricio walked away, clutching on to Cristian. She stood staring until she could no longer see them. Elizabeth came by to tell her that the flight was delayed. Roselia sent Elizabeth to the cafeteria, and she came back with a plate of french fries and one chicken leg. "I saw Papi's friend there," she announced. "He gave me this chicken leg for free. He said, 'Kiss Roselia for me, and when you get to America, kiss Javier, too!' " Elizabeth giggled.

Roselia smiled her half smile. There was no plane. She knew she could go home right now and forget about this. Any one of the taxis outside would take *her* to Camú, even though she wasn't a tourist and wouldn't tip like one. But there was no turning back. They had left Camú and they weren't even in Puerto Plata. They were in the Puerto Plata Airport, a space in between.

She went with Elizabeth to the waiting room and shared her french fries and chicken leg. They watched *Cantaré Para Ti,* a Venezuelan soap opera, which was playing on a television set mounted on the wall. Roselia was trying to keep her suit nice, it was so hard to keep pleats from wrinkling. But when Elizabeth fell asleep across a few chairs, so did she. She woke and saw some mechanics wheeling something out to the plane. One of the other passengers said it was an acetylene torch. They were going to fix the landing gear. A few minutes later someone said they weren't going to fix it at all. Maybe the airport wasn't so different from the *campo*. You didn't know whose story to believe.

At 10 P.M. they heard the announcement. Dominicana de Aviacion's flight to *Nueva Llork*. It was four hours since Mauricio had left. She hadn't been out of the airport, but by now Mauricio had a whole new life. Julio was putting him to bed in a manly, avuncular way. She wondered how Mauricio was, not sleeping with his head on her breast. This was the first night they had ever spent apart, except for the week she was gone to have her kidney stone removed. But Mauricio had come to visit her in Santiago—and he knew she would be coming back.

As they walked onto the plane, Roselia told Elizabeth to sit by the window; it would be too close to the sky for her. Elizabeth picked up a magazine, read about *videos,* popped a piece of gum in her mouth. Roselia tried to put on her seat belt. Was this the same Elizabeth who had been asking everyone, including Víctor, who barely went even to Puerto Plata, if airplanes were really safe? *Ay yai yai.* How did this one piece get into the other side? Roselia was still fumbling as they moved down the runway. Finally, as they took off, she fastened the belt.

"Eliza, this plane is very big, but I thought it would make more noise." She sounded as if she were the child.

Elizabeth slept. Roselia ate her meal—more chicken—and tried to sleep. Her head hurt. It hurt for hours, until she looked out and saw the lights of New York City, one lightbulb after another shining into her face. "We are far from Camú," she said out loud. "Very far from Camú."

Roselia walked off the plane ahead of Elizabeth. She was not going to show Elizabeth, any of the *yanquis,* or Javier, that she was afraid. She knew what she was supposed to do. Javier, Marta, and María had all drilled her. She was not supposed to worry if the officers looked over her papers. They had to make sure she hadn't stolen them. In one hand she clasped two red Dominican passports, two brown envelopes with their birth certificates and medical records, and most important of all, their two white American visas. Trying to look confident—she believed she was succeeding at it—she walked mistakenly onto the line for U.S. citizens.

"*Ay*, Eliza, not here," she said, realizing her mistake. She pulled her sleepy daughter to the line for immigrants. She handed their visa envelope to an immigration officer, who ripped them open and took out copies of their fingerprints.

"Two?"

Roselia nodded, guessing at his English.

He pointed to a room.

Roselia pulled Elizabeth in that direction.

As they walked into the room, Roselia gasped. An officer was putting handcuffs on one of their fellow passengers, a handsome young man who was pushing a large red suitcase on a dolly. The young man looked sheepish to Roselia, not scared. Maybe he had tried this before. A few officers stood around him. One of them pushed him, but another spoke kindly, although Roselia did not understand what they were saying.

Elizabeth was watching the young man when they called their names. Roselia had to nudge her into attention. She knew that her daughter had a friend who had gone to New York on a travel visa and had never been heard from again. Every time the radio played that *merengue* "Elena," about a Dominican prostitute who sold drugs and died on the *sobuey*, Elizabeth talked about her friend. Roselia wished she wouldn't talk about it. They went up to a window where another officer scanned their documents quickly, took prints of their index fingers, and gave them more instructions, which Roselia did not understand because they were also in English.

Customs was easy. "*No frutas?*" the agent asked Roselia.

"*No frutas,*" she said confidently, although she wondered if yellow cheese was permitted. They went to the baggage claim and found their large suitcases. A porter appeared. "Like *burros!*" he said as he lifted them onto his dolly. Roselia and Elizabeth followed him through the doors. American doors. They opened by themselves.

Even if Roselia hadn't seen Javier, she would have heard him.

"*Ay! Qué bueno! Ay, qué bueno, qué bueno, qué bueno!*"

He took her in both his arms. Even in America, Javier smelled like Javier. Like cilantro, cooking oil, and aftershave. He let go of her with one arm and reached for Elizabeth.

"*Ay, qué bueno!*"

He held out a purple jacket for Roselia, made of a soft material she had only seen used for ribbons. "From Marta," he said as he buttoned her up. There was a red woolen one for Elizabeth.

They stepped out into the New York City air.

"*Ay!*" Roselia said. "I'm freezing."

"I like this," Elizabeth said. "The air part. The cold. It will make me white."

At 2:30 A.M., nine hours after Mauricio had left the airport, Roselia walked into the kitchen of her husband's apartment in Corona, *Quins*. She touched the refrigerator first. She moved her hand up and down its length. Then she put her hands on the black burner of the gas stove. It was an entire piece of furniture with four burners. Nothing like the little three-burner cooker she'd had in Camú. She slid her foot back and forth on the linoleum floor. It was smoother than any cement or swept floor she had ever seen in a *casita*, smoother than the floors in the Vista Alegre house. Even her mother-in-law, Demetria, famous for her floors, had not been able to get hers this smooth.

She looked out her first glass window. It was open halfway, and in the yard behind her she could see laundry hanging on the line, although it was the middle of the night. She tried to open the screen.

"You will have to show me how to work this," she said to Javier.

He was smiling at her, as though she were a girl in her father's grocery. "*Sí, Sí, mi amor.* I will teach you everything."

"Eliza. Eliza, we have arrived." Roselia put her hand back on the stove burner. "If only Mauri could see this, he would like it very much."

"You need to sleep," Javier said.

Roselia looked at him.

He pointed to a room with a bed that had a Humpty-Dumpty spread on it. "Where is Ernesto?" Roselia asked.

"Working." Javier sent Elizabeth to another bed, just like it, which was in the living room.

Roselia did not sleep well. She dreamed about Mauricio. At first she could not see him. She could only hear him weeping. Then she focused on his face and he looked the same; he looked fine.

In the morning she believed that Mauricio was in her arms. But it was Javier, who had not changed, either.

"I can assure you I wasn't thinking about American immigration policy, either, the day my mother left for America without me," Mauricio the graduate student says. "I was thinking about how not to cry in front of all those people. My mother was so upset when we wound up going to the airport in different cars. I was upset, too. But it gave me time to think. I remember I saw a dog running after the car my mother was in, and I felt like I was that dog, running after something I couldn't catch. At the airport I wanted to cry again, so I ran upstairs to the water fountain to wash my face. That gold medallion, the one my father sent, was a comfort. It had my father's name engraved on it. My father had sent that medallion to me with a note that I should bring it back to him in America. That I would bring it back to him in America. My view was that if I could bring it back to him in America, I would be with my mother again."

"Family reunification" is a staple of American immigrant policy today, as it was a decade ago. But the phrase is

misleading. What it really means is that immigrants, particularly those from poorer countries such as the Dominican Republic, have to come piecemeal, if they want to come at all. They reunify—eventually. The rationale behind this, as Barbara Tobias stated, is to keep immigrants off welfare.

The rationale doesn't take into account what it might cost later.

Children who are left behind for years, a year, or even months, often stay with relatives. Those relatives, as they tell everyone as soon as their more fortunate brothers, sisters, and children leave, are busy minding their own children. Or, like Fian and Víctor, they are too tired for vigilance. The children who have been left behind, fall behind. Academically—and emotionally. The anger of abandonment is difficult to quell. When, and if, they do come to America, those children are the ones who cannot read even in their native languages, never learn English, and ultimately turn away from school.

In the nineties, the practice has remained common. In 1994, the *New York Times* reported on a Jamaican child-smuggling operation and noted: "In most West Indian immigrant families, the women are the pioneers, traveling here alone to find domestic work, settle into new lives and then send for their families. But even legal immigrants from Jamaica must now wait three years to have their children follow them. For instance, government officials are now processing Jamaican applications filed in 1991. . . ." In 1997, immigration advocates predicted that a new law which sets income requirements, rather than the guidelines Barbara Tobias described, will make family reunification even more difficult.

Splitting up families is a hard practice to beat, though. It is the way immigrants have always come. And not always because of immigration officers.

"I know your list of split immigrant families, know it as

well as I know my own family," Mauricio the graduate
student says. "Montague's family. Your mother's family,
briefly. The family in the movie *Hester Street*. That was
like your father's family, right? What's that story? Your
grandfather came to America to get away from your
grandmother. And then your grandmother showed up a
few years later. He was a drunk, too? He beat your grandmother? We have it all wrong. I should be writing a book
about your family."

21

Early May 1986

"Mami, is Mauri with you? . . . I told you Mami, I haven't seen
it. We only got here last night. I've only seen it through the window." Roselia put her hand on the screen in the kitchen window. "Yes, Eliza has been out. That's all. Where are you? . . . Are
you outside María's house? Listen to what I'm asking you,
Mami. Did you bring Mauri? . . . Good. Good. Can you put
him on?" Roselia held the phone tightly. If she dropped it, it
might break. She realized that she had never heard her mother's
voice on a telephone before. "Hello?" she smiled halfway.
"Mauri, is that you?" She had never heard his voice on the
phone, either. "How are you, son? Did you go to the doctor?
What did he say? . . . Good. Good. . . . Don't cry anymore. . . .
Okay. We arrived okay." She pulled away from the receiver and
looked at it, to give herself a rest. "Who took you to the doctor?
. . . And with whom did you sleep? . . . Okay. Good, son. Don't
cry. Put Fian back on. Hello. Mami? Mami? . . . I don't know.
Out there it seems very big to me. The buildings seem big.
There are a lot of cars. Too many. Look, I'll put Eliza on."

Roselia passed the phone, carefully, to her daughter.

"Hello? Doña? . . . Hey, Doña, how are you? Hey, Doña, I got
to this country by airplane. . . . Good, Doña, good. I went in the
airplane, like a car. And Doña? I called Alexis. And the *novela*. I
saw it on TV. . . . Of course they have it here. What happened

there? . . . That's not what happened here. What happened here
is the girl, Victoria's daughter, was in a car accident. It was with two
cars. The girl . . . Diana's her name . . . Yes? . . . Diana went with
a boy named Gabriel. . . . Diana's in a wheelchair. Luis Alfredo and
Cristal went to see her, and she asked for her daughter . . ."

Javier rolled his eyes, pointed to his chest, and mouthed the
word *yo*.

"Wait, Doña," Elizabeth said. "Papi wants to talk to Mauricio."

"Son," Javier said, drawing out the word into a sentence.
"Are you in a lot of pain? . . . No? Good. And tomorrow they will
wash it out? . . . You have your marks? . . . You passed? Good."

As soon as Javier put the phone down, it rang again. Elizabeth
ran back to the kitchen as the second ring began. She waited
until the tone was complete and then picked up the receiver.
"Alexis!" she said.

Javier rolled his eyes at Roselia. She didn't know what to say.
Didn't he realize Elizabeth was sixteen? She talked to boys. It
was late afternoon and although Roselia had taken a shower in
the morning, she wanted another. The hot water felt so good.
She walked into the bathroom, and while she prepared herself,
slowly, admiring the American tile, she could hear Elizabeth on
the phone.

"Well, I already know I like English. For many people it is difficult. But I like difficult things. *Ay!* Can you call me back
later?"

Roselia knew Javier was not happy that Elizabeth was on the
phone.

"I want to see *Calle Cuarenta y dos*," Elizabeth announced.
Off the phone but still talking. "They mention it in my *novela*."

"You can get anywhere from Forty-second Street," Javier
said.

"*Cuarenta y dos* is where the two main characters meet. But
it's not a date. It's a coincidence."

Roselia peeked out from the bathroom. She held out a plastic basin. "Do they make these any bigger, Javier?"

"*Sí, mi amor,* America has everything."

"Well, where is the gas tank, then?"

"Here it comes in through a pipe, like the water." Javier turned from her. "Eliza, get the Tide!" He walked into the bathroom to take a red baseball cap off one of the hooks. "I'll take Elizabeth with me to do laundry," he said. Roselia looked at the tub. She could do the laundry right there.

Elizabeth was rummaging in the pantry. "Windex, Clorox, shoe *polis.* No Tide, Papi."

"*Sí,* there is Tide."

Roselia took her shower and changed. When Javier and Elizabeth came home, her daughter told her all about the laundromat. "There are so many machines, Mami! You put the soap in the top and it all gets rinsed out. Papi says that's because it makes many revolutions and there's a lot of . . . what did you call it?"

"Velocity," Javier said.

Roselia went to take another shower, just a small one.

The next morning, her third day in America, Roselia went with Ernesto to the supermarket. She walked home and into her apartment like a lady. Ernesto was behind her carrying the packages. "Apples, Eliza," she called out. She took four large, shiny, Red Delicious apples out of a bag. "Apples and it's not even winter." She opened the pantry and lined up her other purchases. A twenty-four-ounce bottle of Mazola corn oil. A one-pound package of country-style sausages. A can of Hunt's tomato paste. A five-pound bag of Vitarroz, extra-long-grain rice. A one-pound bag of Jack Rabbit pinto beans. They would be fine for *habichuela,* although she wouldn't make it yet. Where would she cook it?

"I can cook the beans for a long time and they will be very good," she said to Elizabeth, who had wandered into the kitchen. "This is a lot cheaper than home, but the store was very big and there were a lot of people."

Elizabeth examined the rice. "Am I supposed to clean this?"

"No, it's clean, thank you."

Roselia went to the sink and washed the apples. Then she walked to the refrigerator, opened the door, but turned back to the stove for a dish towel. "I can't put my hands in the refrigerator after I wash in hot water," she said. "I will get sick if I do that." She put up some rice to cook for Javier's supper. Then she went into the bedroom, changed into her housedress, and brought a couple of Javier's undershirts into the bathroom. She put the shirts in the plastic basin, put it under the shower, and ran the hot water.

When Javier came home on that May evening, the apartment was warm. Roselia had raised the heat to eighty-five degrees. He sat down at the kitchen table and Elizabeth took off his boots. She brought out his slippers and put them on her father's feet. Roselia set the table and spooned out rice and sausage she had cooked with the tomato paste. She put out some lettuce and tomato she had found in the refrigerator. Javier liked just a little salad.

"Gracias, mi amor," Javier said.

For dessert, she cut up apple sections.

When Javier was finished, she brought him a piece of paper. "From the airport," she said.

"Welcome to the United States of America," it said in Spanish.

"According to the law every new immigrant and each one of the members of his or her family must obtain a Social Security number. You will need this number in order to work in the majority of positions in the United States, to pay taxes, to open bank accounts and many other purposes. When you are established in your new residence, please call the Social Security office so that you can find out where you should apply in order to obtain your number. You can find the telephone number in the city telephone directory under the Government of the United States. Please bring your passport or travel document, residence card (form I-551) if you have one, and a birth certificate (if you have one) for each member of your family and fill out the necessary applications to obtain your new numbers. Your Social Security card will be sent to you by mail within two weeks after the date of your application."

"The consul said I can get Cristian and Mauricio if I work," Roselia said.

Javier rose, opened the window, teased up the storm window, and pulled down the screen. Roselia watched with interest. Then he sat down and began to read the letter.

"Look at the laundry," Roselia said, pointing to a line strung across the backyard of a two-story, redbrick house. "They hang it out here like Camú. That makes me feel happy. It makes me think of Camú."

"Before you get a job, you should learn a little about the city," Javier said. "You should go out."

"You know it's not like me to go out. I didn't do it at home, either. I didn't go out to discotheques or the restaurants. I don't know why. I just don't like it."

Elizabeth led the way to the Social Security office the next morning. Roselia was grateful. She followed her daughter to the southwest corner of Junction Boulevard and Roosevelt Avenue. Above them was a large train platform, unlike any Roselia had seen. It spread from four street corners and made the neighborhood dark.

Roselia thought they were supposed to go up the stairs to the platform. "Papi said it's the wrong side," Elizabeth explained. She pulled her mother across Junction Boulevard. It was the smaller of the two streets. Roselia was grateful for that, too. But Elizabeth looked up at the platform and shook her head again. She pulled her mother into the center of Roosevelt Avenue. Roselia couldn't read the street signals, but she saw that the white one had changed to red. They both began to run as the cars came at them.

Elizabeth stopped at the next stairway. "Mami, I am too smart to just stand here."

Roselia followed her up the stairs.

Elizabeth held up two fingers and handed the clerk a twenty-dollar bill. *"Veinte pesos!"* she whispered. She collected her change and the two tokens and handed one to Roselia. Then she walked through the steel door. Roselia smiled weakly. The other passengers, she saw, were putting their money into a small box and pushing a wheel-like contraption around to get inside. She did the same. Elizabeth shrugged her shoulders when she realized. "The next time I will know," she said.

Roselia followed Elizabeth up another flight of stairs to an open platform. Elizabeth walked onto it confidently, while Roselia stayed at the top of the stairs, held tight to the banister, and watched her daughter with awe.

"Somebody here must speak Spanish," Elizabeth said. She walked over to a large, elderly woman with red hair. "Doña, how do I get to Seventy-fourth Street?"

"You take the train that comes over here," the woman answered in perfect Spanish.

On the train Roselia stood and hung on to the straps that were on the ceiling, as Elizabeth did, although there were empty seats. Elizabeth almost missed Seventy-fourth Street and she had to quickly pull Roselia out the door with her.

"We need to walk two blocks until we find Seventy-second Street," Elizabeth explained. Roselia peered into the shops. One sold clams, another had ribs that looked good. One had small brown pillows that were some kind of food she could not identify.

"I need to ask again," Elizabeth said, unperturbed. "Somebody who speaks Spanish?" She stopped the first woman who passed them. *"Español?"*

"No Spanish!" the woman yelled.

"What did she say?" Roselia asked.

"She doesn't speak Spanish." Elizabeth turned to the store window behind her. "I want to look at these sneakers."

"Not now, Eliza!" Roselia was desperate. She kept walking, fished in her purse for the paper with the address, and looked at the building in front of her. It was the correct number.

Inside, a security guard handed them forms in Spanish and told them to fill them out. Roselia began to write.

"What race are we?" Elizabeth asked.

"Just write Hispanic," a man who was standing next to them, another applicant, said. "In America, everyone who speaks Spanish is Hispanic."

Roselia was so relieved to hear Spanish that she would be any race the *yanquis* wanted her to be. Going out in New York was too much work. She would never do it alone. Tomorrow she would stay in the apartment all day in her housedress, even though Marta was coming for dinner. She would send Elizabeth shopping for food.

22

Mid-May 1986

Javier realized that Roselia had rejected New York, the New York outside her window, anyway. She was happiest at home, in her housedress, cooking, puttering, and looking out at the neighbors' laundry. At suppertime, Javier could tell if she had spent the day like that because she kissed him, helped him with his slippers, and smiled a full smile. He saw that she went out only to shop for food or cleaning supplies. She did go with him to Marta's, but complained that his sister's furniture was much nicer than what they had. Javier knew that his wife had never been adventurous, even when she was surrounded by her family. But she had at least shown spunk in difficult situations. What would she do in the winter? Marta, when she came for dinner, had put it too clearly: "Can you imagine Roselia in the cold?" Javier was sure his wife would be better if she had the two other children with her, particularly the boy.

He considered asking the newspaper to help him get visas for the children. He didn't object to asking for a favor, or even begging for one. But he decided not to do it. He worried that he was immobile, as he had been in his youth. But if he asked the newspaper, it would look bad, particularly if they turned him down. With his children's pictures on the front page once a month, it would happen on its own. He did not tell Roselia that he believed it would happen. This wasn't as simple as bragging about winning the lottery, the way he used to do. In those days if he lost, he just had less money. Now if he was wrong, they would be at the mercy of the consulate. Roselia would not survive having her hopes raised, only to be disappointed.

Two week earlier, in a tonier Queens neighborhood, Congressman Gary Ackerman had picked up his Sunday *Newsday* and studied a front-page picture of four unhappy people outside a decrepit palm hut, including a young boy who stared intently into the camera. Ackerman read about the Almontes and discovered that their father, pictured riding the New York City subway, lived in his district as a legal resident. Not a citizen, not a voter. Not yet.

Ackerman eventually would become a luminary of the House Foreign Affairs committee, an Asia expert, a broker of peace in the Philippines, and the last American official to talk to Kim Il Sung before the Korean strongman died. But in 1986, the abrasive, rotund Democrat was a two-term congressman whose attempts to lose weight garnered him more attention than his political accomplishments. Ackerman did know his community, though. He had prospered with a string of his own small, local newspapers and had accepted that Queens was becoming a mini United Nations. Instead of trying to fight that, he made a point of getting as many immigrants as he could on his side. He had even flown to Bucharest to convince Romanian officials to let a young physician, the wife of a man in his district, leave the country. Ackerman and his son accompanied the woman back to New York and the congressman was touted as the engineer of a romantic reunion. Then the woman accused her husband of physical abuse, left him, and filed for divorce. The congressman, although embarrassed, still wanted to be a savior. Children, he reasoned, were easier to save. He read the Almonte story again. This, he thought to himself, is even worse than the Romanians.

This isn't some crazy dictatorship. This is us. We're the ones who are separating this family. Ackerman put one of his aides, Fior Rodriguez— a Dominican herself—on the case.

When the phone call from the *congresista*'s office came, Javier wanted to jump, scream, and cheer. He wanted to announce that he didn't have to sell any calves, that he had known all along he would win. But he was circumspect. It could still go wrong. All that the woman who called had said was that she worked for the *congresista* and would try. The woman—he could tell from her accent she was Dominican—told Javier that the *congresista* had read about his children in the newspaper. She said the *congresista*'s own children were the same age and he was "personally embarrassed by the policy of the United States government." Javier was encouraged, but he knew that any number of Dominican politicians could say the same thing and do nothing.

Then the woman who made the call came to his house. Fior Rodriguez was young, well dressed, and pretty. She knew exactly what she needed to take with her to the consulate in Santo Domingo, which was where the *congresista* was sending her to help Javier. Right to the source. "Your pay stubs," Fior Rodriguez instructed Javier. "Give me all your most recent pay stubs so that I can show them how much money you are making now." Javier had never met this *congresista*. He couldn't even pronounce his name. He couldn't vote for him. He gave Fior Rodriguez whatever papers she requested. America was a wonderful country.

Fior Rodriguez stopped by a few days later to tell him that she had called the consulate twenty times but had gotten nowhere. She told him not to worry. The *congresista* himself was going to call.

Two weeks later, Fior Rodriguez called from Santo Domingo with good news. She had gotten a *cita* for the children, for May 29, a week away. *"Guuauw,"* Javier said quietly. He tried to control himself. His children had had a *cita* once before. Fior asked if she could drive up to Camú and bring them down to the capital. "Of course," he said.

A few days later Fior called again to say she was worried. The United States, though, wasn't the problem. "It's our country," she said. "They're talking about a coup." After an eight-year absence, Joaquín Balaguer, aging and blind, had—according to the latest tally—won the presidential election held earlier that month. A lot of people were unhappy about that. Balaguer had last ruled for twelve years, from 1966 until 1978. During the 1978 election, his soldiers beat the witnesses and stole ballot boxes. Jimmy Carter had to push him out of office. Fior said it was her uncle who had heard there might be a coup. Radio Bemba, Javier thought disparagingly, forgetting the times when Radio Bemba was all they had.

"My uncle is a general in the Air Force," Fior said. Javier felt himself sink. He still trusted the pilots.

It's Balaguer, Javier told himself. It's that old man. It would be that old man. A *Trujillista!*

Javier remembered being young and feeling angry about the Mirabal sisters. He remembered voting for Juan Bosch to keep the *Trujillistas* away, even though Balaguer was in exile and Bosch was surely a Communist. Javier had been sure that without Bosch the *Trujillistas* would be back. He would never have voted for a Communist if he didn't think it would keep Balaguer away. But Bosch had been such a disaster. And Bosch was still around, too. He was among the candidates who ran—unsuccessfully—against Balaguer.

Those two old men!

Javier held his breath for a few days. In the end, Fior's uncle, the old pilot, was wrong.

Dominican historian Frank Moya Pons writes that Balaguer organized his own paramilitary right-wing groups, which he claimed were "uncontrollable forces." According to the historian, "More than 3,000 Dominicans lost their lives in terrorist acts between 1966 and 1974."

In the 1990s, Mauricio the graduate student was one of many Dominican-Americans to read *They Forged the Signature of God,* a thinly veiled fictional account of Balaguer and his terror. The book was said to be the best-selling novel ever in the Dominican Republic, and it was given a national book award by a literary panel. But then the Minister of Education rescinded the award, and Balaguer, of course, denounced the book. But that was all he did. Perhaps things *were* improving. Trujillo would have never permitted such a book to be published, and would have killed the author to ensure that.

"This isn't typical," Tobias complained on the day that Mauricio and Cristian were scheduled for their second *cita*. She said that Ackerman used "excessive pressure" to get the appointment, the "pressure" of his office, no doubt. The Almonte children, she said, would be getting ahead of 2,300 other people "because they knew Congressman Ackerman." Tobias was asked why Jonathan Mueller could not simply have told Roselia to get her husband's pay stubs. "We have one hundred forty thousand active files and twenty-one caseworkers," she said. Did Mueller make a mistake? "I don't think it was a mistake," she said. "I think he gave them the best advice he could under the circumstances that were presented to him. . . . I could have said he could have been more complete, but the advice he gave was not wrong." When it was suggested that his advice was wrong, since the Almonte children could have qualified for visas the first time, Tobias balked. "What was available did not meet the requirements the first time. We cannot be omniscient. We cannot know the exact details of every family that applies to us. We have to leave some of the burden of this on the applicants themselves. . . . The burden of proof should not be put on us. We do the best we can. We give it our best shot from what we know."

In the spotlight, the congressman spoke about trying to do something in Congress to help families immigrate together.

But he had nothing specific in mind, and months later he still didn't. Instead, he mused—albeit prophetically—about the United States' burgeoning problems with immigrants and immigration.

"I think it's as much an attitudinal problem as it is a legislative problem," he explained. "It's not really that you need a law that says you should not take the parents away from the children. That's just good common instinct. . . . There's a higher price to pay on different levels when you separate a mother and father from their children. There's the price of pain and anguish and suffering. If you tell a family that they cannot afford a luxury, that's one thing, but if you tell a person they can't afford their children that are already born, that is an absolute outrage. There are poor families who have nine children, and it really doesn't make much of a difference at that point. . . .

"I've talked to some of the people from immigration. . . . But there are members of Congress who agree with them that you should do whatever possible to make it difficult and discourage people from coming into our country."

23

Late May 1986

On the afternoon that he knew for sure the American government was going to give him a visa, Mauricio Almonte sat next to his sister Cristian on a bench at the United States consulate in Santo Domingo. He had been on that particular bench before, and it was still hard and uncomfortable. Mauricio fidgeted in a new pair of stiff Bonjour jeans. With his new jeans, which Mami had bought for him before she left, he wore a crisp, pink shirt.

The day before, his grandmother had brought him into Puerto Plata to talk to Papi on the phone. Papi had told him it would work this time: "You will bring the medallion back to me here, son. Just listen to the *dominicanyorker* when she comes to Camú. She works for a *congresista*."

This wasn't bad at all, Mauricio thought. Mami had only been gone a few weeks. She had left May 2. Now it was May 29.

"In a year we'll be able to read an English newspaper," Cristian said. The polish on her long nails was the same shade of bright pink as his shirt.

"Less," Mauricio argued. He wondered about the English verb that was the same as *ir*. He wanted to be able to say that he was going somewhere, in English. With any luck he really was going somewhere, this time.

The clock on the consulate wall said 1:45 when Mauricio heard their names called. He stood up with his sister, as if they were attached. Cristian bit down on her longest pink nail. He played with his papi's medallion.

This meeting with a visa officer was even shorter than the last one. But they came out smiling.

Later, with white sheets of paper, their visas, in their hands, they walked past Ronald Reagan's portrait.

"I am leaving on Friday," Cristian said to the president of the United States.

Mauricio thought that was very funny.

That night in Camú, Mauricio watched as Cristian sorted through the letters and instructions Mami had sent for them. It felt so good to be getting chores from Mami again, even if most of them were for Cristian. Mami wanted Cristian to take the dagger that had belonged to their dead uncle Mirito and give it to one of her brothers. Papi had left it in the wardrobe. Mami had sent a ten-dollar bill and Cristian was supposed to send one of María's daughters to buy her *dos condicionador de romero* and *cremita bellina*.

"American beauty products," she had written, "do not work on Dominican skin or hair."

All Mami really wanted Mauricio to do was to leave all his toys under his bed. He hoped that meant he would get new ones in America. Elizabeth had a few more orders for him. He was supposed to bring his English books—how could he forget those? But leave his sneakers. "They have better ones here," she had written.

At bedtime Mauricio hugged Fian, who was crying over his departure, although many of her other grandchildren either lived with her or visited for hours or days at a time. Then, for the next to the last time, he walked up the path to his *casita*. Grass had grown high around it. He walked through it and stopped in the kitchen out of habit, but there was nothing there, except a half jug of salt and a hot plate Tío Julio had made from a brick. Mami had given her gas stove to his grandmother, and the *casita* was a man's house now. Nobody cooked much in it, anymore. Mauricio had eaten at Fian's all the time and eaten well. His grandmother bragged that he "ate everything I've cooked for him. All the milk, all the meat, all the beans, all the *tostones*." Mauricio loved his grandmother. But he'd had to be honest with her. When she'd asked if he loved her, he'd said, "I do, Abuela. But I love my mother more."

When he woke, he realized he had one more day in his country. Outside of the *campo,* there was just one person he wanted to see to say good-bye. His teacher, Mercedes Robles. He had only begun chatting with her the last few weeks. But since he didn't speak to anyone much, particularly teachers, she became important to him. Since school was already out, he would have to go to her house in Puerto Plata.

She lived in a *bloque* house. He knocked, and his teacher opened the door and enfolded him in her arms.

"I am going tomorrow," Mauricio said quietly. A motorcycle sped by and he knew that its noise made his voice harder to hear than usual.

"What, *mi amor*?"

"I am going," he said, trying to speak up.

Mercedes touched his shoulder. "Well, you see, all your dreams have come true. Can I go with you?"

"If I could, I would take you," he said, a big smile on his face.

"How do you feel about going so soon?"

"Nervous but happy."

"Go. But remember Quisqueya."

Mauricio nodded. He would remember the "Mother of All Lands."

"Vaya con Dios. Vaya con Dios. Mis saludos a Javier y Roselia."

Víctor stood on his porch the next morning and waved good-bye to Mauricio and Cristian. Fian, in a clean, pink dress, was with them. This time she was going to the airport. The caravan of cars and pickups that accompanied them seemed even longer than the one that had sent off Roselia and Elizabeth. As soon as they arrived at the airport, everyone began to say good-bye to him, although it was a while yet before they had to leave.

"We'll see you there soon," one of María's daughters called out as the flight was announced.

Fian hugged Cristian. "Go without any sadness. Everything will be good."

"Don't be nervous," Tío Julio said to Mauricio.

Fian hugged Cristian again and began to cry. "She's leaving me all alone," she said, her voice shaking. Three of her little grandchildren clung to her skirt. Fian bent down and gave Mauricio a long, loud, smacking kiss. He looked up at Fior Rodriguez, who just arrived. *"Vámonos,"* he said.

On the way to the plane a large man in a khaki airport security uniform got up from his chair and, ceremoniously, walked over to Cristian. His stomach hung over his pants and he held his belly, proudly. Mauricio thought he looked familiar.

"A farewell kiss?" the security guard asked Cristian.

Cristian looked behind her and primly gave him her cheek.

Mauricio saw that the man handed his sister a piece of paper.

They traveled American Airlines. Papi had paid extra for it. He had said that he didn't want them to go on Dominicana because it was always delayed. But this plane left on time and landed on time, although Mauricio felt that the trip had lasted forever. *"Juan Kenadee* Airport," he sighed as the plane finally began to descend. He saw a skyline he had only seen once in a picture.

Large buildings covered with lights. It occurred to him that America might be fun. "Ah," he said, "what a beautiful city."

Mauricio followed his sister and Fior off the plane. He was looking for his mother, but the first person he saw was a round American man with curly black hair who was waving two small American flags. "The *congresista*," Fior explained. The man handed a flag to Mauricio and another to Cristian. Mauricio squinted because his picture was being taken by two photographers who were trying to get him and Cristian near the *congresista*. The *congresista* said something to him, in English, which he didn't understand. He wished he did. He thought this man was funny.

Mauricio followed his sister, Fior, and the *congresista*, quickly, through customs and immigration.

"Do you like baseball?" the *congresista* asked him, in English.

Mauricio was so proud. He understood and he knew what to answer. "Basketball," he said, giggling. Then he looked up and saw his parents running toward him. With his flag still in one hand, he opened his arms wide.

His father did the same with his arms. They stood for a second looking at each other, grinning as though their team had just won. Then Mauricio hugged his father, in what he believed was a strong, male way. Cristian and his mother were hugging, too.

His mother, his mami, let go of Cristian and grabbed him by the head. She cradled his chin in the crook of her elbow and he felt his head being taken in both her hands. He held his mother around the waist with both his arms, but he kept his fist closed around his American flag.

His father hugged his sister. With her high heels on, she was a bit taller than Papi.

Mauricio started to cry. He was still hugging his mother.

"Mauri, do you like this airport?" Elizabeth asked. He hadn't noticed Elizabeth. She was hugging Cristian.

He pulled away from his mother, but he was crying so much, he couldn't answer.

"Did you get your marks from school?" Elizabeth asked.

Still crying, he pointed to his report card, which was sticking out of the back pocket of his Bonjour jeans.

"There are many things. It's very pretty," Cristian said.

The *congresista* shouted something about a baseball game.

"You were the one who told us that Gary Ackerman said he was going to take us to see the Mets," Mauricio the graduate student says. "You said he wanted to take me and his son. I had no idea what he was talking about, although I did hear the word baseball. He never took us, though. Fior came over a lot, but we never heard from the congressman. I'm not sure I would have wanted to go to a baseball game with a congressman, anyway."

For a month in the *campo* and for hours on the plane, Mauricio had imagined America as a place where he could be with Mami. When they arrived at the brick house that was now his home, he looked into the bedrooms. His Tío Ernesto's clothes were in one. In the other he saw a small bed with a Humpty Dumpty cover on it and wondered how he and Mami and Papi would all fit.

Later, after dark, he went into the bedroom and began to take off his clothes. He was so tired. All he wanted to do was sleep with his head on Mami's breast.

She came into the room and put her arm around him. "*Ay,* Mauri," she said.

Mauricio looked up at his mother, expecting a half smile. But he didn't see it.

"Mauri, here you'll sleep in the *sala* with your sisters."

"Mami?"

"I am sorry, Mauri. But you have to learn how to become a man."

He spent a lonely night on that hard sofa in the strange apartment with its new appliances and electrical smells, listening to his sisters giggle together in the single bed.

24

May–September 1986

For three days Mauricio strained to read every English word he saw. He read words from the television screen, from signs he saw when his father or Tío Ernesto took him out for walks. He tried to read the package of bubble gum his uncle bought for him to find out why it came with baseball stickers instead of baseball cards. But the words swam past him, like the fastest little fish in the river Camú. There was only one solution. On his fourth day in America, he asked Cristian to come with him to the school he had seen on their way home from the airport. Fior had said it was a *primaria*. School Diez y Nueve. She told Mami they gave free English lessons there.

"I know how to get there," Mauricio said, surprised by his own courage. "Please, it's not far."

Ten minutes later he was walking down the street, his older sister behind him. They passed a group of boys sitting on the front steps of a house like his. Mauricio eyed one of them, the one who had a bicycle, and wished he had friends. He kept walking, stopped at the corner, and looked carefully for cars, the way Papi and Tío had shown him. Then he ran across, his head turning back to make sure Cristian was following. At the next corner, he did the same but with less fear. In the distance he could see the redbrick building, P. S. 19. He slowed as he got closer, and when he was directly across from it, he stopped altogether. *Guau.* He hadn't realized the school was so big. What if they didn't let him in? He should have brought his report card. His last English mark at José DuBeau had been a 90; it was his best mark. Did he need a uniform? He'd had uniform at José DuBeau. Why had he left it in Camú? Next to the school, a boy in a blue-and-white-striped baseball shirt threw a rubber ball against the wall of a house and caught it with a real baseball glove. On the next throw the boy missed, and the ball went rolling into the gutter. Mauricio looked at Cristian. She nodded. He retrieved the ball and threw it back across the street. As the boy caught it in his glove, Mauricio motioned for his sister to cross the street with him.

The front doors of P. S. 19 were metal, painted brown but scratched and heavy. Mauricio strained as he pulled one open. Cristian followed without saying a word. The hallway was dark; it was a cave. At José DuBeau he had been able to walk out of his classroom, directly into the open air.

Inside, a police officer stood next to a woman who sat in a chair with an attached desk. It was as if the woman was being guarded.

"Can I help you?" she asked, in English.

Mauricio didn't understand.

The woman opened her mouth and nodded knowingly.

"Have you just arrived?" she asked in Spanish.

Cristian nodded. "We want to learn English," his sister said with a giggle.

"Of course, then," the woman answered. "You can sit in on the classes. Anyone can. But they're only on until the twenty-sixth. Monday, Wednesday, and Friday from nine to ten in the morning."

Mauricio's brown eyes were puffy from sleep when he and Cristian arrived at P. S. 19 a few mornings later. They stood in the dark hallway with Mami behind them. Mami had insisted they needed her to register and had followed them to the school, her purse clutched in one hand, their visas and passports in the other. Mauricio looked up and down the hallway. When the teacher came out alone, he was relieved. He didn't want any boys his age to see him with his mother.

The teacher had large, flashing eyes, brown like his and an enormous smile. She spoke Spanish as fast as a Dominican. But with a different accent.

"Are you ready for class?" she asked Mami.

Mauricio was annoyed. Why wasn't the teacher speaking to him?

"*Sí,* I'm ready," he interrupted.

They walked through another dark hallway to a large, stuffy

room that smelled of soap powder. Students, women mostly, were
sitting around rectangular tables. So many mothers, Mauricio
thought. Did everyone bring their mami? His eyes checked
each table. No, this couldn't be. Almost everyone in the class was
a mother. There were a few fathers. But no boys his age. There
weren't even any girls his age. He looked everywhere for a boy
his age, someone like the baseball player he had seen the other
day. But he and Cristian were the only ones who weren't adults.

Baffled, he sat down at a long table with his mother and sister. The teacher asked the class something in English.

"El Salvador," answered one of the mamis.

Mauricio understood that.

The teacher asked another question. Mauricio heard the
words "El Salvador" again. But that was all he understood. She
asked another question he couldn't understand at all. The students were all answering in English.

"Yes?" answered another mami.

Mauricio knew that meant *sí*. This was like watching a television program that kept turning on and off. At least in Camú
when the power went off, it stayed off for hours. Mauricio tried
to translate. Either the woman was from El Salvador or was
going to El Salvador. Was she going home?

"Ay em goween to Domeeniecan Reepooblic," another woman
said.

Mauricio saw that his mother was smiling at the mention of
their country. Around him people were whispering their own
answers.

The teacher began a conversation with a woman who looked
Chinese. She said something about Cuba to the woman. Mauri-
cio guessed that the teacher was from Cuba. She held up the
Chinese woman's pencil.

"This is her pencil," the teacher said.

"Ah," Mauricio thought. *"Lápiz. Penseal."*

"This is her pencil," she said. She waved her hand in the
direction of her own mouth.

"This is her pencil," the students repeated. Mauricio tried to mouth the words, and as he spoke he turned to his mother and was amazed to see she was doing the same.

"This is his pencil," the teacher said, holding up a man's pencil. Cristian's lips were pursed. The teacher took three pencils in her hand. "Long, longer, longest," she said. "This pencil is longer."

Cristian was trying to mouth the words. Mauricio was surprised, again.

As they walked home, Mauricio saw that his mother was still holding their passports and visas. They hadn't needed them. "This is very important," Mami said. "I won't learn all of English. But I'll learn a little. A few words." Mauricio thought it was strange to hear his mother worry about school.

"I didn't get a bicycle until I was a teenager," Mauricio says. He sounds wistful and needy, not at all like someone on full scholarship. "Almost as soon as we got to America, Papi's landlady tried to throw us out. She was Greek and didn't speak much English herself. But she told the Dominican woman who lived in the basement apartment to say that she was sorry. I remember her exact words. She said to say that she was sorry, we were nice people—and clean, too. But she had rented to two brothers. Not a family. The rent was already six hundred dollars a month, and she wanted to raise it to eight hundred dollars. Papi was so worried about finding us a new place to live that I didn't have the heart to bring up the bicycle. Of course, the bicycle he eventually bought me was a teenage bicycle. Seven years later I came home from college and found the bike I had wanted when I was eleven. Papi had bought it for Julito, my sister Cristian's son."

Later that week, on a day so bright that sunbeams poked through the elevated train tracks like shiny pillars, Mauricio took the subway into Manhattan with his sisters. There were no English classes that morning, and Papi had given them *dólares* before he left for work. "Get off at Times Square," he had said. "You can get anywhere from Times Square." As the train rattled through Queens, Mauricio tried to picture those tall buildings he had seen only in photographs. It was Cristian's first time in Manhattan, too, and Elizabeth was *loca* over the idea of showing them how much she knew. Mauricio reminded himself that his oldest sister had only been to Manhattan once, before they had arrived and all she had seen was was Times Square, some shops, and the lobby of the Hilton Hotel where Fernandito, her favorite Dominican *merengue* star, had stayed. It wasn't as if she had seen his room, or anything like that. The truth about Elizabeth was that she bragged too much. She wasn't even afraid to get lost. She said that Papi had told her if you want to know Manhattan you have to get lost.

"We'll get off at Times Square and walk to the Empire State Building," Elizabeth explained. Alexis, a boy from home who now lived in *Bruckleen,* had told her what to do. Mauricio peered through the dirty train window and tried to understand what he was seeing. One *bloque* house after another, one *bloque* building after another. Red *bloques,* like the ones in Corona. Big buildings, too. Large signs, most of them in English. He had to strain to look at the pictures and guess what they said. He watched the doors, too. They opened and closed so quickly.

Then it went dark and he jolted. "We are underground," Elizabeth explained.

The train arrived at *Calle Cuarenta y dos* and Mauricio grabbed onto Elizabeth's elbow, petrified that the doors would close and separate them. When they got off there were so many people in front of his eyes. He tried to look at just one thing. He tried looking at his sisters' shoes but there were four of them. He tried looking at one of the English signs. But there were so many of those. He tried looking at one American face. But there were more of those than signs.

"I have been in New York a month," Elizabeth called out, as they walked. "Already I know how to go to the store, go to the supermarket, get on the subway and know where to get off, go to the laundry. If this continues I will make a lot of progress."

"I'll know more than you soon," Cristian said to her.

Outside, the buildings were even larger than the ones in Queens, and they shined more brightly, too, as if someone had just washed them all.

"After the Empire State Building, we can take a subway to Central Park," Elizabeth said. "Alexis told me to go there, too."

"Alexis is the one who keeps calling you," Cristian said.

"You better be quiet."

Mauricio walked to the music of his sisters' bickering, familiar music. How strange to hear it in this large city. Elizabeth grabbed them both. "Pray to your saint," she cried out as she pulled them across a wide street.

"I'll know more than her soon," Cristian muttered when they were safely across.

At the Empire State Building they rode the elevator to the observation deck on the eighty-sixth floor, same number as the year. They walked outside, and Mauricio decided that he wanted to look down at everything. All those wonderful buildings—there were so many of them—had become minuscule, and little toy cars moved around them faster than any toys he had ever seen. If only he could lean over and lift one up, as though he were a giant. Thinking about that made him dizzy. "You'd need an airplane to get higher than this? Right?" he asked. Before he could get an answer, they were in an elevator, speeding down the way they had sped up. It was as if he had dreamed it all.

In Central Park, Mauricio climbed a rock, stood on tiptoes, stretched his long, skinny arms. He looked up at an American flag that flew from a skyscraper beyond the General Motors Building, at the ornate trim of the Plaza Hotel, at a sign for the Essex House, which confused him because he translated it literally and could not imagine that a house could be so big. English phrases he had learned at José DuBeau, and even a few from P. S. 19, tumbled out of his mouth: "It's okay. . . . Let's go. . . . So long! . . . See you tomorrow."

"Mira! Policia!"

A man was being put into handcuffs. Mauricio wondered if this was over marijuana. In Camú he had heard the grown-ups say that there were a lot of *drogas* in America.

When the adult education classes at P. S. 19 ended, Mauricio and Cristian enrolled in a summer program for new immigrants. The classes were held at the Leonardo da Vinci Intermediate School, also in Corona. But this time the only adults were teachers.

Mauricio loved summer school, and not just because there were boys, lots of boys, his age. His teacher, Mr. Olivares, was from the Dominican Republic, and he played the guitar. On their first day, Mr. Olivares spoke softly—and in Spanish—to all of them, even the students who were Chinese. He explained that they would be studying English and mathematics—and going on trips all over New York City. "Bring your lunch those days," he had instructed them. "But just a simple sandwich. There's no need to bring meat. Or beans." Mauricio was so excited to hear his own language in a classroom again that he forgot to laugh. "The first year is hard for all of us," Mr. Olivares reassured them. "You miss your family at home a lot."

During the weeks that followed, Mauricio and Cristian saw the United Nations, the Bronx Zoo, the New York Aquarium, the Statue of Liberty, and the South Street Seaport. "I think you like the trips better than the school," Papi said each time they came home from another excursion. On the last day of summer school, Mr. Olivares spoke to them sternly: "It is very important to finish school," he said. "You leave school and you get a job in a store making a hundred dollars a week and you think, Four hundred dollars a month. That's terrific. A lot of my friends did that. When they're twenty-one or twenty-two they get married and have children, and maybe they get a raise to one hundred and twenty-five dollars a week. That means they're making five hundred dollars a month. Here that isn't even enough to pay the rent." Then Mr. Olivares played "Guantanamera" on his guitar. Mauricio believed that Mr. Olivares himself was *un hombre muy sincero*.

Muddy Cup

★ ★ ★

By September, Mauricio felt American. At least he thought he was American until the morning of the first day of school. He walked though the streets of Corona, wondering why he felt so nervous. He was on his way back to Leonardo da Vinci, and Mr. Olivares might be his teacher again. He had to repeat seventh grade, but he didn't think he was nervous about that. Was he nervous because his family had moved over the weekend? Was it his fault they had to move?

Their new apartment was nice. It had two bedrooms and was on the first floor, like the last one. But now Tío Ernesto slept in the basement, where the landlord rented a few rooms to single men. That meant that Mauricio and his sisters could share the second bedroom. They didn't have to sleep in the living room anymore. This was the house where Papi had lived when he first moved to Queens; this was Frank Corona's house. Papi had said that Frank would never throw them out, that he treated Javier like "family." The landlord now lived in Santiago. But his wife and daughter still had a room in the house, and another daughter lived upstairs with her own family.

Mauricio stopped on the pavement in front of the school. He put his Adidas book bag on the sidewalk and looked up at the four stories of white bricks of the junior high. Why, now that it was September, did it look so big? The white bricks glistened and hurt his eyes. The kids who swarmed the building without noticing him seemed so American. He played with the medallions around his neck and looked for someone he knew.

He felt in his pocket for the pencil sharpener attached to a miniature globe. "Your own little world," Cristian had said, with admiration, when he showed it to her. Mauricio had bought the pencil sharpener and his book bag in the same store on Junction Boulevard, and he had been sure they would make him feel like he belonged at Leonardo da Vinci Intermediate on the first day of school. Why did he keep hearing his mother blessing him as he walked out the door? *Dios te bendiga, m'hijo.* He wished he was home, even though he wasn't sure what was home anymore. This morning the only thing familiar about the place where they lived was the clip of his mother's voice, rushing him out the door, telling him he would be fine since he had already spent two months in the same school. She didn't understand that summer school was different. It wasn't really school, just a lot of kids like him who couldn't speak English. ("Recent arrivals," was what Mr. Olivares called them.) He wasn't even the most confused one there. The Chinese kids were definitely more confused. In class their heads popped back and forth between people talking English and people talking Spanish, and since Mauricio couldn't speak to them he never found out if they knew which language was which. But he had wondered about that.

He kept searching and saw a boy he knew from the summer. He didn't go over to him because the boy was there with his mother.

When the bell rang, the metal school doors seemed to open by themselves. Mauricio watched the other students grab their backpacks and their book bags, lunch boxes, and briefcases and walk quickly inside. No running allowed, the teachers on the steps said. At least that was what Mauricio guessed they said. He picked up his Adidas bag, turned his back to the doors of Leonardo da Vinci, and headed for home.

Fortieth Road, he said to himself.

He was afraid he would go to the old apartment. The new apartment wasn't that far away, only a few blocks. But it had a whole new address. It was in Elmhurst, Queens, instead of Corona, Queens. Fortieth Road, Elmhurst, Queens, New York, U.S.A. The new apartment was six blocks from their old apartment, three blocks from Junction Boulevard instead of eight; twelve blocks from Leonardo da Vinci instead of seven. It was a yellow two-family house and Papi liked it.

Tío Ernesto answered the doorbell.

"There was a long line. Everyone else was with someone bigger, a brother or a mother," Mauricio told him.

"We needed some things, some *yuca*," Tío Ernesto said. He

was cheerful as always and happy to see Mauricio. "Mami went to Top Tomato."

"I thought I wouldn't be able to go in alone."

Mauricio followed his uncle down the short, dark hallway. They walked past the staircase up to the top floor and past the staircase to the basement where his uncle slept.

In the kitchen his uncle mixed a large spoon of white sugar into his cup of dark coffee.

"You'd better go to school and try again," Ernesto said.

He felt silly walking to school again. But he didn't know where else to go. He counted the blocks. Twelve instead of seven blocks to Leonardo da Vinci. The sidewalk outside the school was empty now. He took a breath, marched up the stairs, and found the crowd inside. "You're late," a teacher said. "Go to the auditorium." He understood that. In the auditorium, he looked for his class sign—Seven bilingual Two—and joined the line. Another boy got on behind him. He was the same size as Mauricio but he had *pelo bueno* combed even straighter with water. His skin was darker, but to Mauricio he still looked like he might be better at sports and more popular.

"Are you new here, too?" Mauricio asked him.

"Yes."

"Do you know English?"

"No."

Mauricio giggled. "Me neither."

"Welcome to this school, Leonardo da Vinci," said the teacher who stood on the stage. She started out in Spanish. "You are in a bilingual program. You are going to learn in Spanish and English, and I hope that after three years you will speak perfect English. . . ." When she switched to English, Mauricio lost her and grabbed on to his new friend, who said his name was Waldir and that he was from Medellín in Colombia. Mauricio clung to Waldir all day. He hung on to Waldir's book bag like a dead weight and let Waldir maneuver him around the building. They got lost together, and the other children laughed at them, mostly at Waldir, who wasn't afraid to ask dumb questions. Mauricio hardly said a word.

In one class the teacher asked Waldir a question, and he stood up to answer. Mauricio guessed that was how they did it in Medellín. But here, it was a mistake. Two boys, Dominicans, began to laugh.

"You don't have to stand up in America," the teacher said.

At lunchtime, they followed the others into a big, bright room, the cafeteria. Mauricio watched his classmates. They were all getting trays filled with food. Nobody was paying. Mr. Olivares—who they did have for math—had said that lunch would be free. Mauricio thought he was joking. At José DuBeau he had bought his lunches, *chimichurris*—cooked meat sandwiches—from a street vendor. He got on line, took his tray, and sat down. He had milk, an orange, and a small brown puff that could have been a *chimichurri* but was lighter in color. Mauricio squeezed it open and scooped out the filling. Ah, *papas*. Then he noticed his classmates biting into the whole thing. He looked at Waldir and giggled.

"How was school?" his father asked him that night. Outside the air had begun to get chilly, but his parents turned the heat so high his mother was in a sleeveless shirt.

"*Bien,*" Mauricio said.

"I went back to school that day," Mauricio says. "But my mom never did. Those adult education classes at P. S. Nineteen ended with summer vacation, and by September she was working in a small clothing factory and too busy— she said—to return. For years she claimed she would go back, eventually. She was still saying it when I started college. But that was because she felt me slipping away from her. I was more comfortable speaking English than Spanish, and I was more comfortable reading it. I never said that to her. But she knew. She heard me on the telephone. She saw the books I brought into the house, books

with titles she couldn't read. Although maybe it was better she didn't know that what I was reading at fifteen was *Lady Chatterley's Lover.*

"I wouldn't call my father an English speaker," Mauricio says. "That's why he can't get his own contractor's license. But my father knows more English than he lets on, and has for a long time. My first summer in America, when we needed a new apartment, I walked the streets with my father, looking for 'for rent' signs. I found a sign written in pen on a loose-leaf paper and taped to a door. I couldn't read it, but I was so proud, so sure I had found a new apartment for my family. I brought it to my father. *"Ay, m'hijo,"* he said. "That's not it. It says that their doorbell is broken." I don't know why my father never speaks English. He might be uncomfortable about his accent, or maybe he doesn't want to embarrass my mother. I think all he cares about is that the three of us speak English, which we do.

"Are my parents typical? They might be typical of people their age. My aunts and uncles are the same. But I don't know that they're typical of immigrants. That class at P. S. Nineteen was so crowded. That's why they held it in the cafeteria. None of the classrooms were large enough. Elizabeth went to night classes at the Louis Armstrong Middle School so that she didn't have to go with us and Mami, and it was just as bad, if not worse. And Louis Armstrong was only a fifteen-minute walk from P. S. Nineteen."

Seven years later, in 1993, the *New York Times* reported that the city's free English classes were still as crowded, if not more so. Many prospective students had to wait months, even years, for a place.

Pinelawn National Cemetery in Melville, Long Island, stretched for *tareas* and *tareas* with its laser straight rows of small, white, rectangular tombstones, each one looking like a ghost itself. The tombstones were all the same size and shape, and they spread out on a flat blanket of green grass. Mauricio walked with Papi, ahead of his other relatives. He had never seen grass so green and straight or land so flat. And so many tombstones, all the same. All they had in the *campo* was a hilly little graveyard hidden in the *cordillera*.

Papi put his arm around him, and Mauricio hugged back. The cemetery was interesting, but it didn't have to be. Mauricio didn't care where he was, as long as he was with Papi. He had not felt like that right way. Certainly not his first night in America when, heartbroken, he had padded to the couch. He was set then to be angry at Papi forever. But during the days that followed Papi talked to him, just to him. "Are you happy to be here, son?" his father had asked. "Or would you rather be in the *casita* with Tío Julio?" Papi was laughing, but Mauricio had given him an earnest answer. "No, Papi, an uncle is not the same as a father." His father smiled, and Mauricio remembered how this man had looked in Camú. He remembered how it used to be when he was a little boy and Papi came home for supper and crowed at him or took him to see the animals.

Arm in arm, separate from everyone, they walked through the cemetery, following Tía Marta. She had arranged the trip, arranged for a friend to drive them out so she could make her annual visit to her husband's grave. "*Ay,* here it is," his aunt said, and she crossed herself. "Javier," she announced. "This is where I want you to bury me." Even in an American cemetery, Tía Marta was the boss.

Mauricio examined the stone. It was a simple rectangle like the others, but it had a funny kind of star etched on it, one made out of two triangles. He read his dead uncle's name: Murray Gordon. All Mauricio knew about his tía's husband was that he had been in the Army and that he had been a lot older than she.

Tío Ernesto was the next to pay his respects. "*Quede con Dios, Murray,*" he said.

Mauricio didn't think his uncle had ever met Murray Gordon. He knew Papi had never met him. But Papi was right behind his tío.

"*Quede con Dios,*" Papi said. "*Gracias,* Murray."

Mauricio didn't know why Papi was thanking Marta's husband. He guessed it had something to do with the idea that dead people were never really gone. In the *campo* people always said they could still see their relatives sitting on their favorite chairs, riding up the *cordillera,* swimming where they had drowned, or cutting their *caña.*

Papi hugged Mauricio and kissed him on the cheek. "You are in America, Mauri!"

25

July–September 1986

On a summer evening, weeks after her duties as a "tour guide" for her brother and sister had ended, Elizabeth brought her father's slippers to the kitchen table and helped him take off his work boots. She tried to break the news to Papi gently.

"I saw my school," she said. "It's very good, but it's going to cost five hundred dollars a quarter."

"*Guauuw.*" Papi did not sound happy. "Five hundred dollars just to learn English? Forget about it!"

"It's not just English, Papi. It's English as a second language. And I can take my other subjects in Spanish."

"I thought this was a city college."

"It is, but they told me I haven't lived here long enough. I'm not considered a city resident yet. That's why I have to pay so much."

She turned to the stove, dished out her father's supper, and waited nervously.

"Elizabeth, it is my opinion that you should repeat your last year of high school. That way you can learn English for free."

Elizabeth knew all about her father's "opinions."

Tía Marta and Tía María visited that weekend, and Papi

asked their "opinions." They both agreed that Elizabeth did not need to start La Guardia Community College this year. Elizabeth was exasperated. Didn't her aunts want to help her? Didn't they understand that the last thing she wanted to do in America was go to high school with Cristian? She hadn't come to America and given up all her friends just so she could wind up back in *secundaria* with Cristian. Maybe Cristian would have to stay in high school for years. But not her. She tried appealing to her father again.

"I am very young because I've been going to school since I was very young," she said. "It's not my fault that Americans don't finish high school until they are eighteen. That's the fault of their parents." Elizabeth had a low opinion of American parents, formed after she saw teenagers smoking marijuana outside the Louis Armstrong Intermediate School where she was taking night classes in English. "Papi, you're the one who told me to fall in love with a career first. That is what I am trying to do."

"You can fall in love with a career when you learn English," he said.

Elizabeth had a talk with herself. She could let Papi stop her or find a way around him. "Elizabeth," she said to the bathroom mirror, as she fixed her long, black hair. "You are not the kind of person who does nothing. If you were that kind of person you would still be stuck underneath Abuelo Víctor's pickup truck."

She put on jeans and a T-shirt she had bought at a store on Junction Boulevard and went to a City University office in Manhattan to speak to more college counselors. Maybe this time she would get better answers.

"My aunts want me to go back to high school," she explained.

"Nobody learns English in high school," the first counselor said. "Besides, you've already graduated from high school."

"I hated high school," added the second counselor.

Finally, she thought, people who see it my way.

"Why don't you apply for financial aid?"

She hadn't known such a thing existed.

Clutching a pile of applications, Elizabeth rode the Flushing line back to Junction Boulevard.

Back home, she told her father not to worry. His wages might be high enough to support all of them in America, but he still qualified for financial aid for his children. She filled out the applications and took the subway to Long Island City and the La Guardia campus. Elizabeth realized that it wasn't really a campus, just a renovated office building on a desolate stretch of Thomson Avenue, across from the elevated tracks that made their way from Queens into Manhattan. Thomson Avenue was the last stretch of desolation before the lights of Manhattan. Once she was inside her school—she hoped it was her school— she forgot about that. Even the hallways were exciting: high tech, with disturbing bright orange metal railings, orange pillars, yellow bolsters on the ceiling, and white-outlined skylights. The counselor she saw this time said that she needed a copy of her father's income tax return. If I only get to know all the counselors, I'll have a lot of friends, she thought.

She calmly got back on the Flushing line. This would be easy. Her father paid income tax. He would have a copy of his return.

When Papi came home that night she took off his boots and put on his slippers.

"*Sí*, Eliza," he said to her. "I had a copy of my income tax return. But I sent it to the consulate for your *cita*." Elizabeth couldn't believe that was her father's only copy. But he said it was. She was beginning to understand what had happened to her brother and sister's *cita*. "This family and papers!" she said to herself. Papi, she saw, had heard her and he didn't look pleased.

For a few days she mulled over the income tax problem. There had to be a copy somewhere, unless her father just didn't want her to go to college. She went through the mail one afternoon and saw a letter from José DuBeau. She took it from the pile and waved it in the air. Finally. Her diploma. Further proof that she deserved to go to college. She thanked her saint, ran to the kitchen table, sat down, and ripped open the envelope.

There was no diploma, only a letter from her old principal.

"*Ay,* no," she cried out, when she read it.

When Papi arrived that evening, Elizabeth took off his work boots, put on his slippers, and told him she had not quite graduated from José DuBeau, as they had believed. "It's not a big problem," she said, trying to avoid her father's stare. "I only failed my literature final. Well, I took it while I was trying to pack and get my teeth fixed. Remember you wanted me to get my teeth fixed before I came to America."

"*Ay,* Elizabeth!"

"There's a problem with algebra, too." She spoke as quickly as she could. "My teacher gave me the wrong test." She wasn't going to explain any more than that. Math was supposed to be her best subject. Besides, they had more important things to discuss. She needed a plane ticket back to Puerto Plata so that she could take her tests over again—the principal had offered to let her do that. She had, after all, been one of the school's best students and she had a chance to go to an American college. "I'll even fly Dominicana, Papi," she said. "It's awful but it's cheaper."

"*Guaaauuuw,*" her father said.

On July 13, Elizabeth Almonte boarded a Dominicana Airlines plane back to Puerto Plata. She had been in America for only ten weeks and one day. She had sworn she would not go back until she had a college degree in computer science. Now she was going back without even knowing much about America. Forget about computers! She took a mirror out of her handbag and checked her plastic yellow heart earrings, which had come from a package of twelve different-colored heart earrings that she and Cristian had bought for a dollar on Junction Boulevard. Junction Boulevard had become their shopping mecca because it had so many bargains. She examined the uneaten bag of popcorn, which the airline had given its passengers as consolation for a two-hour departure delay, and put it in her carry-on bag. Someone in Camú would be happy to have airline popcorn from New York, she thought.

As the plane took off, she looked down at Queens, still

unable to identify the different squat neighborhoods that made up the borough or find any of its landmarks. She wished she could find La Guardia Community College. That was what this whole trip was about.

She slept, and when she woke, she knew she was home. She saw a green roof, a white stack spewing smoke into the green countryside. Montellano and the sugar mill where her grandfather brought his *caña*.

The plane landed and someone in the back began blasting *merengue* from Radio Puerto Plata.

"Excuse me," Elizabeth said in English to a passenger who was in her way.

Víctor laughed out loud when he saw Elizabeth walking up the hill. Fian ran out of the house and clapped her hands without making a sound. "Tell me everything!" Víctor said. "This is very quick to come back. Very quick."

Elizabeth stepped onto the porch and touched her grandfather. Víctor held her by the waist and walked her to the breezeway between the house and the kitchen. He picked up the bottle of rum he had left on a bench, poured himself a capful, drank it, and then gave one to Elizabeth, which she gulped.

"You look so skinny," he said.

Elizabeth handed him the Dominicana Airlines popcorn. Fian, dressed in a blouse with leopard spots and spaghetti straps, stuck her hand into the bag and ate some. "Do you have a boyfriend?" she asked Elizabeth.

Elizabeth giggled and pulled out a pair of white Trax sneakers for her grandmother.

"Tennis shoes," Fian whispered. "I love them."

"Tell me again why you are here," Víctor said. His brown eyes were fogged and his smile showed he had no front teeth.

"I have to a take my algebra test over again," Elizabeth told him. "They gave me the wrong one."

Víctor motioned for Elizabeth to come with him into the living room, where they had business. He was going to sell some

tareas of his land to Javier. Elizabeth peeked into the kitchen and
saw that her grandparents had a refrigerator. Their first. She
guessed they had bought it with the first money Mami sent
them.

"You are very pretty now and whiter," Luis Felipe Pérez, the
principal of José DuBeau, told her. Elizabeth was wearing blue
jeans and a black T-shirt from the Robbins store on Junction
Boulevard. In colored letters the T-shirt said SINGLE AND LOOK-
ING TO MINGLE.

Felipe, which was what everyone called the principal, wore a
silver identification bracelet and a loose white *guayabera* shirt
with white embroidery.

"You have been a good and respectful student," he said. "I
want to help you so that you can study in the United States. So
I am going to give you a special kind of test, the kind they give
in the universities. It's called an open-book test."

"Oh, thank you, Felipe."

Elizabeth went to take the test in the school library, which
had fewer books than José DuBeau had students. The literature
test consisted of true-false and matching questions, each one
about her country's early history. Gonzalo Fernández de
Oviedo, the sixteenth-century Caribbean historian. The diaries
of Columbus. The Taíno Indians. *Areítos.* Elizabeth did not
even need to look at the textbook.

The algebra final had nine problems.

Felipe stood over her, whispered, and once showed her
where on a page she could find an answer.

"These two I can't do," she said.

"Don't worry. Those two are too long and take too much
time. You have passed."

Before returning to New York, Elizabeth called the consulate
in Santo Domingo to see if she could pick up her father's tax
return. She was told that the woman who handled such matters
was on vacation. Back home, in early August, a secretary at

La Guardia told Elizabeth that her father should see if his accountant had a copy of his tax return. None of the Almontes had thought of that.

Javier took the next morning off from work, went to see the accountant, and brought the copy home.

Elizabeth called La Guardia the day after that and found out that it was too late to apply for financial aid for the fall. The secretary had not told her that. "I never thought it would be so hard to go to school," she said.

Within a week after school began in September, Mauricio was walking into Leonardo da Vinci as if he had been going there all his life, although once inside he still clung to Waldir. Cristian was taking the subway and then a bus to John Bowne High School in Flushing without complaining about the long ride or her classes. Only Elizabeth wasn't in school, unless she counted night English classes at the Louis Armstrong Intermediate School. "They don't count," she told herself. It wasn't that she didn't like those classes. She loved them. (At her very first session, when it was still funny, she had learned to say, "I am un-em-ploy-ed.") She had been thrilled to learn who Louis Armstrong was—and that he had lived in Corona. A famous musical star from her neighborhood! (Who needed Fernandito and the Hilton? She had Louis Armstrong, right here in Queens.) But the classes were at night. Everyone who went did something else during the day.

Her brother and sister left her each morning and came home each afternoon with their homework. "I can say it in English," she complained. "I am un-em-ploy-ed." Elizabeth stared out the window and thought that the air looked colder. She was convinced that winter would be terrible because the overcoats she had seen in the stores on Junction Boulevard were so beautiful. If winter wasn't so terrible, these *yanquis* wouldn't need such beautiful coats. For her, winter would be even worse if she had no school to go to. She stood up, got a cup of Tío Ernesto's coffee from the stove, and wondered if she should have stayed in the Dominican Republic. If she had stayed she would be at college with Tío Julio and her friends.

"I'm the only one who doesn't know which school to go to," Elizabeth moaned to herself or to whoever would listen. She stayed home, worried, plotted, and prayed to her saint. Then she looked at a school calendar and realized that college classes had not begun. She decided to go La Guardia anyway and hope for a miracle.

She found a different college counselor and told her what had happened. The counselor arranged for a "tuition deferment" so that she only had to pay $150 until she received an answer on her financial aid application in November. Elizabeth had never heard of a tuition deferment, either, but it sounded almost as wonderful as financial aid. She was sure her father would give her $150. "It will probably take you two and a half or three years to finish," the counselor cautioned her.

Elizabeth began community college on September 20. She registered for English as a second language, in which Spanish was strictly prohibited; a freshman orientation course, which was taught in Spanish; and a basic mathematics class, which was taught mostly in Spanish with some English. She walked into her English class and looked around, relieved. These people were like the grown-ups who went with her to Louis Armstrong. They were not high school students. She wasn't in high school. Finally, she was em-ploy-ed.

She examined her teacher, who stood in the front of the room. Her name was Linda Kunz. She had blond hair, looked nice enough, and wore a button on her lapel, which said something about a *víctima*.

Linda Kunz wore a "Victim of the Press" button on her lapel. On the first day of class, she wrote this on the blackboard:

"The purpose of all education is to like the world through knowing it—Eli Siegel."

And then this question: "Can grammar, which is the structure of language, tell us anything about the structure of the world—including ourselves?"

Elizabeth strained to understand. She didn't.

"I'll ask you at the end of this week, the end of next week, are you learning anything more about the world, about yourself through grammar. That's my purpose. Does anybody have a brother or sister in public school?"

Elizabeth watched the other students raise their hands. She didn't because she did not know what the teacher was asking.

"Tomorrow is a big day in public schools in which all students will be taught about drugs. . . . Many homosexual people think they can't change. The newspapers say it and it's not true."

Elizabeth thought that her teacher might have switched topics.

"Any homosexual person who doesn't like it can change. My best friend was homosexual for twenty-five years, and he found out, not through the newspapers, that he can change and he's married now and his wife is having a baby."

She explained that she was a devotee of Aesthetic Realism and a follower of Siegel, the late beat poet and self-styled philosopher. He taught that you could teach dyslexics to read, stop drug abuse, and "cure" homosexuality by teaching children—and adults—to "like the world" and appreciate "opposites." "I want you to know what my method is and why I wear this button," she said.

Elizabeth's eyes were tense, darting. Linda Kunz handed out yellow cards with helping words—she also called them "x-words"—written on them in black marker. "Am, is, are, was, were, did, does, have, has, had, can, could, will, would, might, must, should (ought to), shall, may."

Some of the students understood that they were supposed to make a sentence with the word on their card.

"You can play the piano," offered one student.

"Oh, that's a good question," Linda Kunz said. "Switch it around."

"Can you play the piano?"

Elizabeth remained quiet.

"These are wonderful small words," Linda Kunz said. She held up a card with "was" on it, as though she were on a shopping expedition. "This is one that people try, but it doesn't go with 'you.' These are the key to English because they will give you some of the great opposites of the world. They will give you questions and answers. They will give you self. They will give you the rest of the world and they will give you active. They are the key to English."

Elizabeth walked out of the classroom and realized that she had understood more than she thought. But much less than she needed to understand. She gave herself a pep talk:

"Elizabeth! You can't expect to understand it all. You understand a little. That is good. It doesn't matter that all of your friends are in school in Santo Domingo. When you are done with this, you will be able to work in two languages, you will earn more money than they do. When they come here, they will have to go to work in factories for a year to learn English. Elizabeth! You have to crawl before you can walk."

She walked into class one day during her second week at La Guardia wearing an outfit she had assembled from the stores on Junction Boulevard: black loafers, red sweat socks, black jeans, a red NEW YORK T-shirt, and a red blazer.

"I liked that class last Friday," she told Linda Kunz in English.

"Which class?"

"Your."

Her teacher gave her a big, toothy smile. "And you say, 'I liked the letter I got from my boyfriend in the Dominican Republic.' "

Elizabeth knew her teacher wasn't prying into her life. She just wanted to give her another example of how to use that verb. She laughed out loud. She had understood.

The teacher wrote some opposites on the board. "Firm-flexible." "Hard-soft."

"Think about your mother. Is she firm?"

She talked about the bindings of books, backbones, and fingers.

Then the verb "to paint" went up on the board—with helping verbs.

Elizabeth went to the board and put the word "will" in front of "paint." Other students followed with correct answers.

"This is a teacher's happiest moment," Linda Kunz said. "You know more English grammar than you think because your eye says, 'Hmmm, it sounds good,' or, 'I don't like it.' " She showed them rigid helping words: "They are: 'have, has, had painted.' I swear. I cross my heart. You can count on them."

"This is advanced work, but I'm going to show you this one. 'My apartment looks nice. I didn't do it. Somebody else did it.' "

A Chinese man raised his hand. "Was painted," he said.

"This is advanced-level work," Linda Kunz said.

Mauricio did not know it was a "big day in public school." Nothing seemed different. He held on to Waldir, and they made their way though the crowded hall to art class. Mauricio was so grateful that he and Waldir were in the same classes. For the first time in his life he had a friend who wasn't also a cousin. Waldir. Waldir Gianny Sepulveda Moiza. Mauricio knew things about Waldir now. He had come to Queens from Colombia two months before Mauricio. His mother had brought him here. But then she left, and told him he had to live with his older sister. Waldir said that his mother hadn't liked America. Mauricio felt so sorry for his friend. He wondered why Waldir never cried. Usually, Mauricio was the one who cried over a small discomfort or insult. Mauricio knew that annoyed Waldir.

They reached the door to their art class, unhooked arms, and took their seats in different parts of the room.

Their teacher, who spoke only English, announced: "Today we are having a special lesson on crack," she said. We are going to work on some posters. We are going to make a slogan to the public that represents crack as a harmful drug. Who doesn't *comprende?* Raise your hand."

Mauricio raised his hand and looked to see if Waldir was raising his.

"You're going to do *expresiones.* How do you say 'against'?"

"*Contra,*" yelled out a few of the other students.

"*Contra* crack," the teacher said.

Mauricio understood that. He got up to borrow a ruler from a boy at the next table. All around him students were writing their slogans in Spanish, not all of them spelled correctly.

Mauricio wrote his in English. He wrote big letters shaped like bubbles, which spelled "No More." Under them was a circle with a line drawn through it. Inside the circle he drew a cigarette box and the word "Crack."

The art teacher looked at it. "Try to make the letters work with the design. Do you know what I mean?"

"No," said Mauricio. He did not understand the teacher.

"Those letters look happy. If you were a person taking crack, would the letters be happy?"

"No." Mauricio still did not understand.

A classmate, a Puerto Rican who had been in New York for a year and a half, began to explain in Spanish.

26

July–October 1986

In July, energized by the arrival of her two youngest children, Roselia had decided to go to work. She was hired as a companion and a nursemaid for a *vieja,* an old woman from Colombia who lived two subway stops away. On her first morning, Elizabeth went on the train with her. The next morning Roselia rode by herself, cowering close to the door, unsure whether she would be able to get through the morning rush-hour crowds on their way to the city. She was not sure whether the train would stop in the same place it had the day before. She wasn't in the same car she had been with Elizabeth. Or was she?

The *vieja* was fat and an invalid, and it was Roselia's job to bathe, dress, and feed her. Roselia's head hurt and she felt the pains in the spot where the doctor in Santiago had removed her kidney stone. She remembered he had told her not to lift anything heavy. In the evening, when she left, the *vieja* would cry out from her door.

"Roselia, Roselia, don't leave me."

Roselia had just left her own mother; she had almost been separated from her youngest children. It would be better to work for someone who could at least walk. She had enough problems without hearing the voice of an old woman crying out for her in the night. Why was she working at all? There were no visa officers asking to see her paychecks. After her first week of six eight-hour days, the woman's daughter paid Roselia $130. Roselia held the money in front of her face and remembered that she was Víctor González's favorite daughter. She didn't have to do such hard work for such low wages.

After her second week, Roselia quit. For two weeks, she baby-sat for a little boy. When the boy's mother took him to see relatives in Argentina, Roselia spent her days cleaning, watching television, and cooking. Javier had bought her a Singer sewing machine. But she didn't feel like sewing. She only wanted to watch television—Spanish television—and cook and taste her food. She would taste her chicken, rice, and plantains or her *sancocho* while it simmered. Sometimes, she tried the airline food Ernesto brought home on plastic trays from his maintenance job at La Guardia Airport. Javier came home to lavish meals, but Roselia was too full to eat by then. She could tell she was putting on weight. One day on Spanish television she saw an ad for a cream called *matagrasa*. And that's what it did: killed fat. She thought she might send away for some.

Each time she walked to the butcher that summer, Roselia passed a brick house with large windows. Through the windows she could see rows of women working on sewing machines. On a September morning when she felt colder than she had ever been in her life, Roselia walked over to that brick house and knocked.

"I need work," she explained to the woman who answered. Roselia followed the woman inside. Material scraps covered the floor and rose so high, they buoyed her as she walked. She was shown to a machine and the woman who had let her in put a pile of cotton shirts in front of her and demonstrated how to sew the sleeves.

She worked five days from nine to six, with a half hour for lunch. On Saturdays she worked from nine to twelve. She sewed sleeves, seams, and buttons, ironed pants, put blouses and skirts on hangers, and made $100 a week. But she liked her bosses, a husband and wife from Ecuador. She had heard stories about immigrants making 30 cents an hour, $14 a week, and was grateful she could bring in so much without going on the subway.

One Autumn afternoon, Javier came home from work early and slashed at his front garden with a *machete*. He had cut Víctor's sugarcane with the same kind of long, curving blade; now he was murdering weeds in his patch of city soil, a space barely large enough to lie in. Someday, he thought, he would plant a vegetable garden in the small backyard, too. Frank Corona would like that. As he slashed, Javier tried to spare the *yerba buena*. Roselia might want to make tea from its leaves. She had told him it was longing that caused her headaches. But that was before Mauricio and Cristian came. Then she blamed her job taking care of the *vieja*. Now she blamed the clothing factory. It was true that the Ecuadorans worked her hard. But why was she sick all the time? Back in the *campo*, Fian would have diagnosed a simple, albeit prolonged, case of *nervios*. She might have even told Roselia to go see Fransica, the *bruja*. *Yerba buena* might not be enough, but with a potion and a prayer or two, Fransica could cure it. Of course, Javier would never have given Roselia permission go to the *bruja*. But he did miss his mother-in-law. She would know how to handle Roselia's moods.

He kept slashing, looked at his watch and realized that he had been home for more than an hour waiting for Roselia to come home from her factory and make his dinner.

He kept slashing.

Finally, he spotted his wife walking down Fortieth Road and was comforted by the familiar pattern and style of the black-and-turquoise-checked dress that cinched her at the waist. He remembered the teenage Roselia in her old checked dress, working alone in Víctor's provisions shop, shying away from his exclamations.

"You are beautiful, Roselia! I love you!"

He was sure he remembered being that bold. Even when he had nothing.

He could make the case that he still had nothing. He still didn't have a car, and that bothered him, although he told his children that he thought immigrants who came here and spent all their money right away on cars were irresponsible. He had no car. He had nothing but bills sticking out of the plastic grape centerpiece on the kitchen table, more than a hundred dollars each month in utility bills and Elizabeth still would not stay off the phone. Money worries, and worries about Roselia. Consolidated Edison. New York Telephone. And Roselia.

And Elizabeth.

His daughter said she was going to get that financial aid. If she didn't, the tuition would be a thousand dollars, a thousand dollars two times a year. *Ayyyy*. And they would have to pay it eventually.

"Papi?" Eliza had asked him. "They want to know if you have any investments?"

"Investments! Tell them I invest in the subway every morning."

He sounded like a New Yorker or like someone who had lived in a city all his life, and he knew he wasn't like that. He was an optimistic person. He had been optimistic that they would find a place to live, and the optimism transferred into luck, into the luck of the apartment on Fortieth Road, where they now lived. This arrangement was like living with family. It was his friend Frank Corona's house. But Frank had gone back to Santiago and his wife had given their apartment to Javier and his family. She had moved into a small room in the front of the house and said she would charge him only $500 a month. Less, if he could do some work on the house. She might even put him in charge of repairs. Soon, she would be going back to the Dominican Republic. Frank could be mischievous. Javier knew that and admired him. An injured longshoreman, missing an arm and a leg, and he was still strapping and handsome with enough of a wandering eye that his wife had to go home to watch him in his retirement.

Roselia stopped at the garden gate, bent over it, gave Javier a kiss on the lips, and walked past him up the stairs and into their apartment. He had to teach her so much. She hadn't really learned how to look for work. She refused to take the subway again, even for a few stops, so she was stuck working for minimum wage or less at this clothing factory. It wasn't even a factory, just a storefront. He had to watch her headaches, watch that she did not become too lonely.

Elizabeth was already inside. So were Cristian and Mauricio. But it was Elizabeth's job to start supper. She was the oldest.

Javier finished slashing and went in. His wife and daughter were quietly seething at one other. Javier sat down; Roselia served him from a pot that had pig's ear mixed with tomato sauce and cilantro. Leftovers. Javier looked at the clock. He had been home working outside and waiting for dinner for two hours.

He held up the cup of beans his wife had placed alongside his plate.

"I don't like these. They're canned. From now on, I only want fresh beans."

After dinner, Roselia went into the bedroom and looked in the mirror at her tired face. She had spent eight and half hours putting blouses on hangers. Her boss was nice, and so were the other Ecuadorans she worked with. But shades of red, blue, and black swirled in her brain; she was tired of all those colored blouses. The day before it had been woolen jackets in size 44.

She had been in New York four months and this was her third job.

She looked at snapshots of Víctor and Fian. They had been taken recently, but to Roselia, they seemed to be old photographs. She had never thought that Javier would notice if she served canned beans. Wasn't that the way things were done in America? There were no fruit trees outside her door. Didn't that mean she could serve canned pineapple, too?

Elizabeth did not understand why her father was making such a big deal over beans. He wanted her mother to cook even though she was working. And her mother wanted her to cook even though she was trying to study. She was trying so hard to learn English from a teacher who was strict about no Spanish in the classroom. After school she had found a job tutoring Spanish, and she still went to Louis Armstrong two nights a week. If Mami wants me to cook, I'll have to cook from a can also, she said to herself. Her mother didn't understand what it was to study. Her mother was so worried about her job; she thought it was the only job in America. Her mother had no sense of humor anymore. One night Elizabeth had been dancing when Mami came home from work. Elizabeth was having such a good time, twisting her shoulders, raising her arms above her head, clenching her fists, mouthing the new English words: "I'm your *Venna*. I'm your fire." But her mother yelled at her to turn off the music.

27

October 1986

Mauricio and Waldir both adored Mr. Olivares, Mauricio's summer school teacher, whom they had for math. Mauricio was bolder now and sometimes he cracked jokes in class or wrote notes to his neighbors. Once, Mr. Olivares threatened to change his seat. But that was as bad as it got. Mr. Olivares always taught with a good mix of language. Enough Spanish so that Mauricio could do the math. Enough English so he could learn new words. Not all of their teachers did that.

It was hardest to learn when the teacher only spoke English. But when Mauricio left the classes where only Spanish was spoken, he felt disappointed. He and Waldir were in the least advanced group in their English class. The other groups were given long, melodic English words to use in sentences: words such as "century," "liquid," "flowers," and "tomorrow." Mauricio wished he could use those words in a good English sentence. He loved to write and was keeping a diary entitled "Mauricio, a boy." In his diary, he wrote, "I imagined a New York that was like a city which had many castles and palaces and also had princes and kings." But that was in Spanish. In English he was still at the "My name is Mauricio. His name is Waldir" stage. So was Waldir.

Two mornings a week, before homeroom, Mauricio met with *Meester* Cohen, a retiree who volunteered as a tutor. *Meester* Cohen wore brightly colored polo shirts and Mauricio considered him his American abuelo. Mauricio didn't know if *Meester* Cohen really was an abuelo. But he knew he could ask him, if he wanted to find out. *Meester* Cohen spoke Spanish and occasionally broke the rule against using it while he tutored English.

"*Meester* Cohen, how do you know Spanish?" Mauricio had asked him, in English. He had thought about how to say that for a long time.

The tutor explained, in Spanish, that he had learned it as a boy. His parents had been Jewish immigrants from Turkey and at home they spoke only Ladino, which was a combination of Spanish and Hebrew. "I still had to study Spanish over the years, too," he told Mauricio.

When Mauricio tried to sound out the word "shoe" and couldn't, *Meester* Cohen, his bifocals slipping on his nose, shook his head in sympathy and gave a speech, in English.

"That's insanity. It reminds me of George Bernard Shaw. He left money to a society that was going to reintroduce spelling phonetically."

Mauricio nodded. He liked *Meester* Cohen even when he didn't understand what he was saying.

★   ★   ★

"I was only twelve, but I had a sense that my school, although earnest, didn't have a real plan to teach me English," Mauricio the graduate student says. "Waldir agrees with me. I don't think either of us really learned English until we got to high school."

The two boys went to International High School, a public school for immigrants housed in the basement of La Guardia Community College. "We learned English there because we had no choice. We could only speak English. But a lot of effort went into helping us do that. It was immersion. But it wasn't unkind. It was the school's mission to teach us English."

A decade after Mauricio began his bilingual education, the debate between methods still rages. Do children learn English, or any language, better if they are immersed in the language and not permitted to hear or speak anything else? Or should they be introduced to it gradually, while keeping up with their studies in their own language?

The debate is complicated by extremists: Those who want all subject classes to be entirely in the foreign language versus those who believe that bilingual education will lead to the eradication of the English language in America. It is complicated as well by the varying capabilities of students. Some flourish even in the staunchest, most traditional "English only" settings. Others retreat from the strangeness and fall behind in all their classes.

"I knew Waldir and I would learn," Mauricio says. He now has a teaching license and has substituted at International High School, the first of its students to come back as a teacher. "The kids I felt sorry for, the ones I still feel sorry for as a teacher, are the ones who are illiterate in Spanish, too. Do you remember that boy at Leonardo da Vinci?"

That boy, a thirteen-year-old from the Dominican

Republic, had been in America for a year. Back home he had never learned to read Spanish, and none of his teachers expected him to pick up English. They shook their heads and offered him as a sad specimen. "Ask him to read for you," they challenged a visitor. When asked to read the Spanish word for wind, *"viento,"* the boy just shook his head. The word *"quieres"*—you want—was pointed out for him. "Does it say *'vivir'*?" he guessed. "I don't understand the letters." Before coming to America, he had been to school for three years.

In 1985, there were 67,000 Spanish-speaking New York City public school students, who were entitled to receive bilingual education or instruction in English as a second language. About 6,000 of them had problems with Spanish, as well. At Leonardo da Vinci about 25 students out of the 259 in bilingual programs were identified as either illiterate in Spanish or very slow.

"In different circumstances, I could have been that kid," Mauricio the graduate student says. "I was a good student. But I was so timid. If I had been separated from my mother at an earlier age, and for longer, I might have never gone to school. Do you think Fian would have pushed me? How many years of schooling do you think Fian and Víctor had? In summer school I was friends with that kid who couldn't read. It scares me to think where he might be now."

The day before Halloween, the bilingual coordinator came into Mauricio's Spanish class.

"I don't really have to come in and tell you this because I know none of you are going to come in with eggs tomorrow, but if any of you do, if I see one egg in your possession, you're going to be suspended. No eggs. No shaving cream. No hair spray. And, if you do go around in your neighborhood, you have to be very careful not to eat any candies that are not wrapped well. As a matter of fact, I don't think you should eat any of it. You should go just for the fun of it. If you get an apple, cut it up into pieces because people put horrible things in it."

Until he heard that, Mauricio had thought he was prepared for Halloween. Tío Ernesto had said that Halloween was like the twenty-seventh of February, Dominican Independence Day. Mauricio had been anxious to wear a costume again. He had grand visions of himself dressed as a devil, attacking other children with a pigskin balloon and asking for candy—an American improvement. But what, Mauricio wondered, was the point of going around your neighborhood asking for candy if you couldn't eat any of it? And why didn't they have the day off from school? They always had off on Dominican Independence Day.

Mauricio's classmates, the ones who had been in America longer, didn't seem worried. They bragged about the quantities of candy they would get and eat. A girl Mauricio knew produced a can of silver glitter hair spray from her book bag. On a desk in another class's homeroom, he spied a pair of notes:

"Radi: Let's meet tomorrow at Newfield's (104th Street) to go to buy eggs and throw them. Okay. Answer me. Ok. Billi."

"We should buy them tomorrow at 'Top in the Queens.' They'll be cheap tomorrow. Afterwards you go to your house at two. We will buy them and go to the school. Okay?"

If the teachers didn't expect them to throw eggs, why, when Mauricio showed up on Halloween morning, did they all say they had parked their cars two blocks away from the school? Nothing particularly bad happened all day, but it seemed like something could at any moment and nobody got a lot of work done. Mauricio wondered why they had bothered to come at all. Secretly, he hoped that someone would invite him to throw eggs after school, but no one did. Waldir said he was just going home. Mauricio began walking by himself toward the apartment on Fortieth Road.

Then he had an idea. He stopped in a store on Junction Boulevard, found what he wanted, and went home to wait for his mother to finish work.

★　★　★

He heard her key in the outside door and then in the one that led to their apartment.

She opened it, screamed, and put her hands over her eyes.

"Trick! Treat!" Mauricio shouted.

Mami laughed out loud. She laughed hard.

Mauricio was wearing a rubber witch mask with a flashing rubber cobra growing out of the head. Next to him, one of Tía María's daughters who had recently arrived in America was laughing behind a glittering bandit mask. She had painted her face with big black freckles, the way they did on the Malecón.

"Maribel says she will take me trick-or-treating," Mauricio said. Maribel Corona was the landlady's daughter, a young woman in her twenties who had lived in New York since she was a child and was making the Americanization of the young Almontes her hobby. She had taken Mauricio to sign up for a library card and had showed the girls how to dress fashionably for winter by layering sweaters over shirts.

His mami was smiling halfway.

"Please?" Mauricio said.

Mauricio ran down Fortieth Road, with Maribel, Cristian, and his cousin behind him. He was so happy that he was singing English words without realizing it:

> I gave it away.
> You what?
> I gave it away.
> What did you say?

"What's that?" Maribel asked.

"*Inglés,*" Mauricio told her. "Jazz chants from school."

He hopped up the steps of the first house, his witch-head cobra flashing.

He rang the bell.

No one answered.

He went to the next house and rang the bell.

No answer.

From across the street Cristian called out, "They're throwing eggs down there."

Mauricio ducked into a side street. Maribel followed him.

"Mauricio, try this house. My friends live there," she said.

No answer.

Mauricio pointed to another house across the street. "Let's go there, the lights are on."

As soon as he got there, the lights clicked off.

"Maybe we can go to the *bodega*? They have lots of candy there," Mauricio said.

"I guess we came out too late," Maribel said. "Nobody wants to open their doors." It was 6:15 P.M.

Mauricio looked in the direction of the *bodega*. Then he saw it, across the street, an open door. A Chinese man was handing out lollipops to other trick-or-treaters. The man shut the door. Mauricio raced over and rang the bell. The man answered.

"Trick or treat!" Mauricio said.

The man dropped two lollipops in his bag.

Back in the street Mauricio examined his meager treasure. "At least the last people opened their door."

Roselia laughed again when Mauricio showed her his candy.

"Look, Mami, two lollipops. Orange and green."

He was so happy that he could still make Mami laugh.

28

October–November 1986

At 6:30 on a Monday morning, too early for school, too late for the roosters to crow, Papi came into their bedroom.

Cristian and Elizabeth were sleeping head to toe in one single bed, Mauricio was in the other.

"Wake up!" he cried out, joyously. "Wake up!"

"*Bendición,* Papi," Mauricio said sleepily.

"*Bendición,*" Cristian said. She shoved Elizabeth, who was always the last to wake.

"*Ay, bendición,* Papi," Elizabeth yawned.

"*Dios les bendiga,*" Javier answered.

"It's early, Papi," Elizabeth said.

"I know. I have something to tell you, all of you. I fell asleep last night and I could hear you listening to a *novela* on the television, an *Espanish novela.* It made me wonder if people dream about the last thing they hear before they go to sleep."

"What, Papi?" Elizabeth asked.

"I want you to dream in English."

Mauricio thought this was interesting. Cristian didn't dare say a word.

"I have something to tell you," their father continued. "Now, this is not a punishment. It is for your own good. I want you to do well in America. So, from now on you may not watch any Spanish television. Maybe you can listen to a little Spanish music once in a while, on the weekends. I've been thinking about this. If you study in English in school all day and come home and watch Spanish television you are going to forget everything you have learned."

Elizabeth was now awake.

"What about you, Papi?" she asked.

"I can watch it," he said. "My mind is not growing like yours."

"This one doesn't speak English. She only speaks Spanish," Anna Corona, Maribel's mother, said as she sat at the Almontes' kitchen table one evening after dinner.

Cristian, who was at the sink washing dishes, shuddered. She hated when they talked about her like this. She felt under so much pressure, even at home. Elizabeth and Mauricio were speaking so much more English than she was. Maribel and her mother had noticed. They were very sweet. But they were the same as any of her relatives. When they weren't hiding secrets, they could be very blunt.

"It's hard to say how many times I would cry," Maribel went on. "Oh, I didn't want to go to school."

"Cristian, you have to practice." Anna Corona continued. "That's why I don't know English. When somebody has a husband to care for, she doesn't have time to go to school . . ."

Cristian thought about the idea of having a husband, of not having time to go to school. Why were they bothering her? At John Bowne she was passing all of her subjects. She had never done that at José DuBeau. She even became nervous if she got an answer wrong.

She was trying to learn English. Eliza and Mauri were not a big help. If an English word or phrase accidentally slipped from her mouth, they applauded. But it wasn't nice applause. It was sarcastic. Each afternoon she came home from school, took a pint of ice cream from the freezer, stuck a spoon in it, and sat down to watch American soap operas. Wasn't that what Papi wanted her to do? He still wasn't satisfied, and Elizabeth always spied on her to make sure she wasn't watching a *novela.* Nobody was perfect. No matter what Papi thought, Elizabeth listened to Fernandito. During the week! Mami had never gone back to P. S. 19. Papi had been here almost four years and he still didn't speak English, although he did watch American movies like *Agnes of God* and *Bye Bye Birdie* with them.

Cristian didn't mind watching American soap operas. If she wanted to see a real Spanish *novela,* all she had to do was look at her own family. Sometimes, she felt like a permanent audience. They were all so dramatic. Mami with her up and down moods, Elizabeth with her never-ending financial aid saga. Even Mauricio, in his own quiet way, was an actor. Each night, with a flourish, he gathered all his books on the sofa and sat with his head buried in his homework, looking even more serious than he had in Camú. He would look up only to catch Papi's grateful smiles. Sometimes Cristian wondered whether anyone remembered that she had come to America, too. She had accomplished things but they were small. She worked during her lunch hour in John Bowne's bilingual office. She had joined the Spanish Club and written a newsletter article about the Dominican Republic. She didn't dress like a *campo* girl anymore. She wore hanging earrings instead of those plastic hearts Elizabeth had insisted they buy when they first arrived. She had let her *pelo malo* go wild since nobody in America cared if your hair was straight. And, for the first time in her life, she could say, truthfully, that she liked school. Her school even had a farm, although every time she mentioned it to her brother and sister they looked at her as though she was crazy. But they really had one, an agriculture department, they called it. *Tareas* of land behind the school with fields of corn, berries, flowers, and vegetables.

Maybe it was better that she was her family's second thought. She had secrets she needed to keep.

In November, it became very cold, and Roselia's depression worsened. Javier tried to remember the last time he had seen her laugh. He thought it might have been on Halloween.

"I don't have a perfect marriage," he announced one afternoon, while Mauricio was taking off his boots. Roselia was not home from work yet. "But who does? We understand one another and that is what is important. It is important that a husband and wife understand one another and that they do not argue in front of the children. If they have a disagreement they should go into another room and quietly discuss it. Children pick up everything."

When Roselia came home, she told him she wanted to go into the bedroom to have a discussion.

"I wish I could go home," she told him.

"*Ay, mi amor,* you just arrived. It's too soon to take a vacation."

"I want to go home for good."

"Why, *mi amor?*"

"I am always reminded of home. The news on *Espanish* television is always about Santo Domingo, Javier. Everyone is buying tickets and going home. My sister Ramona is going home."

"*Sí, mi amor.* But that's just for Christmas. Ramona's boys have their *cita.*"

"I just want to go home."

He didn't know what else to say.

On a Saturday after work Roselia walked into the apartment wrapped in her trench coat, her hair pulled back in a careless ponytail. In the living room she put down her plastic Top Tomato bags and saw that her sister Ramona had arrived from *Nieu Yersey*. Ramona was in the kitchen, at the stove tasting the *sancocho* Roselia had cooked that morning before work. Her sister was wearing white leather boots, skintight blue jeans, an oversize rose-colored blouse, and an orange jacket.

"I don't feel well," Ramona said, as they hugged. "I'm very nauseous. I'll have to leave soon."

Roselia knew that it was the *cita* that was making Ramona ill.

"Good luck," she told her younger sister. "Tell everyone that we are fine. Make sure they know about this new apartment. Make sure they have the address!"

As her sister left, Roselia saw that the name of the taxi company where her husband was a driver was on the back of her jacket. She remembered that Ramona's husband had his own car, a big red one with cartoon stickers pasted on the glove compartment. Later, she wished that she had told her sister that she would not have any trouble with the visas because her husband had a car.

Javier brought Roselia flowers. He went to a clothing shop in Jackson Heights and bought her a low-waisted, calf-length turquoise dress with padded shoulders. It was Roselia's color, but it looked more like something Ramona would wear. Roselia loved it and said that she would save it for the turkey dinner they were planning to celebrate their first Thanksgiving.

A few weeks later Roselia sat down on their bed while Javier talked on the phone. She put his head on her lap and then she lay down next to him.

"I am going to find another, a fifteen-year-old," he said, teasing.

"That's okay, go ahead, but if you do I am going to go to another country."

"Santo Domingo?"

"No. I won't go there. I'll go to a brand-new country altogether."

On November 26, Cristian's fifteenth birthday, her parents made her a little party, a *quinceañera,* at home. She had really been born in September, but she always celebrated on November 26, the day Papi registered her birth in Puerto Plata. He had often told her about the floods of Juan de Nina that came right after she was born.

Cristian was determined to look like an American teenager, so she set her hair to make it even fuller, frizzier, and sexier. She put on a tight knit dress, which was also sexy, even with its high collar. At school she had heard about other girls who had grand *quinceañeras* in rented halls with bands, but this was just going to be with her family. She was feeling older. That was all that mattered. At school a boy she knew had walked over to her, his black-and-olive satin jacket open and hanging just right, and kissed her on the cheek very close to her lips. It was strange to be kissed by a boy who was young like her.

Her parents, sister, brother, and Tía Marta sang to her, and she remembered the secrets she was keeping.

On the day of her science midterm she had felt the right side of her head pounding and was convinced she would fail. I am going to do so badly, she had thought. I can't hand in a paper with a question that doesn't have an answer. I'd rather get this wrong than hand it in blank. But I don't want to get it wrong. I hurt so much. This must be the way Mami's head hurts. She tried putting her hand to her head to soothe it; she looked up. The science teacher was in the front of the room with her back turned. Cristian glanced quickly at the paper of the girl next to her. The answer to the question she couldn't even guess at was 433.2. She copied it down quickly.

She told herself that she was probably going to get caught.

"What I gave you," the science teacher announced a few days later, "is called an alternate-row test. Every other row had a different test. Those of you who copied will get a small *c* next to their marks. But if I catch you again, you're in trouble."

There was no way she would tell her parents about her 75c.

Or about Julio Santini in Puerto Plata. Julio Santini was a lot worse than her 75c. He was fourteen years older than she, the fat, ne'er-do-well son of a prominent Puerto Plata family. But she loved him. She had met him in Camú, when she was thirteen years old at a party for one of Mami's friends. She and Julio sneaked out in the middle and drove to a hotel in Puerto Plata. The romance continued until her visa came through and she had to go to New York with her brother. Two days after she arrived in New York, Julio called to tell her that he was there, too. He had gotten on a plane and followed her. She told him not to call again. There were newspaper articles being written about her. The last thing she needed was a picture of Julio Santini in *Newsday*.

He called a few more times. Once Elizabeth was in their parents' bedroom and answered the phone. Elizabeth had been living with a phone for a month by then and she knew all the tricks, more than Cristian did. She handed Cristian the phone, ran to the kitchen, and listened in on the extension. "Aha, Cristian," Elizabeth said when they came face to face in the living room. Cristian did not tell her anything. For two days, whenever she caught her alone, Elizabeth would whisper, "Aha, Cristian. Aha, Cristian." She whispered it one day when they were alone in the kitchen, and Cristian became so angry she took a spoon and hit her sister on the head as hard as she could. Elizabeth screamed. There was a drop of blood on her head. Mami came running into the kitchen, and when she saw Elizabeth's head, she took a mop and hit them both.

"Blow out your candles, Cris," Elizabeth said.

29

December 1986

Elizabeth had not settled her financial aid problem. Her application had been sent back without a decision and with a note from some anonymous person in the federal government, another Jonathan Mueller coming back to haunt her. Why hadn't her father claimed her mother as a dependent on his 1985 tax return? How was she supposed to know that? She asked Papi, and he didn't know why, either. An adviser at La Guardia told her to resubmit the application and say that her parents were not living together anymore. Elizabeth thought that was stupid. Her parents had gotten married a few years earlier so they could get visas. Now they were supposed to get "separated" so that she could pay her tuition?

The only thing for her to do was to keep studying and learning English.

She had not been satisfied with her midterms. On one of them she had written this about a short story her class read:

"It was a history very sad and very interesan. Where Suzanne go to the Lima Airport with your mother. The plane was late and going to Pulcalpa. Went 80 passengers. And take Gate number 5. It was a Christmas day. After the plane climb up and up Suzanne found a seat proximity to the window for look at the jungle."

Well, she had only been in the United States six months. Linda Kunz gave her a grade of "almost passing." On Elizabeth's paper she wrote: "I think you can pass at the end of the term if you trust *(confiar)* your own English and make sure you use your exam time carefully and finish both parts."

Her next composition was better, although the subject matter would not have thrilled Javier:

"The opinion that I have is the in Dominican Republic things are different than here. Because in my country they critized if they see someone kissyn in the park or in ony public places. The reason they critize is that the towns are small and they know each other. In the United States are different because is more liberal, is more advanced, and more civilized. The people from here lives their life in their own way. They don't like nobody to get on his business. In the few months I have here, I'm beginning to like this country a lot. Because of the freedom. I like to do things in my way and not being critized by nobody."

Elizabeth wanted to go dancing with Maribel at the Palladium discotheque in Manhattan. Javier would not permit it. But he did say that she and Cristian could go to a party at the home of one of her La Guardia classmates, a married woman who had a child.

On the night of the party the sisters were finishing their hair when their father arrived home.

"Papi!" said Elizabeth. "We need money. They asked us to bring rum."

"The liquor store is already closed," Javier said. It was only 6 P.M. "Bring some soda."

Wearing overcoats borrowed from Tía Marta over their good dresses, the girls arrived at the party with bottles of Coca-Cola and orange soda. Elizabeth went to the kitchen to talk to the hostess. Cristian, wearing her tight *quinceañera* dress, sat on the couch.

"Do you ever talk?" a boy asked.

"I'm very shy," she replied flirtatiously.

"I can't believe you're younger than Elizabeth. You look so much older."

As if to prove the point, Cristian stood up and got herself a can of Budweiser. She took a few sips, but put it down to salsa with the boy. He was another of Eliza's classmates, but he seemed young to her, too.

Elizabeth was in the kitchen watching her friend, the hostess, who was Colombian, slice a meat loaf that had a center of carrots and eggs.

"I like the ways of American men," the friend said as she continued slicing. Her Colombian husband was in the living room. "They don't have that *machismo*. They don't tell their wives they can't go out at night without them."

Elizabeth nodded vigorously.

"I'm trying to get my husband to be more like that. If he says those things to me, I'll give him one of these." She put the meat loaf on the table and did a karate kick.

A week later, the Salvation Army band on Fifth Avenue was playing "Joy to the World" as Mauricio walked down the promenade at Rockefeller Center. He passed floating angels and boutique windows stocked with presents. Christmas in Camú had been simpler. People roasted pigs and drank *habichuela*.

Mauricio looked up at the giant tree with its spread of red, blue, green lights, its star that really did seem to be in the heavens. He hadn't meant to look down, but when he did, he pushed as close as he could get, hooking his head over the shoulder of a tweed coat in front of him.

People were ice-skating: moving, swirling, spinning on white.

"Elizabeth, I want to go skating," Mauricio said.

"Brother! You can't go. You'll fall down. You don't know how to do this."

"Well, if I fall down, I'll just get up again."

Ten minutes later he was on the ice, his delicate ankles wobbling on rented skates, size 6, his long legs and arms sprawling and flailing like elastic. For a moment he froze in front of a woman with neatly coiffed blond hair and a short red skirt. She made him think of Nancy Reagan.

"Don't stop here," she scolded him. "This is an exit."

He moved, wobbled, and turned to wave at his audience: Elizabeth, Cristian, and Maribel. He bent down to touch the ice, to see if he could figure out what ice was. He had never seen so much at one time. He went around and around, never really getting far from the rail or skating. But never falling, either.

He came out of the locker room as "Guantanamera" was blaring over the sound system. Elizabeth put her arms around him and Cristian. Maribel joined them. And they all sang.

Then they went to McDonald's, where they huddled together in one booth, ate french fries, and drank Cokes. Maribel told Mauricio to stop playing with his straw. "Shaddup!" he told her. In English. He said it as though it were one word. He unwrapped a pile of straws and attached them until he had a chain two feet long. He put it in his Coke. "With something like this you could be in one place and drink in another."

At home there was a new, green artificial tree that cost $55. They decorated it with yellow and red balls, plastic strawberries, and lights. On the top they put their own flashing silver star; on the bottom, a crèche Javier had bought during the years he was in New York alone.

On December 30, they all went to see the Empire State Building. Mauricio led his father who, unlike his children, had never been there. They walked through the marble first floor to the elevators. Mauricio could see that Papi liked the floor. They rode the elevator to the observation deck, but it was snowing out and Mami wanted to stay inside.

"Do you want ice cream?" Papi asked her.

"Later," she said, nervously.

"Ah, Papi, if only there was sun," Cristian said.

"Yes, it would be better."

They looked out of the windows and waited for the sheets of fog to pass and reveal for seconds, minutes if they were lucky, the lights below.

"I can see the city more or less," Javier said. "But not very well. There's too much fog."

With her hand, Roselia wiped the window for him.

"What happens if you fall down from here, Papi?" Mauricio asked.

"Nothing, you only die."

"That's terrible," Mami said.

Mauricio realized she was talking about the height.

"It is terrible," she said. "It's a lot more terrifying than Camú. There's nothing in Camú this high."

Javier put his arm around Mauricio.

"I'm afraid," Mami said.

Papi looked at her. "In the plane you were higher than you are now. Why are you afraid?"

30

January–February 1987

Elizabeth walked down a construction ramp outside La Guardia Community College. Her first year in America was more than half over, and she still had not received her financial aid. But she was managing. Papi had given her $350 to pay her first-quarter tuition; then she had been given another deferment for the second quarter. It was late afternoon and the wind was attacking her face, freezing her ears, making her eyes tear. She still didn't understand how to dress for the cold. She had forgotten to take a hat. She hated the cold and she hated it even more when people who had been here for longer made fun of her. If one more person said, "You think this is cold? You haven't felt cold yet!" she would scream.

She had struggled through Linda Kunz's English class and earned a C. But her second-quarter English class, which began after the New Year with a teacher named Mimi Blaber, was harder; the students were more advanced, too. They spoke English in sentences, called out answers, and corrected one another. They could talk back to the teacher in English.

Mimi told them she didn't want them returning late from their breaks.

"Where are we going to go?" asked one of the young men in the class, motioning toward the stark hallways of the old Execu-tone building and Thomson Avenue beyond. All Thomson Avenue had to offer were hot dog vendors.

Mimi had assigned them to write a speech, in English, of course, and deliver it in class. Elizabeth went home to practice. She practiced the entire weekend, for hours in the small bedroom she shared with Cristian and Mauricio. She practiced even when Cristian and Mauricio were there. The room was smaller than the bedroom in their *casita* had been. But along with two beds, the three of them had squeezed in two closets, all their clothes, books, and tapes. Elizabeth thought she would go crazy.

On the morning of the speeches, she put her fingers to her temples and listened to her classmates, the ones who had volunteered to go first.

With stammers, pauses, and lapses into Spanish they described their first days in America; their first skyscrapers, subway rides, escalators. One student said the cold air had made him feel as though he were living inside a refrigerator.

Each time Mimi looked at her, Elizabeth flinched.

"You're ready, Elizabeth?" she asked.

"No."

"Okay, let's take a break, but don't come back late."

A year earlier, in the Dominican Republic, English had been a game for Elizabeth. She had learned what she could in her noisy classroom at José DuBeau, taken lessons after school, and shown off mercilessly for her brother and sister. Even nine months earlier, when she had first come to America, English had been a game. *"Mekdonnas!"* she had shouted when she wanted a hamburger. "I am un-em-ploy-ed," she had said in her Louis Armstrong class, without shame. On the street she had walked up to strangers, regularly, and asked for directions, without a worry about her grammar.

But now that she had spent four months in an American college, she felt that she was expected to speak correctly. She did not want to make any stupid mistakes.

After the break the only choice she had was whether to speak standing or to remain in her seat. She sat. She put her fingers to her temples and took a deep, loud breath. She sighed.

"I want to talk about . . ." She paused. "I want to explain how a person shoulda study in order to get a good grade."

She paused again, as though she had just done a day's work.

"Can I give example?" "Example" was her new favorite word. Mimi nodded.

"For example, we are studying here because I don't know how to speak English. And . . . we are . . . we come to try. For the future. And we have to study every day, even, and we have to do it. I don't know how to say it. Sacreefeese?"

"Sacrifice," said Mimi.

"We have to do a sacrifice."

"We have to make a sacrifice," Mimi said.

"We have to make a sacrifice for don't speak Spanish in our home, in the street, at school. And don't watch the TV in Spanish. Don't listen to the radio in Spanish. *Ayyy.*"

"Only speaking English!" called out one of her classmates, a young woman named Ana. "Okay!"

"If have homework, we have to do every day." Elizabeth stopped. "Nooo. We have to study every day at home. In my home my parents speak Spanish. They don't know to speak English. But I need. I canna talk Spanish. Only with them. But my sister and my brother are studying English, too, annnddd . . . we have a good practice, every day, every afternoon and every night, and the weekend, the weekend."

Elizabeth Almonte's first speech in English, which lasted two minutes and forty-eight seconds, was then applauded by her classmates.

"Very good," said Mimi, smiling.

"Very excellent," added Ana.

"Excellent," agreed Mimi.

"You can try to speak English to your parents," offered a student named Yocasta, a Dominican who had been in the United States three years. "Because my mother doesn't know English and sometimes I try to her. I say, 'Mami, I wanna water.' She say, 'No speak.' But she understands. But sometimes my brothers they yuk. Yuk?"

"Yes," encouraged Elizabeth.

"They say, 'Oh, she wants to be an American person.' "

There was laughter.

"My parents told me is difficult for them. They are very, very old," Elizabeth continued. She was conversational now. She had lost her nervousness, seemed to have forgotten she was not speaking Spanish. "They told me that but I don't believe. My parents are working, and when they come back to my home, they are very tired. Is *obligación*."

"Obligation," said Mimi.

"Yes! Is obligation to speak Spanish with my parents."

Mauricio's social studies teacher told her class she wanted to build their poise and confidence. Each student was supposed to prepare a theatrical presentation—an imitation of a movie star, a singer, or teacher, if they had the nerve.

Mauricio knew what to do. On the way home he stopped at a store on Junction Boulevard and bought a short, black, curly wig. Then he went home to rehearse.

In class, he was the second to volunteer. He marched to the front of the room and began imitating the Spanish singer Rocio Durcal. It was a song about the end of love.

"Dejame vivir que tú no comprendes. . . ."

His high-pitched, adolescent voice was sweet; he shook his head to the music. He could see that Waldir was laughing hysterically.

As he returned to his seat, hands shot out from every seat in the aisle. "Hey, Mauricio, Mauricio, slap me five," his classmates called out to him in English. "C'mon. Slap me five."

Cristian still did not speak much English.

Roselia was at her second factory job now. The business the Ecuadorans had run shut down just before Christmas. But finding another low-paying job in a clothing factory in Corona was not difficult. The factories were scattered throughout the neighborhood in private homes, behind storefronts, in concrete-block buildings with no signs. In a mammoth brick warehouse filled with different factories, Latin and Asian women sat at machines and sewed blouses, skirts, dresses, even "doggie beds."

Roselia saw a sign in Spanish outside a building. They needed sewing machine operators. She went in and they put her to work. This time she was paid for each piece she sewed. There was a scowl on her face when she said the word *peezwurk*. It was one of the few English words she had tried to learn. She disliked this job so much that she did not even keep track of how many hours she worked. Roselia was paid $76 in cash her first week, but she sometimes did not stay all day.

On a Sunday in February, a year after Cristian and Mauricio's first visa applications were rejected, all the Almontes went to a *merengue* festival at Madison Square Garden to celebrate Dominican Independence Day. They bundled up and each in a different way remembered when they used to be warm in February.

They all remembered the Malecón in Puerto Plata. Mauricio thought about the boys from school who were not his friends and their devil costumes. Javier remembered looking for city girls, the eels who walked the promenade, when he was in the Army. Elizabeth remembered jogging on the Malecón, running with her girlfriends, walking when they were winded. At the end someone would yell, *"Marineros,"* and they would start doing jumping jacks and other calisthenics in the middle of the sidewalk. Boys they knew drove by on motorcycles or piled into old cars. Sometimes the boys stopped to watch. Roselia remembered how she had hidden at the house on Vista Alegre and tried to stay away from the noise. Cristian remembered being at the Malecón with Julio Santini.

At the Felt Forum, the Almontes, together for a day, a Sunday, stood for the Dominican national anthem. Roselia and the children did not sing, but Javier boomed, *"Quisqueyanos valientes . . ."* Nobody recited the Pledge of Allegiance or sang

"The Star-Spangled Banner." But the Almontes remained standing for those as well.

They stared at the familiar *merengue* stars, who performed on smoky stages dressed in multicolored lamé capes, shirts, and pants. Elizabeth screamed. Each group was her favorite, and only Javier's presence kept her from rushing to the stage.

The music was loud and blaring, but Roselia, the queen of headaches, smiled through it. Sometimes it was a large smile. Sometimes her half smile. Sometimes her half smile crooked. But for three hours the smile endured. She even stood up to cheer for some of Elizabeth's favorite stars. It was good to be with Elizabeth. In the Dominican Republic she had felt Elizabeth was her best friend. But now they hardly saw each other. She had never seen La Guardia Community College. Elizabeth had not seen the factory where she now worked.

At home Mauricio took out a sheet of paper from school that had the Pledge of Allegiance printed on it. He sat on the living room couch, held it out in front of him, and recited, "One nation, under God, invisible . . ."

PART THREE

AMERICANOS

31

November 1988

Cristian's "first year in America" had faded into memory, into a photograph of her at-home *quinceañera*, old loose-leaves from her sophomore and junior years at John Bowne High School, love songs the American radio stations called "oldies." She had been glad when that year was over. The shocks, surprises, the uncomfortable newness of everything, had been too much. She liked a predictable life and a private one. She was so happy when she didn't have to tell the newspaper what she had done all day or change the way she acted because she was being watched. It was hard enough to keep secrets from her family.

Mami, she knew, felt the same way she did about the newspaper. Although Mami didn't have any secrets, at least not like hers. The rest of the family missed the attention. That was what Cristian suspected. Even Mauricio. He used to hate it when the newspaper came into his classroom. He said he might as well have his mother at school every day. But now that the attention was gone, he missed it. Mauricio had changed. He had grown tall, almost as tall as Tío Julio, and *chulo* like a rooster. He thought he was very smart. To prove it he had hung a poster of Albert Einstein on the outside door to the bedroom the three of them still shared, as if everyone in the house wanted to look at his hero. Why couldn't he hang up a rock star like a normal person? Even a *merengue* star would be better than Albert Einstein. "Albert Einstein was an important man," Mauricio said. Who cared? He was *feo,* too, ugly—very ugly.

Papi certainly missed the attention. Now he had only the four of them and Tía Marta to listen to his speeches. Elizabeth missed it, too. But she had found a way to replace it. She would. She had found teachers who helped her through every problem and listened to her every word.

Cristian didn't need that. She just needed her predictable life. She hadn't done great in school. No one had expected her to do great. But she had earned enough credits so she could graduate this January, instead of waiting for June. She didn't know what she would do then. She had a job after school at Youngworld, a children's clothing store on Junction Boulevard. She would probably work there when she graduated, unless she found someone to marry.

Cristian did not see him come into the shop, although later she thought it must have been a sight: that tall, bulky, confident, perfumed man she knew so well from Camú squeezing himself past racks stuffed with little snowsuits and sweaters and jeans; past all the frilly dresses. Julio César Santini wading through the narrow aisles of an overstocked, brightly lit store on Junction Boulevard, politely saying, *"Discúlpeme,"* as he brushed into strollers parked alongside Latina mothers searching for ways to dress their sons and daughters, their precious *hembras* and *varoncitos,* their *guapitos,* their *futuros,* better for less. Cristian could imagine those mothers being charmed by Julio—the way she was—even though he was so large and not really a romantic type.

He found her in the middle of the store, behind the cash register. She worked with her head down; it was the only way not to lose her place or the rhythm of sales. Youngworld was an important store on an important street, and this was her only after-school job. While the manager watched Cristian, she watched the hands of customers as they placed merchandise on her counter. They were women's hands usually. Mothers' pretty hands with long, painted nails, rings, and bracelets.

Julio Santini slapped a baseball cap on the counter.

Cristian froze at the familiar sight of his large, white fingers. She could smell him, too.

"What are you doing here?" she whispered.

She had never told him where she worked. But that wasn't what she meant. Julio knew so many people. He knew people in Camú, Puerto Plata, and Sosúa, where he now owned a car rental agency, even in Santiago and New York. She had always assumed he could find her if he wanted to. She had just not expected him to come looking for her.

"*Hola,* Cristian." Julio smiled. His stomach protruded proudly, as always.

"I have days off," she whispered, again. A line had formed behind Julio; her boss was still watching.

"You should come to my house one of those afternoons."

She was not sure why she had invited him.

A few days later, Cristian cut her last class at John Bowne and rode the subway home. She got off at Junction Boulevard, walked over to Fortieth Road, where Julio Santini was waiting for her. She didn't think anyone would see them. Elizabeth and Mauricio would be in school, her parents would be at work, as would all the other people in the house. Even Tío Ernesto had been leaving for work earlier.

"How are you?" he began. "I am interested in you."

This was not news. He had been interested in her, and she in him, since she was thirteen years old. Now a lot of boys were interested in her. She was not as thin as she used to be, but the boys she knew were like their fathers, like Papi. They did not like women to be too skinny. And she had a good *busto,* too.

"I am not thinking about doing anything bad to you," he assured her. "Don't listen to what people say about me."

The things people said about Julio Santini were not new to her, either. Cristian had been hearing them since the day she first spoke to Julio, at Mami's friend's birthday party. Julio was twenty-seven then and almost as large as he was now. She had been barely a teenager.

She had not seen him again until this past summer when her parents sent her and Mauricio to Camú to visit their grandparents. It was the first time either one of them had been back, and Cristian picked up her old habits. When she needed a ride or some information, or some other kind of help, she called Julio. When the lights went out in Puerto Plata and Cristian was stuck at the dentist, she called Julio. That was natural for her.

They sat on her parents' new couches, which were maroon and protected with clear, plastic covers.

"I would never do anything bad to you," he told her again. "What I am thinking about doing is marrying you. You don't have to come back with me, but what you have to know is that I feel something great for you. I am not fooling around. I know you are studying. I know you are working. I know you are just starting your life."

Now she was seventeen and he was thirty-one. It still didn't sound good. Even her parents were only eight years apart.

"I don't know," she told him.

Julio Santini stayed in America for three weeks. That was, he explained, as long as he could be away from his business. He slept at a friend's apartment in the Bronx and drove to Queens, to Youngworld, every day that Cristian worked. He always bought something, usually bits of clothing that Cristian knew he would bring back to his children. She wasn't sure how many children he had, but she did know that more than one woman was involved. That was Julio Santini's reputation.

She saw him after work, too. And when she wasn't working. And when she was supposed to be in school. "I *kuttaclass,*" she would tell Julio, proud of her English. She knew more of it than he did.

He was the secret of her life. Sort of a secret, since everyone from Eliza to Fian had suspected for years. In 1986, her mother left for New York suspecting. That's why she told Fian she wanted Cristian to sleep with her every night. Cristian did not think anyone had seen her with Julio this time. But she knew she wasn't being careful.

"Cristian, why haven't you left for school?" Mauricio asked her one morning. "It's already eight-thirty and your first class is at eight forty-five. You're never going to make it." She wondered when her baby brother was going to start to get into trouble.

That night, Elizabeth caught her alone in the kitchen:

"Cristian saw Santini today and I bet they had a fight," Elizabeth sang out to her.

How did she know?

"Cristian, what are you thinking of doing?" her father asked her.

"Nothing," she told him.

Elizabeth swore she hadn't said anything.

When Julio left for Camú, he gave Cristian $200 to buy a plane ticket and his business card—that's where he had his phone. Although his family was from Puerto Plata, he lived in Camú, and there still weren't any phones there. Cristian knew why Julio lived in Camú. People there called him *licenciado,* even though, unlike all of his siblings, he wasn't a professional and didn't have much money of his own. All that mattered in Camú was that Julio was a Santini. In Camú nobody would ever imagine that a Santini would want to marry a daughter of Javier Almonte. More likely he would hire her to be his maid.

She kept remembering what he had said: "You don't have to do this." She was in her senior year at John Bowne and told people she was two months away from an early January graduation. She thought about Julio for two weeks, and when she couldn't stop thinking about him, she decided to go back to Camú.

Cristian knew that if she wanted to leave Queens, she would have to do it when her parents were distracted. Particularly Papi. He noticed too much. She planned her departure around a weekend when her father was going into the hospital to have an operation on a finger he had injured at work. On Friday, November 18, after she was sure that her father had checked into the hospital and that her mother was with him, she cut what remained of her morning classes at John Bowne and went home to pack. She brought her clothes to a friend's house and bought a plane ticket for the following Monday at Corona Travel. Then she went home to wait out the weekend.

Cristian was afraid that Elizabeth would notice that there was suddenly room in their closet. But Elizabeth was too busy with her schoolwork and friends. On Sunday night, Mami went to the hospital in a taxi and brought Papi home.

On Monday morning Cristian kissed her mother when

Roselia left for the factory. She gathered her books and told her convalescing father she would see him later. Then she walked to her friend's house and left her textbooks there so that they would be returned to the school. It was bad enough they would tell her father she was a dropout. He didn't have to hear that she was a thief, too.

She called a taxi to take her to the airport. She looked very good in the white shirt and tight black jeans that she wore to go home to Julio Santini.

Late that afternoon, the phone rang in Elmhurst. Javier picked it up with his good hand.

"Javier!"

"*Sí.*"

"It's Edito."

"Brother. How are you?" Edito was Roselia's brother. He was a police officer in Puerto Plata.

"Javier, do you know where Cristian is?"

"What are you talking about, she's in school."

"Javier, Cristian is here."

"Cristian is at John Bowne. In Flushing. She went this morning."

"Javier, she is here. In Camú."

"What?"

"I saw her going into Julio Santini's house."

"You tell her to call me! Tell him to call me, too!"

"She has a father, a mother, and a home," Javier said calmly into the phone, when Julio called later that night. "If you want to fool around with her, then send her right back here. But if you love her, then she can stay there with you."

Cristian stayed.

Mauricio the graduate student sighs when he speaks about his sister Cristian. He does not understand why she left, why she left for Julio Santini. Why, right now, Autumn 1996, she is still with Julio Santini.

"Or should I say back again with Julio Santini," he says.

"My father believed it was the worst thing that ever happened to him in his life. He was still recovering from his operation when he went to John Bowne and told them she would not be coming back. He called you when it happened? Right?

"I know he said that to you. That he could not have felt worse if he had told them at John Bowne that she had become a prostitute. Now? He accepts it. Of course he accepts it. She is still only *junta,* but she has two sons with Julio Santini. Julio Santini is the father of his only grandchildren. My father and Cristian are on good terms. You know what he says? He says it to you all the time. 'With children, communication is important.' I think he watches too many talk shows on Spanish television. Now whenever Cristian has a fight with Julio Santini—and it's usually because he's been with another woman—she comes home to Mami and Papi. The last time she was here for a year. But she always goes back to Camú. I wonder if she's returning to Julio Santini—or to Camú?"

32
1988–1992

International High School was an odd bird, a new New York City public school hidden in the basement of La Guardia Community College. It specialized in lost souls, or souls about to be lost. Students were immigrants "at risk"—teenagers who had lived in the United States less than four years and who ranked lower than the twentieth percentile on a standardized English proficiency test. IHS was not a school that accepted success stories. Instead, with hubris that was both dangerous and unheard of within the New York City public school system with all of its quirks and despair, IHS claimed it would make its own successes. It claimed that its students would be fluent in English by the time they graduated.

Students from different countries, who spoke different languages, were put into the same classrooms, where they had to help each other figure it out. Teachers acted as language instructors, regardless of the subjects they taught. The school was offering what some believed was the antidote to bilingual education—full immersion. But with a modification—a community atmosphere with fellow sufferers. School administrators liked to emphasize that their school was dedicated to teaching language, period, and tried to convince their students to keep speaking and reading their native tongues. An assistant principal who one day found a Spanish-speaking student poring over *Don Quixote* in English was quick to point out the advantage of being able to read Cervantes without translation.

It was Mr. Olivares who suggested that Mauricio apply to IHS. The boy had told him how frustrated he was; that he felt his English should be better after two years in America. After school Mauricio went home and tried to write his diary entries in English, but he didn't think they would make sense to anyone else. He watched Elizabeth, whose English compositions and speeches got better all the time and wondered why that wasn't happening to him.

Mauricio asked Mr. Olivares if the teacher could help Waldir with an application, as well. He couldn't imagine going to a different school than his friend.

At the end of the school year, Mauricio and Waldir celebrated—they both had been accepted to IHS—and went their separate ways until September. They were not far from each other; Waldir had moved to Bayside with his sister, but it was only twenty minutes by bus. Mauricio was busy, though, working six days a week at a *bodega* on Junction Boulevard. Waldir's family had cautioned him not to work. He was in the United States on the same tourist visa his mother had used to bring him over two years earlier. It had long since expired, and they did not want him to risk being deported.

In mid-August, Mauricio went back to Camú with his sister,

their first trip back since they had come to America. He stayed three weeks with his grandparents and returned happy to be living in New York and ready to start high school.

Years later, Mauricio would hear that when his friend Waldir saw him on their first day at International High School, he believed Mauricio had become somebody else. Mauricio had grown taller during the summer but looked as if he had made a lot of money. He had bought himself new clothes, and for the first time, his pants were as long as his legs. He still wasn't as handsome as Waldir, who had thick hair, well-developed muscles, and chiseled features. But even with his baby face atop his lanky body, Mauricio looked tougher and sensed that Waldir was keeping his distance. Mauricio kept his, too. Years later, it broke Mauricio's heart when Waldir told him that even when they weren't speaking, he continued to tell his sister that they were best friends. On Saturday nights, Waldir and his sister would watch the *Sábado Gigante* show, the part in which relatives were asked questions about one another. "If we ever go on that and they ask you who is my best friend, say Mauricio Almonte," Waldir would remind his sister.

As freshman year progressed, Waldir became involved in student government, and finally, he was speaking English. Mauricio's English improved as well. He had known more of it than Waldir when he left Leonardo da Vinci, and now that he was in high school, he felt ready to tackle anything. His English teacher wanted her class to keep a log about their reading experiences. Mauricio came to school with a copy of *The Stranger.* He wasn't sure if he would understand it, but the idea of an author named Camus tickled him. He could tell his teacher was impressed. The others in his class had selected books by Judy Blume; one or two had *The Diary of Anne Frank.* One very smart girl had a book by Hermann Hesse.

Mauricio had another problem, though. He was scared of something he could not identify—petrified—and he didn't know why. He didn't feel he could confide in anyone except

Waldir. But he and Waldir were so estranged. He tried to soothe himself by trying out for *Grease,* the musical his English class was presenting. Mauricio was given a part as a gang member.

He liked the part so much that after the play was over he joined a real gang, a group of Dominican boys at La Guardia who lived in the Bushwick section of Brooklyn. Back home Mauricio would not have dared to befriend such boys. But at International he was quickly accepted because he was Dominican. They were not as bad as they could be, he told himself. No major drugs or major crimes. They cut class, drank Vicks Formula 44 syrup to get high, and, without using any weapons, mugged students in the bathroom. (Students who deserved it because they weren't Dominican and showed off their money.) At any other high school in New York City, Mauricio's new friends wouldn't have even qualified as gang members. And Mauricio was the meekest of the crew. When the boys from Bushwick said, "Let's go to the bathroom, mug the Indian kid, and get five dollars," Mauricio would go and watch. He didn't participate or help the victims. But he always felt bad for them. They looked so pitiful to him, giving up their after-school earnings without a fight because they were scared, just like Gallina on his old program *Lucha Libre.* When Mauricio's friends weren't in the bathroom mugging kids, they cut class and hung out in the halls both at IHS and upstairs at La Guardia Community College. "Denizens of the Halls," was what his English teacher—the woman who had directed Mauricio in *Grease*—called them. Those halls, particularly upstairs at La Guardia, were still high tech. But if you missed the elevator and took the stairs, you would find an old-fashioned carved banister. The Denizens of the Halls dressed like punk rockers—and Mauricio had begun to look a little like that himself—but really they were old-fashioned juvenile delinquents.

Years later, Mauricio would find out that his English teacher had been monitoring his behavior. At first she didn't say anything. She felt that students were entitled to some rebellion, as long as it didn't get out of hand. And, at the time, she didn't know about the muggings.

Then, there was a fight in the cafeteria; the Bushwick boys had started it. Nobody was seriously hurt but chairs were thrown, and after it was over, some of the mugging victims found the courage to complain.

Mauricio's English teacher called him aside. "There is talk," she said, "that you should transfer to another high school."

Mauricio did not know how he would explain that to his father, so, gradually, he came in from the hall.

In September of senior year, only a few days after school started, Waldir's sister was murdered. She was in a Colombian social club in Jackson Heights and was caught in the cross fire over a bad drug deal. Mauricio heard about the murder in class and remembered that this was the sister who had raised Waldir when his mother left him in America. It seemed that every night in the news there was another report of a drug murder somewhere in the world. Mauricio thought about all the reports like that, particularly the ones that came out of Medellín, and wondered if Waldir's mother had believed that in America her children were safe. Although he had hardly spoken to his old friend in months, Mauricio joined a contingent of International High School students who went to the funeral. When he saw Waldir he shook his hand, hugged him, and expressed his sympathies. Then he looked him in the eye and remembered their old friendship at Leonardo da Vinci. This was his first friend, the boy to whom he had clung so hard.

By winter the friendship was completely reignited, and Mauricio had a new interest: school politics. He was elected senior class president, the school's first. Waldir, who had been student body president the year before and was touted as the school's best orator, served as Mauricio's trusted adviser.

In the spring of 1992, two "memorandums" were hung on the senior bulletin board at International High School. They were mean, racist, in terrible taste, and the two students responsible needed to be reprimanded. Officially, the school's administrators disapproved heartily. Unofficially, they couldn't help being impressed.

The grammar and spelling were good enough, and the satire, while not always subtle, was well aimed. (One of the targets, a student named Andy, vigorously claimed that his father was a Mafia don, and everyone was tired of hearing about it.)

But the most gratifying thing about the memos was that they were written by students who had come to America only six years earlier, knowing almost no English and virtually nothing about their new country.

And now those two students could imitate David Letterman.

"Top ten Reasons why Andy is so peculiar"

By Mauricio Almonte & Waldir Sepulveda.

10) Discovered that the Coleone [*sic*] family was just a movie.
 9) Can't afford to get a godfather ring.
 8) Discovered that his raincoats were really made in Honk [*sic*] Kong.
 7) Has seven raincoats and they all look alike.
 6) Rejected as a superhero.
 5) It's his third year as a senior.
 4) Has yet to discover GAP stores.
 3) Work [*sic*] for Genovese family at the drug store.
 2) Mr. Ling is his counselor.
 1) He is a teenager and it is only normal.

"Top ten Things students say in the lounge."

By Waldir Sepulveda & Mauricio Almonte

10) Stop Smoking.
 9) When are you going to pay me those $20 you lost to me in Black Jack?

8) Are we beating the security guard today, or shall we wait until tomorrow?
7) Duck, here comes Van Cooten.
6) When will these dam [*sic*] stop smoking?
5) When is student government going to talk with Mr. Sisco?
4) What ever happened to that soda machine?
3) Go to class? You kidding, I am a senior.
2) It's not paradise city but, It's all we've got.
1) What's the deal with the air conditioner?

When the memos came off the bulletin board, one of those administrators put them in his files so that he could illustrate what a creative student Mauricio had been. By that time, more than 90 percent of the school's students were graduating, and a comparable number were going on to college.

Mauricio and Waldir often wondered about Mr. Olivares. Waldir saw Mr. Olivares once on the subway and they looked up and smiled at each other but did not speak. At a social club on 108th Street, Mauricio heard that Mr. Olivares wanted to know how he was doing. But they never saw each other again.

Mauricio the graduate student speaks wistfully about his friend Waldir, whom he has renamed Waldo, because it sounds funny. The two young men went to different out-of-town schools, but remain close friends and correspondents. After college, Waldir returned to Colombia. "He's staying," Mauricio says. "He has a job teaching English."

Mauricio never imagined that after graduating from Vanderbilt University in Nashville, his friend Waldo would want to go back and be Waldir in Medellín. Later, he heard that Waldo planned to go to graduate school himself in Colombia. And that he wanted to study literature, as well. "It was when we were in college that Waldo told me his mother had brought him to America because

she was afraid he would be recruited by one of the drug cartels," Mauricio says.

"Uh, do you think that's enough for now?"

Mauricio is trying to be polite. He has taken phone calls the day after moving into his apartment in Bowling Green, the day a woman he is interested in comes to spend the weekend, the day before his debut as an old Caribbean storyteller in a Spanish-language "murder mystery" theater. He has gone to the library and looked up obscure information about his country: why do boys dress like devils on the twenty-seventh of February; where is the source of the river Camú; how do you mine amber; why did Robert E. Lee want to annex the Samaná Peninsula, which is in the east and nowhere near Camú? Most of the information he was sent out to find will never be used. He knows that, and up until now has remained as patient as he was when his class was invaded at Leonardo da Vinci by someone who could have been his mother. He only complained to his sisters about that. Now, a decade later, he has had enough. He is still polite about it, though. "I can't talk to you for a few days," says Mauricio the graduate student. "Maybe a few weeks." He has his own writing to do. A graduate paper on "The Fantastical in Latin American Literature." He is writing it in Spanish. That is what his course requires, although he says he would prefer to do it in English. "I'll be back by the time you get to my citizenship ceremony," he promises. "Meanwhile, can't you get that far on your own? Don't you have a study from somewhere you can use? Can't you call my father?"

Abuelo Javier is asleep by now.

In 1995, the University of Southern California published a study on language proficiency. USC had studied 5 percent of the population in its region—a remarkably large sample—and found that the percentage of school-age Latino immigrants who had learned English had, in ten years, almost doubled. According to the study, in 1980 a third of Latino immigrants between the ages of five and fourteen spoke English. In 1990 more than two-thirds of the same group were proficient. In contrast, among their parents' generation, proficiency levels were only a third as great.

33

February 1993

As predicted, Elizabeth took three years to finish La Guardia Community College. She earned an associate degree in computer science and parlayed a student internship into a temporary job as a "computer assistant" in the mailroom of the Port Authority of New York and New Jersey. The mailroom was in the basement of One World Trade Center in Manhattan, the tallest building in the city. Elizabeth remembered when she thought the Empire State Building was the tallest building in the city. She hadn't even known that the World Trade Center existed.

Mauricio was away at an upstate college now. Cristian was in Camú with Julio Santini. Elizabeth, who liked to be called Liz, still lived with her parents in the apartment on Fortieth Road. She had her old bedroom to herself, but she had gotten rid of one of the beds and put in a bunk to make more room. She had to admit that she missed her siblings, particularly Mauricio. Albert Einstein still hung on the door, and the poster reminded her of the late-night conversations they used to have. She knew her parents would be surprised to hear how grateful she and Mauricio were to have been children in Camú. They agreed that their parents, however inadvertently, had timed their immigration just right for their children. When they were young, the three siblings had Camú with its space, security, nature, and relatives. Then, as their educations and careers became important, their parents got them out of there. True, it hadn't worked for Cris. But she was not doing so badly. She was living with Julio and their baby son in her parents' old *casita* while they built a house next door. True, they were building it with Papi's money. And Cris had become, by Elizabeth's standards, "too fat—and I used to be the fat one." But it wasn't as if her sister was living on the street.

Elizabeth loved working at the World Trade Center, even though she was only a clerk. To do any better she knew she would have to go back to school and get a bachelor's degree. But, as she told her father—who hadn't wanted her to stop school to work—she needed some time off to make money. And to have fun.

She felt comfortable in her office. Her boss, Tony Oliver, was a Cuban-American with Puerto Rican roots who was trying hard to make Elizabeth a permanent employee so that she could qualify for benefits. Her boyfriend, John, worked in the mailroom, too. He was a dark, strapping Greek-American from Astoria, Queens, who had introduced Elizabeth to the wonders of hockey: she and John had season tickets to the Rangers. Her immediate supervisor was also named Liz and was her best friend in the office. Liz Millan was Puerto Rican, married, and more matronly than Elizabeth, but she knew how to have a good time. The two women called each other Nellie, a pet name the origin of which neither of them could remember. It made them giggle to say it, as if they had a code of their own. Their office was on B-3, right underneath the B-2 parking lot, and whenever a car screeched or a tire blew, they would hold their ears.

"Imagine, Nellie, if one day they put a bomb in here," Liz Millan liked to joke. "They're going to destroy us. We'll come out of here in pieces."

"You might be right," Elizabeth would answer. "You never know."

Often they lunched together, quickly eating salad and breadsticks at Wendy's so they could run back to the shopping concourse in the World Trade Center to see which clothes were on sale.

Like a true New Yorker, Elizabeth believed that there was a lot more crime now than there used to be, and too much of it was in her own neighborhood. She worked out every night at the gym on the other side of Fortieth Road, where they played *merengue* in step aerobics classes. Every evening when she left class, cars were lined up outside the Mexican restaurant next door, more cars than could ever be buying burritos. There had been a few burglaries on Fortieth Road, and her father had put bars over the front downstairs window of the house. More drug deals than ever were going down on Roosevelt Avenue, and undercover cops regularly patrolled the neighborhood, looking for men carrying brief-cases into travel agencies. Roosevelt Avenue was flooded with travel agencies: some blocks had as many as three or four, and a lot of them were just drop-offs for drug dealers. Even in Corona, Elmhurst, and Jackson Heights, with all their immigrants, there weren't *that* many people going on trips. As if that wasn't enough, the city had launched a vice cleanup in Times Square, and a lot of houses of prostitution that used to be there had moved to Roosevelt Avenue. Washington Heights had always had a lot of crime. But not Elmhurst. Elizabeth wondered where she and Mauricio would be now if Papi had decided to live in Washing-ton Heights instead of Elmhurst.

She didn't let her fears stop her from enjoying the city. Most Friday nights, if there was no hockey game, she and John went to the Houlihan's across from the World Trade Center to share a basket filled with small bottles of Budweiser. Occasionally, she and Liz Millan and another friend from work, three garrulous Latinas, slipped away to see the male strippers at Chippendales. They each had one or two Lite beers, an Absolut and cranberry juice, or if they were feeling rash, a Long Island iced tea. Then they danced with the Chippendale men in ways they would not want any of the men in their lives to see, bought souvenirs they would hide, and went home laughing about it all.

On the morning that the World Trade Center was bombed, Fri-day, February 26, 1993, Elizabeth woke up late, skipped breakfast, as she usually did, and put a pair of tight blue jeans on her well-exercised body. She tucked in a mustard-colored silk blouse, tied her rubber-soled oxfords, and took a green leather coat. Fridays were "dress-down" days. This Friday was payday, too.

She left the apartment on Fortieth Road at twenty to eight, her usual time. She rode the No. 7 train to Times Square, transferred twice to other trains, and got off at Cortlandt Street.

She and Liz Millan were in the middle of a rush job for the Port Authority's transit center. They had piles of brochures to insert into envelopes and the computerized labeling to finish. Elizabeth took a break at ten-thirty and rode up to the forty-third-floor cafeteria, for a cup of coffee and a bran muffin. She went to the Citibank window and cashed her check. Four hundred and fifty-seven dollars for two weeks' work. She had a Citibank savings account but no checking account, so she purchased money orders to pay her bills. She owed money to *Sports Illustrated,* Victoria's Secret, and New York Telephone. She now paid the phone bill for the apartment on Fortieth Road, an arrangement she liked since it ended years of disputes with her father.

Her business completed, she returned to the glass-enclosed office she shared with Liz Millan. She sat at her desk, facing the door, and kept stuffing and labeling. Liz Millan was right outside the door. At one o'clock they had planned to go to lunch.

At 12:15 there was a noise that was like thunder. But thunder that was louder than any Elizabeth had ever heard. Thunder in the building.

The lights went out. Thunder right over her head. Every light was out and Elizabeth smelled gasoline. She could not get any part of her body to move.

The thunder stopped and the sound of shotguns started. One bang after another. (She would later find out those were tires exploding.) Elizabeth stood up from her chair without moving her arms or her feet. "Liz! Liz!" a voice called out to her. The door opened. Liz Millan was shining a flashlight at her.

Elizabeth felt Liz Millan pull her by her silk blouse. "Nellie. Nellie, let's get out of here." Liz Millan pulled her to the back of the office, to the emergency exit light, which was still on. The rest was dark, and all Elizabeth could hear was Tony

Oliver, her boss, and his assistant calling the names of the people who worked with her.

Two lights flickered on. Everyone was walking to the exit. Elizabeth looked for bodies. She didn't see any. But she didn't believe that there weren't any.

"*Ay, Dios,*" she said.

"Everyone hold hands," Tony Oliver said. Elizabeth clasped Liz Millan's hand and the hand of the man behind her. There were people linked in front of her and people behind her. Her boss was in front. His assistant behind. She thought she saw John, her boyfriend, ahead of her.

Tony Oliver led them up the stairs through smoke. Elizabeth held tight to Liz Millan and tried to breathe in, but she smelled more gasoline and almost gagged. They wound up through more smoke, and when they got to a door, two maintenance men directed them, "Through here. Follow here."

They guided each other out a door onto the concourse level.

John was there. "I have to get home," Elizabeth told him.

"Are you all right?"

"I was so afraid." She was shivering. John took off his black leather jacket and draped it around her. She had left her coat, her handbag, the money orders she hadn't mailed, everything, in the office.

Firemen were rushing them out of the building. By the revolving door people were waiting patiently, peacefully, to go, as if they were too shocked to push ahead.

On the street Elizabeth could see dark smoke. She looked up as high as she could and saw what looked like office chairs being smashed through windows. She thought about friends on other floors. Christine on sixty-one. Jackie on sixty-nine.

"You know what this was," the man whose hand she had held said. "It was a bomb, a car bomb."

Two men from their office were missing.

"I'm going back down," Tony Oliver said.

He returned with the two missing men, who walked so

stiffly they could have been mummified. Their faces were the palest Elizabeth had ever seen.

"I just want to get out of here," she said to John.

They rode the subway to Times Square and changed to the No. 7 train back to Elmhurst. Elizabeth did not speak. John sat with his arm around her.

"What's the matter," a woman asked him. "She didn't have a jacket?"

They both just stared at the woman.

But she persisted. "Is she sick? What's the matter?"

Ay, Elizabeth thought. What a time to be asking questions.

At her factory, Roselia heard on the radio that the World Trade Center had blown up, and the tears came quickly in a flush. She tried to call Elizabeth's office. No one answered. She was sure that her daughter was dead.

Elizabeth did not have her keys. She rang the bell and Frank Corona's brother-in-law, who lived upstairs, answered. He had heard it on the radio. Tío Ernesto came running up the stairs from the basement, dressed in the maintenance uniform he wore at La Guardia.

"I'm running late, Eliza," he said.

"Tío, do you know what happened?"

He shook his head.

"I have to call Mami."

She kissed John good-bye and ran upstairs with the landlord's brother-in-law.

"I'm home. I'm okay," she told Roselia. She could not get out anything else.

Later she found out that her friends on the other floors were safe. But two people she knew, acquaintances from other offices, people she said hello to every day, had been killed.

Tony Oliver, who had spent hours pulling out victims' bodies and rescuing the wounded, had also taken a big sack down to B-3 and retrieved everyone's coat, bags, and what they had left of their paychecks.

A few months later, Elizabeth and John were at the Houlihan's across from the World Trade Center, sharing their basket of Budweisers.

"In Camú they used to call me the little black girl. But I love my skin," she said, patting her arm.

John was a quiet man, happy to sit back and listen to Elizabeth talk.

After the explosion she had not been to any of the counseling sessions offered to employees. She felt she understood what had happened and her feelings about it. If she ever saw any of the people who planted the bomb, she swore she would take them in her bare hands and strangle them. But something else nagged at her.

"God knows what reasons they had to do that, you know. What they had to have done to them that forced them to do it. You know what I mean?" she asked John. "You gotta look at it both ways, understand. But the wrong people were paying for something."

With the distance of time, she had come to view the bombing as a very personal event, a sign about her future. She talked about the accident with Víctor and the pickup truck.

After the bombing she had remembered another incident. Víctor was teaching her to ride a horse and she fell off. "Maybe I'm never going to die from an accident," she said.

34
1992–1993

Mauricio grew tall but didn't realize it. He came home from college in October, for the Columbus Day weekend, and thought that his mother's surprised expression was a reaction to his long hair. After he went back to school, Roselia raised her head, as if her only son were standing in front of her instead of four hun-

dred miles away at the State University of New York College at
Fredonia. *"Más grande que Julio,"* Roselia bragged to her sister-in-
law Marta. Taller than my brother.

Mauricio heard about this and could not believe that in
comparison with Tío Julio his mother gave him the edge. Tío
Julio, the first in the family to go to college, was the tallest man
in Camú. Mauricio didn't think he was that tall. He thought he
was five foot nine. That's what he told people. Is that why they
looked at him strangely? He measured himself and discovered
that he was six foot one and a half.

His height, at first glance, was his most obvious feature, but
he also had a round, dimpled face, the sweet smile of his childhood years, a modest beard, and a chest that hollowed. He
looked like an elongated little boy and still ate the way he had as
a child, like a Taíno. Those might have been liabilities if he
lived in the Dominican Republic with Tío Julio. But an innocent, sensitive demeanor was not necessarily a bad thing for an
American college male in an era of date-rape jitters.

At Fredonia, a lot of girls liked Mauricio Almonte.

He was only interested in Kristina.

She was a petite, blond, green-eyed junior. She was not pretty,
although Mauricio believed she was beautiful as well as handsome, attractive in a strong way. Her hair was short, in a modi-
fied crew cut, and she wore a gold or silver ring in her left
nostril. Mauricio never asked her why. He had asked that question of a girlfriend in high school and she'd broken up with him.

Kristina grew up in a New York City suburb, where her
stepfather was chairman of the English department at the local
high school. Like Mauricio, she read a lot. She liked Bob Dylan,
too, and had lived in South America as a child; her parents had
taught there. Mauricio liked the idea that Kristina could speak the
same language as his mother.

They'd met in October on the Amtrak he'd taken back to
school after the Columbus Day break. Kristina reminded him
that she had been on line behind him at the student center
delicatessen a few weeks earlier than that. "Are you together?"

another student, a black guy named Lamont, had asked. Lamont and Mauricio were two of only a few nonwhite students at the school. Mauricio remembered that he had looked at Kristina with her blond crew cut and her nose ring and thought she was too tough for him.

After their train ride the romance quickly became hot and exclusive. When Kristina's parents came to visit, they took Mauricio out to dinner. During Christmas break, the two saw each other often, although Mauricio stayed with his family in Queens and worked in his old *bodega,* while Kristina had a job at a bakery near her house. They went to each other's homes, met in the city, and stayed overnight in hotel rooms. On New Year's Eve they saw Blues Traveler at the Paramount in Madison Square Garden.

They were old-fashioned lovers: they wrote letters.

"Do you realize that 2 weeks (actually less) from Christmas, it will be 3 months for us," Kristina scribbled on a card that had two parka-clad bears decorating a Christmas tree and hugging. "That's beyond exciting and I beyond love you. I was surprised the day we realized that even though we have a lot in common, we have a lot more not in common. But nonetheless we love each other, we respect each other, and learn so much from each other especially because we are so different. P.S. If we were two bears we wouldn't have to worry about BAs or money or jobs or anything. And I bet we could travel, just not on the road. [At Mauricio's urging, she had read Kerouac.] We'd stick to the forest and we could snuggle in a cave all winter to avoid hunting season. . . . Happy Holidays to you, and your whole family. I love you. *Te Amo. Adiós.* No, see ya *mas tarde.*"

By February, snowdrifts slowed them down on the way to class. What they didn't have in common was getting in the way of the little they did. It wasn't so much their cultural differences as how those differences meshed with their genders and upbringings. Despite his years in America and what he believed was his sophistication, Mauricio craved the tenderness he had received as a child in a small place that was full of relatives. In Camú, people crowded next to each other all the time, on their porches, in their *casitas,* and in their beds. Mauricio wanted to be with Kristina all the time and was surprised to the point of depression when she wanted to do something else. He didn't understand how she could say no to him. On the porches, in the *casitas,* in the beds of Camú, men got what they wanted. Or did they?

"I just don't feel right," Kristina told Mauricio one night after thirteen new inches of snow had fallen. "I just don't feel right about this whole thing between us. I am remembering this relationship I had two years ago, and it was around this time of the year when it all started. I don't know. It might be the weather. I just think that I can use a lot of space right now."

"Don't you have space right now?" Mauricio asked. "It's not like I'm with you all the time or I'm keeping you from doing your schoolwork."

"I know. I know. It's just that I think I would be way better off without a relationship now. Ever since I was sixteen, I've never been out of a relationship, and I don't want to be in one now."

It was about ten-thirty when Mauricio got back to his own suite in Hendrix Hall, hoping that he could blame this on Kristina's PMS. He walked into to the bare common room of the suite and sank into the foam cushions of the yellow couch. He had been sleeping with Kristina for months now, and he had made it a point to memorize, more or less, her menstrual cycle. He thought about this and realized, unhappily, that there was no easy biological explanation for her behavior. He smoked a Marlboro Light. His roommate, Dave, came in and found him. Usually, Mauricio enjoyed talking to Dave, a farrier's son from Beaver Dams, New York. They were not as unlikely room-mates as it had seemed the first day of school, when they mentally compared skin colors and ethnicities. They had both grown up in the country and learned to ride horses before bicycles. And they talked easily about the usual topics: music, girls, and classes. But now Mauricio wanted to be by himself.

Mauricio grunted at Dave, lit a second cigarette, stubbed it out before it was half finished, and left. He went down two flights of stairs, through another hall. An oversize papier-mâché electric guitar, Jimi Hendrix's presumably, hung on the wall. Mauricio walked past the dormitory security station and out onto the cold campus.

He remembered that in the *campo* when he wanted privacy, he sat alone under the mango tree or walked up the *cordillera*. In Queens he took walks, but he never felt the same sense of privacy he had known in the mountains. Now he was again enjoying the luxuries of space and nature. Since there were no nearby mountains, he decided to go into the neighboring village of Dunkirk and down to the Lake Erie shoreline.

He made his way through the architectural potpourri of the Fredonia campus. He had read about all the buildings and could give a tour. He passed the Campus Center, modern and squat; Mason Hall, redbrick and traditional; Maytum Hall, a curved I. M. Pei paean to technical elegance. He went through the outdoor passageway of the Rockefeller Arts Center, through snow-covered grass, out onto the very end of Ring Road, off the campus, and left on Central Avenue. Along the way, he saw students he knew, but he was so distracted and energized by a brewing freshman mixture of fear, passion, anger, and hormones that later he would not be able to remember who they were. He was on Central Avenue before he realized that he was only partially dressed for this adventure. His bottom half was fine. He wore ankle-length, brown leather boots, thermal long johns, and blue jeans. But he had no coat. Only a purple golf shirt and a thin, nylon windbreaker—the dorms were always overheated. He did have a wool scarf. It was still snowing and the temperature had to be below freezing.

He wanted solitude but he didn't really want to use it to think about Kristina. He wanted to blot her out. He tried remembering problems from the chemistry course he had taken, and failed, the previous semester. He was trying desperately to stay in pre-med. His father was expecting that. What he really wanted to do was major in English.

He walked by vintage Fredonia houses: Victorian and Greek Revival showpieces that became less spectacular the farther he got from campus. He passed the D&F Plaza Shopping Center with its Little Caesar's Pizzeria, Chinese takeout, and the doughnut shop that other students frequented. Mauricio rarely craved doughnuts. When he crossed the road that ran alongside the shopping center and which ultimately led to the Thruway and New York City, he left the village limits of Fredonia and found himself in the city of Dunkirk. On the edge of Dunkirk, he saw his first off-campus human, a man shoveling snow in front of his house. The man, who was white, saw Mauricio, his coffee-colored face strangely frozen and snowy, his hair, shoulder length, kinky, tropical, and hard with ice, and moved closer to his driveway.

Mauricio was not the first Latino to walk the streets of Fredonia-Dunkirk late at night. Puerto Ricans had been settling there since they'd been recruited by local vineyard owners decades earlier. Many still lived there; some worked in the factories, some at better jobs, others were on welfare. Mexicans, many of whom lived in a hotel on Route 5 in Dunkirk, now made up the bulk of the itinerant population. But Mauricio didn't know anything about this. He still viewed these upstate towns as communities of white people who went to bed early. At the college, even with its influx of New Yorkers, not to mention late partygoers, it was hard to see it any other way. In the fall of 1992, the school had only 111 black students and 72 "Hispanics" out of a total enrollment of 4,428. Mauricio decided within seconds that the man was scared by either his presence late at night or his race, or both.

From his dormitory he had walked about two miles. He looked behind him and saw an old man in a green Army parka. He wondered if he should be frightened. What would anyone else be doing on the streets? To avoid the old man, he crossed over to Brooks Memorial Hospital. It was quiet there, but two weeks later, while writing a fictionalized account of the night he spent walking, he would put an old Spanish whore in the emergency room doorway, shouting *"Mira!"* at him. Now he was too cold to be imaginative. He kept walking, and when he was sure he wasn't being trailed, he crossed Central Avenue again and wound up in front of Dunkirk City Hall. It was an old building with yellow bricks, spruced up with new windows. Alongside City Hall, on Fourth Street, just before the old-fashioned white globes that lit the entrance to the Police Department, Mauricio spotted a bus shelter. The pristine structure was made from black metal and glass with a white domed top. Mauricio couldn't see a speck of graffiti. But somehow it reminded him of Queens. The metal bench inside was long enough so that he could lie down on it.

Mauricio went in, sat down, and rubbed his hands. He had no gloves, either. He explored his pocket with a numb finger and discovered a cigarette. No matches. Suddenly, in front of his face was the man with the green parka. Up close, he didn't seem so old. In his fifties, probably. Mauricio made a silent accounting of the provisions they each had to get them through a bitter night in a Dunkirk bus shelter. The man had a parka. Mauricio had a windbreaker. The man had blue-and-white running shoes. Mauricio had boots. Mauricio had a cigarette and no light. The man had a copy of the *Leader,* the Fredonia student newspaper. Maybe he had matches, too.

"Need a light, young fella?" the man asked.

"Yeah, sure," Mauricio answered weakly.

Mauricio had lived in Queens since he was eleven, and it didn't occur to him to take comfort from being next to the police entrance. He was frightened. His street smarts were still out of the palm hut. He didn't know what to make of this man. With his dark beard and little granny glasses, the man looked like a skinny Jerry Garcia. Mauricio was still thinking about Kristina but he wasn't worrying about her.

"I can't believe I walked fucking five miles for a damn newspaper and they're calling for more snow tomorrow," the man said.

"They're calling for more snow?" Mauricio wiped his own round, wire-rimmed glasses with his polo shirt. He bent over so that the man could light his cigarette and then offered him one, which was accepted.

"Yep. All day tomorrow. Why do you think they call us snowbirds?"

Mauricio tried to think of a way to make conversation. He noticed the newspaper again. "Did you walk all the way from the college?"

"Yep. And for this piece of paper!" The man slapped the *Leader* with his hand. The front page had a story about Black History Month and the Rosa Parks Scholarship Competition. It would, Mauricio thought, be a very white Black History Month, even if it didn't snow. Mauricio wanted to ask why the man had wanted the paper so badly, but the conversation went in another direction.

"You from around here?" the man asked.

"I go to the college. I just felt like taking a walk. I guess I ended up walking a bit more than I planned."

"That's quite a walk there, fella," the man said in agreement.

"I was feeling kind of depressed."

"Whatcha gonna do? Jump in the lake?"

"No. I'm not that depressed."

"Well, you couldn't jump and sink in the lake. It's frozen. Everything is frozen. My fucking toes are frozen." The man slapped the newspaper in his hand again. His hand looked large to Mauricio. "I worked at the college back in '72. I got fired. What dorm are you in?"

"Hendrix."

"It's nice that they have a dorm named after Jimi Hendrix."

Mauricio was beginning to feel more comfortable. There was something avuncular about the man.

"It's too bad there's no building named after Bob Dylan," Mauricio chimed in.

Jerry Garcia laughed. "I've been driving trucks for years. Once I drove down to Nashville and got robbed. It's full of con artists."

"I have a friend who goes to college there."

"Hey, that's great."

They had complementary clothing for a storm. They both liked Jimi Hendrix and Bob Dylan. They both had tenuous connections to Nashville. Not bad for a bus shelter on a snowy night in Dunkirk, New York.

The man continued, "Yeah, I've been all around this damn country and it's all the same fucking shit. It's too cold in one place. It's too hot in another and you have insects that poison your ass. Other places are full of con artists that want to fuck you up the ass; and south of the border is just fucked-up jungles. I was shot at down there; the only place I will never go back to."

Mauricio listened with interest. Mexico was the place he wanted to go to most in the world. Maybe he had read too much Kerouac.

"And here I am on my fortieth birthday freezing my ass."

"Happy birthday," said Mauricio, surprised that he had been off by a decade.

"My neighbor was supposed to take me in his snowmobile to get the darned paper. He's probably at Demetri's."

There was a pause, and then the man got up and started walking down the street. He hadn't said anything, not even good-bye. He just started walking. Mauricio threw his cigarette on the ground and followed him, uninvited. Demetri's, he had heard, served until late, and it was better than thinking about Kristina. They crossed the avenue together.

"Would you like to go to Demetri's now for some hot chocolate?" he asked the man as they walked.

"Are you paying?"

Mauricio nodded.

He had never been this far into Dunkirk. A lot of Fredonia had a historical look, clean, well-painted buildings that had landmark preservation plaques. Downtown Dunkirk was more quintessential, upstate, gray factory town, where the architectural influences of the 1950s mixed with those of the industrial revolution.

The pair walked by the white-brick Dunkirk Memorial American Legion Post 62 and next to it Dunkirk Exempt. At the next building, Mauricio stopped short. Three-story. Redbrick. Old. Looked like a small Queens apartment house with storefront. A pole hung next to a second-story window, and swinging from it was a red, white, and blue wooden banner with the words CLUB SOCIAL PUERTORRIQUEÑO. Two flags on the banner. One U.S., the other for the Commonwealth of Puerto Rico. Puerto Rico, right across the Mona Strait from the Dominican Republic. How many times had he been mistaken for a Puerto Rican?

"What's the main source of income in Dunkirk?" Mauricio asked.

"Mostly welfare," the man said.

Mauricio realized that because he went to college, the man viewed him as he would any white, middle-class student.

They walked down the next block past the soup kitchen run by the Chautauqua County Rural Ministry, then crossed Lake Shore Drive to the water side. The lake was in front of them with rock jetties that ran parallel to the pier. To the left a Niagara Mohawk power plant hoisted its stacks in the air. In the dark and the fog, Mauricio could barely make out the lake. Demetri's was on their left. On its blue-shingled roof the word "restaurant" was spelled out in white letters. Outside was an arbor, draped with snow instead of grapes, and a balcony with a lake view. Inside was a diner where they served a lot of fish.

In the back, tables faced a bright primitive mural of a Greek village with white stone houses. Mauricio followed the man to the front where farmers and deer hunters in old jeans, flannel shirts, and caps were swiveling on orange leatherette chairs or sitting in the booths. Mauricio took a counter seat and a waitress came over. She bent down, stuck her breasts in his face.

Mauricio jerked his head back. "I'm with him," he said, pointing to Jerry Garcia, who had taken the next seat.

"I'll have coffee," said Mauricio. It didn't seem like the right atmosphere for hot chocolate.

Mauricio's walking companion seemed animated again as he, too, ordered coffee, nodded, and greeted the other customers.

"Hey," Jerry Garcia said, turning back to Mauricio, "do you know the story of the cowboy, the nigger, and the Indian?"

"No, but I'd like to." The words were out before Mauricio could stop himself from being too agreeable.

"Well, there was once this Indian, this cowboy, and a nigger who walked into a bar out West. They were sitting down and the Indian said to the cowboy, 'There were so many of us and there are so few of us nowadays.' The cowboy looked at the Indian and didn't say a word. He just lit up his Marlboro and took a sip from his drink."

The man took a puff from the cigarette Mauricio had given him at the bus shelter. He had saved it. Then he swigged his coffee. Mauricio was growing nervous. He wasn't exactly the Marlboro man himself.

"Then the nigger looked at the cowboy and told him, 'Boy, there were so many of us then and there are even more of us today.' The cowboy looked at the nigger and said, 'That's because we haven't played cowboys and niggers yet.' "

The men chuckled. The waitress adjusted her blouse, looking as though she was trying to ignore them. Mauricio chuckled, too. He was too chicken not to.

He stood, walked to the phone, called his roommate, Dave, and told him the joke and the circumstances, as if sending a coded plea for help. "I might not make it back tonight. I might hitch a ride to Erie to get away for a while." Kristina had not called.

He paid the waitress for the two coffees, left a fifty-cent tip on his napkin, waved to Jerry Garcia, and left silently. The walk back was difficult. But Mauricio didn't stop at the bus shelter. He felt happier, more capable of concentrating on something besides Kristina. The scene in the restaurant was potent enough to distract him, and now that he was out of there, he thought it might make good material for a short story. A bank sign he passed said that the temperature was zero.

Mauricio arrived at his suite, numb and covered with snow. He went back to the couch for fifteen minutes. He didn't know it, but he had walked more than seven miles. It was 1 A.M. Dave came in to tell him Kristina had called a while ago. She said she was worried about him.

Mauricio phoned her back. "Do you have anything majorly important to tell me?"

"No. Just wondering where you were."

"Oh, I'm fine. I just went down for a walk to Lake Erie. I'm just fine. Fine." His fingers were getting their feeling back and hurting.

It wasn't over with her. It wasn't even over for the day. He didn't fall asleep until five and only slept till seven.

Over the next week, when he told the joke to friends, he would sometimes call the Indian a "native American," which of course confused the tone and ruined his point. But in the short story Mauricio wrote over the next few months, he got it right with all its embarrassment. It was a story about a young man confused in love and trying to reconcile who he was with where he came from. The story needed a lot of work. Mauricio's English grammar and syntax were far from perfect, and he called his character "Jesus" and Kristina's "Mary." But the scenes were sharp. He never saw the Jerry Garcia man again, never knew his real name. In the spring he also summoned the nerve to walk into the Puerto Rican Social Club of Dunkirk. He got thrown out because he wasn't a member. But he couldn't be the only Dominican at Fredonia State and not know what it looked like inside.

That summer Mauricio went searching for his Latin roots in Mexico. He was fascinated by the country. It was the place the Dominican Republic might have been, on a smaller scale, if Columbus had found his gold, if Columbus hadn't killed so many Taínos.

He was on a train with two good-looking, blond British women he had met, telling them what he knew of his country's history, when the Mexican immigration officer arrested him.

He was pulled off the train, accused of being an illegal Central American immigrant—and of stealing his green card. From an "immigration detention center" he was allowed to call home. His parents were not there; neither was Elizabeth. (Later he would find out she was visiting the Baseball Hall of Fame in Cooperstown, New York, with her boyfriend, John.) Finally, he found some friends and asked them to see if MasterCard would raise his credit limit so that he could get cash to bail his way out.

When Mauricio arrived home a week later, via a Mexican deportation and a stopover in McAllen, Texas, the friend who had called MasterCard for him suggested that he consider American citizenship. Mauricio had already thought of that.

He practiced what he would tell his father: He had left his Dominican passport at home because he was afraid it would get stolen. He was arrested on a train heading south from Mexico City to Campeche and didn't understand why immigration had bothered. ("I never heard anyone say, 'Oh, I wanna go down to El Salvador and pursue the Salvadoran dream.' ")

No, he wasn't smoking pot on the train, at least not while the immigration officer was around.

Yes, he had some, in the pocket of a khaki shirt he was carrying, but they didn't find it, and he even managed to smoke some in jail.

No, he did not think that bringing it with him was stupid and that smoking it in jail of all places was even stupider.

Yes, he made friends in jail, mostly illegal immigrants from Central and South America, including a pregnant woman from Nicaragua, for whom he felt sad.

Yes, things were stolen from him. A package of condoms and a copy of *Lady Chatterley's Lover,* translated into Spanish, which he had bought in Guadalajara.

And, yes, he was in jail for four days, during which time he thought about, and not necessarily in this order, Kristina, for whom he had bought a porcelain flower bouquet at Plaza Tutili in Ciudad Obregón; his mother; Waldir; why he wanted a daughter but was glad he did not have one yet; famous people who had been in jail, including David Alfaro Siqueiros, Oscar Wilde, and Martin Luther King; the state of his MasterCard payments; Mario Vargas Llosa, because the guards were playing radio serials and he really did want to write one; and finally, whether anyone would be able to get him out.

He decided to tell his father an edited version.

Back in Fredonia in the fall, Mauricio wrote a short story about his Mexican vacation:

"Look, how much did you pay for this?" asked the officer, holding my U.S. resident alien card.

"Me? Nothing," I answered, with very little control over my fingers and smoke over my face.

"But this is a little boy," said the robust officer.

"I was eleven years old when I became a resident," I answered, thinking Marijuana–fucked up, Marijuana = fucked up, while some other voice in my head was saying: "I'd like to see you get out of this one." The officer passed my alien card to the other officer (whom I'll address as officer #2). He looked at it, flipped it, and nodded his head, making a "yes" gesture; he gave it back to officer #1.

"If you have been a resident for eight years, then how old are you?"

"Nineteen," I quickly answered, looking at the burning filter of my cigarette; my legs were still crossed.

He looked at my Bank of New York MasterCard and said: "Credit card, huh?" He looked at my MasterCard receipts and some old train tickets I had kept.

"How much did you pay for this resident card?"

"Don't ask me again. It came from my father. So don't ask me how much."

I looked at him and, in English, in a low voice I said: "How much I paid for my green card? Screw you."

That was what his father had said, a bit more politely, when Mauricio told him the officers thought he had stolen his green card.

35

1993–1994

Mauricio drove his eleven-year-old BMW east, toward home. He had been traveling for twelve hours, much of it through the monotony of upstate snow, and it was a relief to see the sidewalks of Elmhurst, even if they sometimes closed in on him. At 3 A.M. on Roosevelt Avenue, social clubs were open, neon signs glowed above travel agencies that fronted for Colombian drug dealers, gypsy cabbies cut off "civilian" cars, and people climbed stairs to the elevated platform where the No. 7 train, the Flushing line, ran. With all the neon it was as bright as day on Roosevelt Avenue.

Mauricio liked Fredonia, some days he loved it. It was a sweet, comforting little village. Still it was a relief to be back in a place where night life meant more than a produce truck getting off at the next exit. This was his city, his neighborhood, and it no longer mattered that he had been born somewhere else.

He made a right on Junction Boulevard, another on Fortieth Road, and parked in the last legal space on his parents' block. After congratulating his car, and himself, he took his backpack and his Mac Classic out of the trunk and opened the silver chain-link gate in front of his parents' house. The brick steps up to the door needed to be fixed. He had forgotten his key and had to ring the bell.

Mauricio glimpsed his mother's face through the dark glass at the top of the door and felt another kind of relief.

He heard her turn the dead bolt.

"Mauri." She hugged him and he stooped his long, lanky body so that he clung to her. Mauricio could see that she had gone to bed but had not slept. She was in her nightgown and had loosened her ponytail.

Roselia Almonte tilted her head back so that she could see his face.

"Mauri! What hair! You need a haircut."

What was she talking about? His hair was absolutely

respectable this time. A little frizzy maybe. But none of his college friends would have called it long.

"It's not long. It's messy. I left my comb here on Thanksgiving."

She answered him with one of her half smiles. This one was sarcastic, superior, and warm at once, and Mauricio was delighted that she liked his joke. Their salutations were now set to the rhythm of American-style situation-comedy banter, even though Spanish was still all that his mother spoke or understood. She did not bless him. They rarely did *bendiciones* anymore.

He followed her into the dark outer hallway. Mail and packages for Ernesto and members of the Corona family, some of whom still lived upstairs, rested on the ledge in the corner.

His mother opened the door to their apartment, and the heat, set at equatorial level, smothered Mauricio along with the familiar smells: oil, cilantro, soap, and aftershave. He put his Mac on the couch and followed his mother into the kitchen. At the table, they sat side by side. Roselia looked up at Mauricio.

"Are you hungry?"

"No, Mami."

The door to his parents' bedroom opened, and Javier, in his cotton pajamas, crossed the living room, peered curiously at him, nodded approvingly, wiped some sweat off his bald head, and returned to bed.

Mauricio relaxed again. Now his father knew that the BMW had made it home. They had bought the car together, but it had become "Mauricio's mistake." There was no sense arguing with his father when automobiles were involved.

His mother went to sleep with his father, and Mauricio walked into the other bedroom. He was happy to see they still hadn't taken down Albert Einstein, who hung on the outside door. He liked the way Albert Einstein perused the living room and its fruits of American prosperity: the maroon sofas covered with plastic and the leatherette bar.

In the bedroom Mauricio climbed onto the top bunk, careful not to step on Elizabeth, who slept on the bottom. He did not think he had been asleep for more than five minutes when he felt her tugging at his feet.

"Get out of bed," she shouted. His eyes were bleary but he could see that his sister already had on makeup, a silk blouse, and a leather jacket.

"I don't have to be there early," he shouted back.

In his half sleep Mauricio heard his sister get ready for work. She had to be at the World Trade Center by nine. By the time he woke, his mother had left for her factory job. He pulled on jeans and a striped flannel shirt—he couldn't imagine you had to get dressed up just to take a citizenship test—gathered his papers, and went into the kitchen.

His father was there, drinking coffee with foamy milk. There wasn't much construction work in winter.

"Papi, I need my birth certificate."

Javier disappeared into the bedroom. Mauricio played with his coffee. He saw that his computer was still there on the living room couch, where he had left it the night before. With any luck he would get his soap opera for the school radio station finished over the vacation. He wondered if he could tell his father about it. In the *campo,* Javier had grown up glued to the radio. But his father flinched whenever Mauricio spoke about writing. Javier still wanted him to be a doctor, but after two semesters Mauricio had dropped his pre-med major, was using his scholarships and loans to study education and contemplating becoming a literature major. Mauricio thought his father should have understood. Javier had only been as far as the sixth grade, but he was a consummate storyteller. Nobody could talk about Camú the way his father did. The details of those stories about the small Dominican farming village where Mauricio was born competed with America in his imagination.

Javier came back with a wrinkled white slip of paper that identified Mauricio Javier Almonte González as "the son of a Dominican farmer" born August 13, 1974. It was not a birth certificate but a clerk's sworn testimony that the original had been filed in Puerto Plata on that date. Mauricio's real birthday was in June.

"This will work," Javier assured him. "You go a Dominican and come back an American.

"What number president is Clinton?" Javier demanded.

"Forty-three," Mauricio said, not knowing he was wrong. He wished it didn't seem that his father wanted to go with him. He knew that his father was too proud to ask if he could come. And Mauricio knew he should have invited his parents. But he didn't want to. His plan was to get to Brooklyn, to the immigration office, ace the test, and get over to Flatbush Avenue to find Allen Ginsberg. Mauricio had heard that the poet was teaching at Brooklyn College, and he desperately wanted to meet him. He was confident that he could imagine many things, but his father and Allen Ginsberg in the same room was not one of them.

"Take the train to Forty-second Street," Javier continued. "Anything else, forget about it. You can get to Brooklyn from there."

His father thought you could get anywhere from Times Square. It was the center of America, if not the world.

"You can get to Fulton Street, Brooklyn, from there," Javier said.

Mauricio did not go his father's way. But when he got off the train in Brooklyn and asked directions, he found that he was still five blocks from the INS building. He had to walk through the cold. Why, after seven years in New York, including three semesters at a college across Lake Erie from Canada, did he still have a tropical constitution?

The Fulton pedestrian mall was so packed with rushing people that they might as well have been cars and trucks. He walked past phone banks crammed with young men doing street business, and more beautiful black women than he had seen in a long time. He liked blondes, but he found these eel-like women in Brooklyn interesting, too. He passed another subway station, a better connection, which came, of course, from Times Square.

In the narrow building at 505 Fulton Street, he squinted, looking for the elevator.

"Citizenship? Are you looking for citizenship?" The East Indian–accented voice came from the newsstand at the end of the lobby.

"Yes," Mauricio said.

"Second floor." The man, a Sikh, waved a paper at him. "Three dollars for the questions," the man said, pointing to the paper.

Mauricio waved him away. He had already studied for the test. Basic American history. If he didn't pass, he had bigger problems than citizenship.

He got into the elevator. All he really wanted to do was sleep. The week before Christmas vacation they had all gone crazy, cramming for finals and partying. He had eaten even less than usual. Mostly coffee and french fries. He wasn't sure he was in any shape to meet Allen Ginsberg. Ginsberg wasn't replacing Kerouac in his life. Nobody could do that. But he was becoming more interested in the poet. He also liked the modern Irish poets, particularly Seamus Heaney and John Montague, whom he *had* met. And he liked Bob Dylan, who was a poet no matter what anybody said. His professors told him that his taste was eclectic. But that was okay with Mauricio. He was having a good time and thinking about writing poems himself, poems about his family. If he met Allen Ginsberg today, he would tell him how much he liked "Howl" and how reading it made him feel sad because he had missed so much by being born too late. He felt that way when he listened to Dylan, too.

The second-floor INS waiting room was filled with people straining to hear their names. Mauricio sat in the midst of them. The chair was padded and comfortable. But he was still reminded of the U.S. consulate and a very hard bench.

Mauricio waited on the comfortable chair in the immigration office. He couldn't believe how tired he was and how much he had driven the day before. His feet hurt, too. He had on the brown boots he had worn on his walk through the snowy streets of Fredonia the winter before, when he and Kristina had first started arguing. They were wearing out, so Mauricio had colored them a bit with some blue marker to spruce them up.

His romance with Kristina was over. But he and Kristina were burning so much from it that she had gone off to Piedmont to live, romantically, with another woman. At least Mauricio wanted to believe she did that because it had burned so much. He still felt as though she were with him. It was hard not to.

It sometimes amazed him that he could have fun without Kristina. He'd had the most fun the night before last back in Fredonia when he went to his friend Shay's apartment on Center Street. After vacation Mauricio would be moving there because Shay was giving up the apartment; he had a sound-engineering internship in Manhattan and was going to live in the Village. The Fredonia apartment was in a two-story, gray clapboard house and suitably bohemian. Mauricio was going to get voice mail. Voice mail would be a permanent commitment to the apartment, a vote for adulthood and independence, and that meant not being dependent on one girlfriend, either.

The second-floor INS waiting room felt sentimentally familiar to him. It wasn't just his memory of the bench. The room had a whiff of something from the American consulate in Santo Domingo. People waiting without complaint, straining to hear their names, trying to be on their best behavior. But here the humility in faces was tempered by pride. These were the survivors of paperwork, of long lines at consulates in their native lands, of stern interviews with American visa officers. These were people who could maneuver in a bureaucracy. Some were also survivors of clandestine border crossings and false documents, the ones who had managed either through the 1986 amnesty or through other assistance offered or sold by their lawyers and their bosses to accomplish what had once seemed impossible: they had figured out ways to become legal. They were all people who had lived more or less lawfully as official

U.S. residents for at least five years. Most of them were people who could memorize enough simple American history and who knew enough English to answer the questions that would be put to them when their names were called.

Mauricio was in that category, of course, but he had heard that those who weren't, but seemed worthy anyway, would be pulled through the test by visa officers, government-sanctioned coyotes charged with helping immigrants cross the Rio Grande of the citizenship examination. In other words, if you didn't know enough answers, the officers sometimes gave you hints. Big hints.

Mauricio listened to a delicate Chinese man who was being grilled by a Caucasian man who sounded like a lawyer.

"What do you say if they ask you if you drink to excess?"

"No," replied his client.

Mauricio decided that if they asked him if he had ever taken drugs, he wouldn't tell the truth. Why should a little marijuana, most of it shared with people born in America, stand in the way of his travel plans for the rest of his life?

Mauricio surveyed the room. Maybe he would find something he could use in a poem. He examined a poster of immigration officers:

"We will serve with distinction as we administer the immigration and nationality laws of the United States, consistently, fairly, and with respect for all people."

Mauricio remembered his friends in the Mexican prison and the Mexican immigration officer. There was a bald man in the poster, but Mauricio still thought the officers looked too young, too much like his contemporaries, to be deciding who gets into the country and who doesn't.

Mauricio sat and waited for his name to be called for his *cita*.

"Mauricio Almonte!"

He walked in calmly; he was feeling cocky, although he did have flash of Jonathan Mueller, the officer who had denied him his visa when he was an eleven-year-old in Santo Domingo.

But this officer, a woman, seemed nice enough. She asked Mauricio ten questions, and Mauricio answered each one confidently. The officer said she would give him nine points, well above the passing grade. She penalized him for mispronouncing Daniel Patrick Moynihan's name as "Moy-hi-man."

Mauricio was too tired to look for Allen Ginsberg. He went home. Roselia, who had left for the factory while he was sleeping, was in the kitchen cutting orange sections. Mauricio smiled at her and could see she knew.

Javier came out of the bedroom. "You passed?"

"*Sí,* Papi."

"*Bueno!* Now the Mexicans won't think you stole your green card!"

Mauricio sat on the plastic-covered couch and read the mail he had found for himself resting on the ledge.

The ceremony that would make Mauricio Javier Almonte González officially an American was held the morning of February 4, 1994, at 8 A.M. at Brooklyn's Eastern District Federal Court in Cadman Plaza. It was eight months after his nineteenth birthday, and almost eight years after he had been given an immigrant visa to come to the United States.

Mauricio viewed it as an important occasion, meaning another one he had better not sleep through if he wanted to live the rest of his life according to plan. But that didn't mean it had to be austere. And it certainly wasn't exclusive. Scores of other people who also wanted to be citizens would be there, too. Mauricio dressed accordingly. When he woke up in the house on Fortieth Road—he flew home the night before because the BMW had broken down on the way back to Fredonia after Christmas—he put on an old cotton tennis sweater. With its winter white cables and forest green trim, it did have a certain Gap-esque appeal. The big hole on the bottom right side only diminished that a bit, and neither Mauricio nor Roselia, who had gotten up to see him off, chose to acknowledge it. Roselia was in blue jeans and a short-sleeved, orange T-shirt, which was warm enough for the apartment even though this was the coldest winter she'd had yet in America.

Mauricio's parents hadn't asked to come to the ceremony and he had not invited them. He imagined it would be too confusing: emotional and impersonal at the same time and embarrassing for everybody if his parents cried in front of all those people who were also being naturalized and all their relatives. But he was surprised they hadn't asked to come. Were they really that stoic? Did they like to keep their emotions to themselves? Did they want him to stay a Dominican? Or had they just not realized that they could come?

He did not press the issue. He was determined, this time, to look for Allen Ginsberg, and the only thing he could imagine worse than his father meeting Allen Ginsberg was his father and his mother meeting Allen Ginsberg. Mauricio saw that his mother was looking at him with wonder, and it was good that her feelings showed on her face because they did not speak as he walked out the door. Instead, she smiled politely at him as if he were a foreigner, a friendly one but not necessarily a Spanish speaker.

This time he took his father's advice and rode the train to Times Square.

"Let me see your green card. . . . Sir, becoming a citizen? Very good!" A short, pudgy immigration clerk in patriotic colors—a navy blazer and a red-white-and-blue-striped tie—was working the marble floor of the federal courthouse at Cadman Plaza. Towering next to him was a large man from the West Indies who needed help. The clerk pointed to one of two long lines going up two pairs of front steps that lined opposite sides of the light-drenched lobby.

"You don't want to go to the wrong place." Something in the clerk's delivery made it clear this naturalization hearing business was his show and had been for a long time. He was part court clerk, part carnival barker, part schoolmaster and babysitter for the cream of the immigrant class.

"The letter must be filled out to be admitted," he instructed. "If it's not filled out, the officer will not let that person past the checkpoint."

Mauricio got on line and started to fill out the card of questions he had received in the mail, with the notification that he had passed his examination and would be naturalized. As he wrote, the lines began moving up the stairs. Mauricio wrote while he climbed. The woman in front of him, a Salvadoran from Brooklyn, looked at him, took an educated guess, and asked him something in Spanish. She was confused about question six. Mauricio read it: "Has there been any change in your willingness to bear arms on behalf of the United States, to perform non-combatant service in the armed forces of the United States, to perform work of national importance under civil direction if the law requires it?"

"The answer is yes?" the woman asked.

"The answer is no," Mauricio tried to explain, in his Dominican Spanish, which must have sounded strange to her, too. "Even though it sounds wrong. They want to know if you've changed your mind about fighting."

The woman had already written yes and she decided to leave it that way. In the background the court clerk continued.

"Becoming a citizen? You're in the right place!" Mauricio looked at the pictures of Bill Clinton and Al Gore that hung across from the stairs. They seemed small and modestly displayed in thin gold frames with dark blue matting, so unlike the large Ronald Reagan that had loomed at the consulate in Santo Domingo eight Februarys ago. At least it loomed in his memory. He took out the green card he would have to relinquish. On it was a photograph of a little boy of eleven. He decided not to answer the question that asked if he had traveled outside the United States. He doubted the FBI was hooked into that small jail in Mexico, but why risk it?

He was up to the final question: "Have you practiced polygamy; received income from illegal gambling; been a prostitute; procured anyone for prostitution or been involved in any other unlawful commercial vice; encouraged or helped any alien to enter the U.S. illegally; illicitly trafficked in drugs or marijuana; given any false testimony to obtain immigrant benefits; or been a habitual drunkard?"

That about covers it, Mauricio thought, and with a resounding swish of his pen he checked "No!"

Upstairs he went to a table where a big woman in a hot pink shirt sat like a calm, albeit colorful, Buddha and announced quite happily, "We get three hundred people about three times a week."

She took the green card of the Salvadoran woman who was in front of Mauricio and read the answers to her questions with a knowing look.

"Has your position changed?" she quizzed her.

No answer.

"Have you changed?"

"No."

"Okay! Next."

Mauricio handed over the little-boy green card he had almost lost in Mexico. This was the real end of it.

"Have you traveled outside the United States?"

"No." Mauricio always felt bad about lying. She handed him back the paper. "Go to table two." While he waited his turn, Mauricio reread the question and realized that what it was really asking was whether he had left the country since he applied for citizenship. He had applied in the fall after he had come home from Mexico; he felt like an honest near citizen again. He handed his questionnaire to another woman and was given a Certificate of Naturalization that said "Mauricio Javier Almonte." No González anymore. There was a photograph of him with hair that was truly long.

"Sign your name exactly as you see it there," another clerk instructed him.

Mauricio pulled a red pen from his pocket and signed.

"Oh, Jesus!" the clerk said. "You signed it in red. You see why I have all these black pens."

Mauricio chuckled to himself. If he had really been a beat poet, that would have been a symbolic act.

"I couldn't help it," Mauricio said.

"Well, just pick up your materials."

The back of the large courtroom was decorated with a portion of a WPA mural by Edward Laning: *The Role of the Immigrant in the Industrial Development of America*. The immigrants depicted were building the transcontinental railway. The courtroom was becoming as crowded with foreign-born as the mural, and a lot of people were still outside. The court clerk from the first floor reappeared in the front. Now he was an emcee. Seven judicial seats were behind him. He was doing a stand-up routine in the Appellate Division courtroom.

"I understand everyone brought a lot of visitors with them. That's okay. It's a happy occasion. Everyone else in this courthouse is prosecuting, sitting, or going to jail, so I have a happy assignment. But I'm going to have to ask everyone to move down so there's room." He made a sideways pushing motion with his hands and resumed, "You can't take any pictures in here. However, right outside you'll see that eagle that you see on the six o'clock news every night. It makes a lovely picture."

It was nine o'clock. People had been waiting on line since before eight.

"We'll have the Pledge of Allegiance with the oath of naturalization, which we'll be discussing later," the clerk continued. "Now, if Judge Raggi gives the oath, she'll do it. If she's in court and another judge comes in, then I'll give the oath."

A latecomer arrived. All he had missed were the lines. He was wearing Hasidic garb, a fuzzy red beard, and a hearing aid. Something was wrong with his eyes. They didn't focus well. But he found a seat in the back row, turned, and smiled at the man next to him. The man, who could have been Indian, Latin—or Arab—smiled back.

"When the judge is ready, there will be three knocks and you'll all rise."

Another latecomer. An elderly woman with granny glasses. The clerk pointed to the witness box on his right. "Ma'am, you just come in and we'll make you a witness." The audience laughed. "You won't have to testify.

"If you see an error on your certificates come back as soon as possible. One guy came back eleven years later. He came in running, out of breath, and he said, 'They won't give me a passport because my name's backwards.' I said, 'When were you naturalized?' He said, 'Eleven years ago.' I said, 'What took you so long? Were the subways late?' "

Mauricio shook his head. At least this guy was funny.

The warm-up act played for another twenty minutes. The clerk gave travel advice to those who came from countries that accepted dual citizenship: "Don't travel with your foreign passport without your U.S. passport because you might not get back into the U.S. They want to see your American passport. Make sure you have it. We don't want anyone to get stuck at the airport with the investigators."

Or with Mexican immigration officers, Mauricio thought.

The clerk sent people out to put more change in their meters, explaining, "This is a tough area." He warned them to be back in ten minutes and told a story about a man who missed being naturalized because he was getting a sandwich. Mauricio never imagined he would have such a good time at his naturalization. Finally, the clerk picked up the gavel and knocked three times.

Judge Reena Raggi was fresh faced and wore her straight hair pulled back in a headband, the way Hillary Clinton used to wear hers. Mauricio stood for the pledge. He dutifully repeated the judge's words, the words he and Waldir had learned together at the Leonardo da Vinci Intermediate School. He repeated the oath of naturalization, too, but was silent at the part when everyone else promised to bear arms for their new country.

Suddenly, he was a citizen of the United States of America.

"Good morning, ladies and gentlemen," Judge Raggi said. "I am pleased to preside over these ceremonies. It just wouldn't be a ceremony if I didn't say a few words of congratulations to all. This is typical of this district. At least two and sometimes three times a week we have large groups of two to three hundred people because annually almost as many new citizens come from this part of the United States as all other parts of the country."

The judge talked about the Laning murals, which had once hung at Ellis Island. She asked how many people were from Asia, and a small contingent of hands went up. She asked about Central America and most of the rest responded. She called out Europe and nodded as a few more hands were raised.

"That was where our immigrants used to come from traditionally. My own mother was not born in the United States. She had to become a citizen. She was born in Italy. Do we have any citizens from Italy?" More hands. *"Anchela mi mamma,"* the judge said with a respectable Italian accent. The former Italians in her audience laughed. "I hope someday some of you will come back to a courthouse like this and find your son or daughter sitting on the bench and telling the story of this day."

The clerk, Mauricio thought, was the opening act, the stand-up comic. This judge was Broadway, an American musical.

"Citizenship comes with responsibilities, not just privileges. You spoke about some of them in the oath you took today, but I want to talk to you about another duty. The duty that you have, the right you acquire today, is to vote. . . . Make sure that the people who represent you share the same hopes and dreams you have. . . . Finally, I urge you to remember one thing about becoming an American. There really is no single definition of being an American. Americans really draw on the best that all cultures and backgrounds have to offer. In your home and with your families you'll want to maintain many of the traditions and values of your culture. But don't keep them just to yourself. Share them with your fellow Americans. I think sometimes we do this with food in New York; everybody else shares everybody's culinary culture. Everybody eats everybody's tacos and egg rolls and bagels. But even more, share your values.

That's what has set this country apart, that talent for drawing on the best that each of us brings."

Mauricio waited for his name to be called and picked up his naturalization certificate.

Three months before Mauricio became a citizen, the INS announced that naturalization would be encouraged as it had never been before. The Clinton administration embarked on a campaign to make our new masses of foreign-born nationals—the 10 million legal permanent residents, in particular—more acceptable to the rest of the country. "Naturalization helps counter anti-immigrant attitudes," Doris M. Meissner, the new commissioner of immigration and naturalization, told the *New York Times*. "When people become citizens, they accept our values and most Americans are reassured."

"I certainly didn't vote for Bob Dole," Mauricio the graduate student says. "But I'm not all that sure that Bill Clinton would appreciate the American values I accept. Although he might have once. I don't know if anyone else is reassured that I became a citizen. But I certainly am. Now I can travel to Mexico without getting arrested."

Mauricio didn't go home after he became an American citizen. He didn't even call. Instead, he went to Junior's restaurant, a Brooklyn landmark, ate a large piece of cheesecake, and went to look for Allen Ginsberg. He took the IRT subway down Flatbush Avenue to Nostrand.

"What did you say you use to call it where those streets meet?" Mauricio the graduate students asks. "The Junction? Sounds like Queens. But it could be a *campo* name. Hey, Allen Ginsberg now teachers in your old neighborhood. Allen Ginsberg teaches in your Camú."

★ ★ ★

Mauricio walked over to the redbrick campus and went through the visitors' entrance at Whitehead Hall. "I need to see someone in the English Department," he told the security guard. "Boylan Hall," he replied.

On the wall of a building Mauricio passed, on a bulletin board encased in glass, was a banner that proclaimed DOMINI-CAN STUDENT UNION . . . CARIBBEAN STUDENT ASSOCIATION. There were some postcards, including one of the Parque Central in Puerto Plata, where his aunt Marta had, as a ten-year-old maid, pushed Doña Fanny's baby.

In Boylan he stumbled into the Classics Department and asked for Allen Ginsberg. They looked at him as though he were very strange indeed.

"Do you have Dr. Ginsberg's schedule?" he asked a woman in an office around the bend which was the English Department.

"What?" The woman had on green stretch pants. She was very blond and businesslike except for the bright green earrings that dangled from her lobes.

"Allen Ginsberg?" Mauricio asked weakly. "Do you have his office hours. I mean his room number?"

"Whatever's posted."

Mauricio decided to be courageous. "Is he around?"

No answer.

He walked back to the hall and found a bookcase with Ginsberg's *White Shroud Poems* in it. There was also a poster announcing the 1994 Allen Ginsberg Poetry Awards honoring Allen Ginsberg's contribution to American literature. It was being sponsored by a community college in Passaic, New Jersey, the state where the poet was born. The prizes were $300, $150, and $100. Across from the poster a bulletin board listed teaching schedules for the spring semester. Ginsberg's class was up there. Mauricio went into 2307B, the room where the schedule said Ginsberg would be teaching. It had a square, wraparound table, linoleum floors, a poster for the movie *Short Cuts,* a sign that said JESUS LOVES YOU, and a real blackboard not a green one. He had not seen Allen Ginsberg, but Mauricio was not disappointed.

★ ★ ★

He got back to Elmhurst in time for supper. Javier and Tía Marta, who had come for a visit, were in the living room, each one lying down on a couch. Roselia was still at work. Javier and his older sister were watching a talk show that had Spanish-speaking transvestites as guests.

"So is it okay?" Marta asked in English.

"Yes, it's okay," Mauricio said.

"Americano?"

"Yes!"

"Okay?" asked Javier.

"Yes!" said Mauricio.

His father's smile now sometimes mimicked his mother's, and it was delivered with just as much irony.

"Now you can ask for *residencia,*" Javier said in Spanish. Another rib about Mexico. Mauricio knew he would be suffering those for years. "And your passport?"

"No, it doesn't come with it."

"When do you get it?"

"When you apply," Marta explained. She was still La Cabeza, the head of the family, and she'd been responsible directly or indirectly for bringing more than twenty of her relatives to the United States. More were arriving all the time.

"You have to turn in the other and give them money."

Back in Fredonia, Mauricio started and completed a cycle—a "family" he liked to call it—of poems on being an immigrant. He called it "Out & In the Muddy Cup" and thanked John Montague. Montague's poem "A Muddy Cup" was included in a collection entitled *The Dead Kingdom,* which Mauricio had read several times. Montague's parents were from County Armagh in Northern Ireland, and "Muddy Cup" represented the poet's mother's view of America. But Mauricio read it and heard the familiar adult voice of a child of foreign-born parents. When he was writing his poems, he thought of Allen Ginsberg's "Kaddish" and the "King of May" as well.

Mauricio entered his poems in the college's Fifth Annual Rosa Parks Scholarship Competition and received a letter saying that he had won $350 dollars.

He was thrilled by the honor and knew exactly what he was going to do with the money—get his BMW out of the shop. The contest had been started by a Puerto Rican professor who was desperately trying to raise the "diversity" level of the school. Anyone who wrote about minority issues could enter, regardless of their ethnic background, an accommodation that had to be made for the near-lily-white school. Only twenty students entered, though. And Mauricio was the only winner who wasn't white.

On the afternoon of the award ceremony, the college's recital hall filled up quickly with students, faculty, and a contingent of high schoolers from two nearby villages, where Mauricio had a tutoring job. He walked into the auditorium and went over to see them. Three pretty seniors with braces were talking about their boyfriends, and two overweight, blond, light-skinned girls in shorts huddled together. One of them was eating from a bag of bite-sized Bit-O-Honey.

"First!" announced Dr. Donald McPhee, the college president. "*Maw-ree-shee-o* Almonte."

Mauricio walked onto the stage and shook hands with the president. The announcement was followed by fifteen seconds of happy applause from the audience. "*Mawreesheeo* is a prize winner and that carries a stipend of three hundred fifty dollars. A junior secondary education major. Elmhurst, New York. And he will be reading later."

The other checks were awarded and all the participants named and thanked. The school's multiracial, predominantly female gospel choir sang.

Mauricio could have waited for his turn forever. But suddenly he was onstage with the woman who lived in the apartment next door, a theater major whom he had convinced to read Montague's poem and then bang a frying pan with a fork while he read his own poems. When he came up with the idea, Mauricio had thought it made sense, fitting within the context of the poem. Now he wondered. He was wearing off-white pants, which his neighbor had ironed for him early that morning, a white shirt, a dark green flannel jacket, and a tie with a Rousseau print.

"Here is a poem by John Montague," Mauricio said, after his second round of friendly applause died down. The theater major read "A Muddy Cup":

My mother
my mother's memories
of America;
a muddy cup
she refused to drink.

His landlady didn't know
my father was married
so who was the woman
landed on the doorstep
with grown sons

my elder brothers
lonely & lost
Father staggers back
from the speak-easy
for his stage-entrance;

the whole scene as
played by Boucicault
or Eugene O'Neill:
the shattering of
that early dream

but that didn't
lessen the anguish,
soften the pain, so
she laid into him
with the frying pan

till he caught her
by the two wrists,
*Molly, my love, if
you go on like this
you'll do yourself harm.*

And warmly under
a crumbling brownstone
roof in Brooklyn
to the clatter of
garbage cans

like a loving man
my father leant
on the joystick
& they were reconciled
made another child

a third son who
beats out this song
to celebrate the odours
that bubbled up
so rank & strong

from that muddy cup
my mother refused
to drink but kept
wrinkling her nose
in souvenir of

*(cops and robbers,
cigarstore Indians
& coal black niggers,
bathtub gin and
Jewish neighbours)*

Decades after
she had returned
to the hilly town

where she had been born,
a mother cat,

intent on safety,
dragging her first
batch of kittens back
to the familiar womb-warm
basket of home

(all but the runt,
the littlest one, whom
she gave to be fostered
in Garvaghey, seven miles away;
her husband's old home).

The theater major hit the frying pan with the fork.

"Ahhhmmmm," said Mauricio. "John Montague is one of Ireland's best poets. . . . Ahhhhmmmmm, I'm not Irish. You might have noticed that already, but nonetheless I found inspiration in Montague's poem, and my family of poems owes a lot to it. 'Out and In the Muddy Cup.' I want to dedicate this to my seventh-grade best friend and still best friend Waldir Sepulveda, whose story remains untold, unheard."

Mauricio went on to list secondary dedicatees, including a homeless person who used to hang around International High School, the Brazilian taxi driver who was in prison with him in Mexico, his parents—and John Montague.

"The first poem is entitled 'The Man.' "

The man I call my father,
and quietly moved me
from the warmth of my mother's breasts
at midnight

at dinner time:
"What happened to you last night?
You went to bed in one place and woke up facing
    the wall."

Muddy Cup

The man who worked from morn 'til night
a tired yet smiley face, he always brought home.
But this man disappeared.

Waking up in my mother's breasts
I found . . .

strange!

The theater major hit the pan.
"The second poem," Mauricio explained, his voice still
strong, "is titled 'Two plus one equals five.' It's about math that
doesn't work."

> "Sad" would not do justice
> when describing my feelings
> and those of my mother
> when denied an international postage
> my sister and I were
> She and my older sister were not.
> A piece of mint I cut with my cavity afflicted teeth
> ½ to my sister
> ½ for me;
> we now had another thing in common
>
> Just another family torn apart
> Just another "fuck-up."
>
> "Sad" would not do justice
> when describing the feelings
> my mom and I shared
> minutes before
> a loud, hard, insipid flying machine
> would take her somewhere
> I didn't know; she didn't know
> somewhere where my father was
> *"Nueva Llork."*

Tears ran,
visible ones at the time
and for months invisible ones
flooding my thoughts that one day:
everything would be all right!
That one day I would go to bed on my mother's
    breasts
and wake up facing a wall.

Another clang from Amybeth.
"The third poem is titled *'Nueva Llork.'* That's about New York."

Greek Landlords.
know it all next door neighbors,
who paid to file their income taxes
who didn't know English,
but high-chinned, claim otherwise

Old can collecting ladies
kids not much older than me
talking about hurting others.

Cuban barbers talking endless politics
Machismo on four wheels
Spanish & handicapped English in the air;
Baseball hat–wearing new immigrants
to protect them from their fears
long ways from home.

Mom's complaints,
that her chicken doesn't taste like chicken
more like the refrigerator!

After the clang, Mauricio, loosened up now, decided he would give a small speech: "The next and fourth poem was written on location. That is to say, aboard a Mexican aircraft with a highly questionable maintenance record and outside a Greyhound station in McAllen, Texas. It's called 'Cup from Afar.' I guess it's about America from . . . I guess it's about what America looks like from the outside."

> At age nineteen,
> Zigzagging though Mexico
> I! was arrested
> for not having blond hair and gre-eeee-nnn eyes
> by officers in gre-eee-nn uniforms

Mauricio was acting now, making much of his indignation and rolling not only the word "green" but all his "I's" as though he were a king—or a dictator. He had long forgiven Jonathan Mueller, but he wasn't sure he could do the same for Mexico.

> I! was arrested, detained in ancient stations
> jailed in urine perfumed jails.
> I was told that bringing condoms
> into Mexico was illegal; thus, they confiscated my condoms
> (But the officer put them in his pockets)!

In the audience, one of Mauricio's students laughed out loud. This was her tutor!

> I! was detained in a supervised space,
> where I met Lidia, María, Lourdes, Petra,
>   Josefina . . .
> a lot of which with potential creatures in their
>   uterus;
> their crime being: wanting to move up a decimal
> in the long ladder of society
> All Central American men & women

who got caught that day, but tried again the next
    day.

And it was here where I met,
Geraldo—a Brazilian cab driver, father and solo
    supporter
of five children, and a now lonesome wife!
And I! met Pedro, Luis, Manuel, Emanuel,
    Andres
All of which were caught that day
but tried again the next day
to fulfill a dream of not only seeing, but being in
"El Norte."

All deported that night
to Military Governments
even dirtier streets
Guerrilla warfare, and ethnocentric tourists
who look and smile, but speed up when asked for
    money!

And I! was lucky to be deported to McAllen, Texas.
Thanks to a "green card,"
a "green card" I could only thank my father for!

The theater major had said she liked that poem. She gave it
three clangs. "This fifth poem," Mauricio continued, "is titled
'My Grandmother's Eldest Daughter.' I guess it's a long way
around saying "Mom" and talking about Mom, I started writing a letter to Mom and probably three sentences into it realized that she didn't . . ." Mauricio stopped to collect himself.

"She didn't read . . ." Mauricio stopped again. "English. But
I kept writing this and it became a poem to her."

Mom,

You who handwashed clothes
'til your fleshy knuckles bled

You who were and still are
the pivotal glue which makes and maintains a
    family

You who faithfully followed
leaving confused little ones behind
after much optimistic explanations and tears

You who makes in a six day week
far less than what I can make in three!!!

You who shies away from English speaking
incomprehensible mouths

You who surrounds yourself with factory work
from eight to five; walks home to continue your
    Eternal Task
of not only a mother, but a wife
Pregnant occupations, that everyday bear new
    duties

Oh! How dare I not be glad to be
my grandmother's eldest daughter's son?

Without waiting for a clang Mauricio launched into the end
of his reading. "The next poem, the sixth poem and last poem
of the family of poems, is untitled," he said.

An American
An American by naturalization
An American for ninety dollars
An American just like that.
And who am I—I still have two eyes!!

I don't have more ribs than a farmer's
son in Mexico!!
My mother looks like many
women in Central America!!

I don't have more fingers than a taxi driver in
   Brazil!!
(Nor did I get my nervous system at Radio Shack!)

"Thank you very much."

The pan clanged and the audience applauded Mauricio for a whole minute.

He was as relieved as he had ever been. Dr. McPhee came up to him and they chatted. On his way into the reception on the second floor of the recital hall, Mauricio was greeted by a few deans and congratulated. He had changed a few more lines as he read, and he still wasn't sure he liked the poems. The next poems he wrote would be better.

He got his BMW out of the shop the next week. Then, in the true fashion of an American capitalist, he began to think of other ways to make money. He wondered if there was still time to enter the 1994 Allen Ginsberg Poetry Awards.

Mauricio thought about getting a summer job working at one of the vineyards around Fredonia. It would be good for him, he thought, to wake up at seven in the morning and work the land the way his father and his grandfather had done in Juan de Nina and Camú. Then he found out that the grape pickers at the vineyard began at six.

It is morning in Elmhurst when Abuelo Javier's clock radio wakes him for work. He has been gloating for months over Mauricio's citizenship. He himself would not become an American. But for Mauricio, it is very good.

He is impressed with his son's poetry award, as well. "Very nice," he says about it quickly—and in English. He had hoped for a doctor. But $350 for a few poems is not bad money. He has heard that his son considered a farm job this summer but balked because he would have to be in the vineyards by six.

Abuelo Javier remembers the roosters of Camú at 4 A.M. "That," he says, "is not for my son."

PART FOUR

IMMIGRANTS

36
1986–1993

I went to hear Mauricio recite his poems in Fredonia, and as I listened I thought about a spring eight years earlier.

On the night before Mauricio's mother left to go to America, I slept with his sisters, in the bed next to him in the *casita* in Camú. It was the first—and last—time I stayed there. I had finally found the nerve to beg that invitation, and when I did I realized that I could have asked much sooner. Roselia, although grieving, could not have been more gracious. "Of course you can stay," she said. "You can sleep with the girls." For Elizabeth and Cristian it was a slumber party; I was "a new sister." Even without me they were squished head to toe in their narrow bed. But they happily moved closer to one another so that I would have room. As I got in, I remembered another story of my mother's.

As as a teenager in a Brooklyn apartment, she had slept in the same bed with her two sisters—another had been born in America. One of my aunts had a boyfriend—now my eighty-one-year-old uncle—who liked to come over for a goodnight kiss. He usually arrived late, after the girls were in bed. They would wait up for him and, in the darkness, trade places, so that he would wind up kissing the wrong sister. Perhaps it was a good thing that in 1986 I knew nothing about Julio Santini.

Roselia adjusted our mosquito net, and I giggled to myself over that story and giggled with Elizabeth and Cristian over nothing in particular. Then they fell asleep and eleven-year-old Mauricio came in. He was very upset and didn't acknowledge me. But I watched him as he woefully lifted up his own net and, sniffling, crawled into bed. Roselia followed him, turned off the single lightbulb hanging from the ceiling, and went to bed herself. I reached for my notebook and pen and recorded the few words mother and son said to one another, along with Mauricio's breaths, tears, and whimpers.

Even that night, sleeping alongside the Almontes, I still felt like a reporter with them. I can remember the exact moment I stopped feeling that way: 5:30 P.M. the next day, May 2, 1986— the moment at the airport when Mauricio said good-bye to his mother and his sister, Elizabeth.

He hugged his mother. Then he turned and hugged me with comparable desperation. He molded his body so close to mine that I didn't know how we could ever be separated. I had no children myself then, but the last thing I wanted to do was get on that plane without Mauricio. I felt I understood how Roselia felt, how a mother felt. I was ready to go home and do as my husband had insisted, send my series to every congressman in New York.

It turned out I didn't have to. Gary Ackerman got to me first.

Weeks earlier, when I had first met Javier, he had asked me why a woman my age didn't have any children. I had the usual excuses about career goals and independence, none of which he appreciated. I didn't know the real reason myself. But as soon as Mauricio arrived in America, I told my husband that I would like to have a baby. The night that Elizabeth and Cristian went to Elizabeth's classmate's party with soda instead of rum, I went with them and wound up lying in the bedroom too dizzy and nauseated to get up. The sisters—who knew nothing about my "at-home efforts"—came in to check on me and exchanged knowing looks. They were right. I was not ill but pregnant.

Some of the sweetest moments I remember from that first year I wrote about the Almontes involve the meshing of our families. I remember Election Day 1986. It was so clear to me that day that the children, Elizabeth and Mauricio, at least, were shedding old alliances and fears and trying to become American. We were on the way to my parents' house in Brooklyn. My parents were ailing, but they had insisted I drive them to their polling place. I don't think my parents ever missed an election. I asked Elizabeth if she knew who was running for governor. "It's Señor Cuomo, but I am an enemy of politicians," she said. I knew she would never have said that in the Dominican Republic. "I know who's running, too," Mauricio called from the backseat of my car.

"Herman Badillo," he said, naming the Democratic candidate for comptroller, "and Mario Cuomo." Cristian smiled a little.

It was the first time any of the Almontes had met my parents, although my parents had been reading about them. My mother opened the door and hugged each of the children, as Fian had hugged me. Then she motioned for them to sit at our dining room table. The wooden table and chairs, like the rusty red rocker out back, had been there as long as the house.

"Watch yourself on those chairs," my mother cautioned Elizabeth. She made hand motions to make sure she was understood and then went into the kitchen and came back with a plate of bagels and a tin of cream cheese. "I have some rice on the stove, too," she added. "A bit of our food, a bit of yours. But really, I eat a lot of rice." She came back with the pot. "I'm an immigrant, too, you know."

My mother began to tell the story of the time she hid in a haystack in Felshteen. I tried not to groan. For as long as I could remember, my mother had told that story not just to her children but to anyone who would listen, as if she, herself couldn't believe it had happened to an everyday woman from Brooklyn. She asked me to translate. I did and the Almonte children were spellbound. My mother decided to tell more stories.

"When I first came to America a little girl called me a greenhorn." I translated that as best I could, laughing because I knew what was coming next. "I didn't like that so I punched her in mouth and broke her glasses. My father had just arrived and we were very poor. He had to buy her a new pair of glasses. But I was glad I did it."

Elizabeth, I could tell, liked that story.

"I can see my mama and papa after we came to America," my mother continued. "And I can see them in this house. Papa in the yard, planting his flowers. Mama in her kitchen."

Years later, I sat with Elizabeth at Houlihan's across from the World Trade Center and, over a basket of Budweisers, she repeated with startling accuracy those immigrant stories my mother had told her on an Election Day almost a decade earlier.

★ ★ ★

When the year was over, I was amazed by how well the Almontes, all the Almontes, had endured. They had been watched by a newspaper reporter during one of the most stressful, undignified periods of their lives. And they had survived that yearlong invasion of their privacy with more grace than I would ever have been able to muster. I knew there were times when they hated my intrusions. I saw the way the other students in Mauricio's class looked at him when I showed up. But Mauricio never told me to stop coming, although I did stop for a while after I heard one of those students say, "Mauri, your mami is here again."

The only family member I ever had words with was Roselia and that, I suppose, was inevitable. She resented my presence in her house. I couldn't blame her. Javier loved to be interviewed and spent a lot of time talking to me. Her children as much as said I was their "American mother." Now that I am a mother myself, the thought of that makes me wince. At that difficult stage in her life, competition was the last thing Roselia needed. To Roselia's amazing credit, she only tripped me up once in retaliation. I told her that I wanted to come watch her at work. I kept asking her if I could come, and she kept telling me another day would be better. One day she inexplicably changed her mind. What she didn't tell me was that she had changed jobs and was now at a new factory. "Roselia doesn't work here anymore," her old boss told me when I arrived. I was in the first trimester of my pregnancy and too sick to go traipsing around every storefront factory in Corona looking for Roselia. That evening I waited for her at home, and we wound up screaming at each other on the sidewalk outside the house on Fortieth Road. We were so loud and vicious that Javier came out to calm us down. Our words were about why she had lied to me. But what we were really fighting over was my presence on her turf.

As far back as Election Day, I had known that when the series was over, my husband and I would be moving to Mexico City.

He had been given a job as *Newsday*'s Latin America Bureau chief, and I planned to go with him and freelance, as I had done in Ireland. *Newsday* gave us a gala farewell party at a jazz club in SoHo. Elizabeth, Cristian, and Mauricio came, and to my astonishment Roselia came, too. (Javier was sick with the flu.) She looked no more out of place in that downtown setting than my elderly parents, and the three of them finally met, although there was so much noise and music that I don't know if they were able to say anything to each other in any language.

My father died a week after that party, and my mother passed away three months later, just before I was to give birth to our first son, Daniel, in Mexico City. An hour before I was told the news about my mother, I was trying to nap but not asleep and I thought I heard her voice calling to me from the sky above the trees in our Mexican garden. I was sure I had imagined it, but later I couldn't help thinking about my mother's own ghosts and the ones the Almontes sometimes saw and heard. The ghosts of parents and grandparents.

In the massive emotional confusion I felt during that time, it was, oddly, Roselia's voice on the phone that helped anchor me. We spoke only about the children, not the dead parents or their ghosts. But Roselia knew what I was missing, reassurance from my mother that I was doing a good job. I brought Daniel—we called him Danny—back to New York for a visit when he was five weeks old and one of the first places we went was the apartment on Fortieth Road.

"Ay, qué lindo!" Roselia cooed when she saw him. He was a good-looking blond baby, and she kept on telling him how handsome he was: *"Danielito. Guapito."* Then she took him in her arms, sang to him, and although I hadn't yet put him on solids, fed him mashed bananas and mango. I didn't argue. She had raised a lot more children than I had. He began to cry and she tried to soothe him, but did not take offense when her rocking didn't work. "Bárbara," she said. "He needs the warmth of his mother now, *el calor de su madre.*" She sent me into the room her three children still shared to nurse him.

Javier held Danny, too. I hadn't known that you could safely wrestle an infant before I saw him do it. It was the most gentle wrestling I had ever seen.

"El gran mejicano" was what Javier called my blond son. A Latin man, like himself.

During the two years we lived in Mexico, I spoke to the Almontes often on the phone. Our conversations usually revolved around children. We felt that we had common ground. When Cristian ran away with Julio Santini, Javier called. "This is the worst thing that has ever happened to me in my life," he said. I could see that it would be.

I was in New York again that spring. Cristian had still not come home, and nobody was expecting her. Javier seemed happy, though. Good weather meant a lot of work for him, and he was enjoying the tail end of the eighties construction boom in New York.

"Go with him to *Yunshun*," Roselia instructed me, pointing toward Junction Boulevard. "We never gave you any presents for the baby."

Pushing Daniel in his stroller, I followed Javier and Elizabeth down to Roosevelt Avenue. We crossed and walked one block to a store with large windows and a lot of chrome: Youngworld.

"Did you ever go here when Cristian worked here?" Elizabeth asked.

I shook my head.

She and her father selected an array of clothes. They held each piece up against Danny's small body to measure it and then conferred on size and style.

"It's too much and nobody is asking me what I like," I complained. They laughed and kept on going until they had collected about a hundred dollars' worth of clothing, although it seemed it should have cost more. The clothes Elizabeth and Javier picked were not like the ones other friends had sent: those were mostly simple good cottons from Hanna Anderson or soft, elasticized Guess baby jeans. But these Youngworld offerings were gimmicky, with prints of boats or animals on them; tiny striped, man-tailored shirts; jeans with zippers "just like Papi's." I would never have believed it, but they lasted a long time.

In 1989, my husband had a new assignment and we moved to Hong Kong.

One afternoon a year later, I was resting in the master bedroom of our fourteenth-floor duplex, overlooking the South China Sea. I answered the phone and heard a familiar, high-pitched, delighted screech.

"Bárbara! Isn't it ready yet?"

"Marta. How did you know?" I was about to give birth to our second child.

"Javier told me. *Ayyy*, Bárbara, make sure you call me as soon as the pains start."

"Why? Are you going to deliver it?"

Marta was not exactly Doña Layla, the Juan de Nina midwife, but she did make me feel as though we were, at least, in the same village. From my window I saw junks and sampans, but as she spoke, I could hear roosters crowing into palm huts, taxi brakes screeching on Junction Boulevard.

"*Ayy*, Bárbara! Do you know that Cristian might have her first baby the same day as you? The same day as your second."

"I know. Javier told me."

"And Danny? Is he okay?"

Marta felt proprietary toward Danny, too. During the first months of that pregnancy, when nausea was still a big issue, I spent a day at a veterans' hospital with her trying to undo a glitch in her Murray Gordon benefits.

"Yes, although I don't know how he's going to take the competition. Marta, have you ever called anyone this far away?"

"No, Bárbara."

We moved back to the United States eight months later, as Mauricio was finishing his junior year of high school, but I didn't see the Almontes, or even let them know I was back, for a long time. Something bad had happened and I couldn't face them. It wasn't Jack, my Hong Kong baby. He was fine.

It was Danny.

The easiest way to explain it was to say that he was three and a half and had stopped talking. But that didn't explain it. It was as though he had been hit by a phantasmal truck, which, instead of leaving physical wounds, killed his will and his humor and even his dexterity. He looked like the same handsome, blond child. But he didn't play; he didn't laugh. He wet his pants and he didn't care if you took his toys and threw them in the garbage.

Trying to describe this and answer the questions it begged was almost as exhausting as living with it, and it was even more difficult with people who liked and understood children. They were the ones who asked the most questions.

"What do you mean he stopped talking?" Javier said when I finally found the energy to call the apartment on Fortieth Road. "You mean he's gotten shy?"

"He doesn't say a word."

"What?"

"He lies around, he doesn't look at anybody. We took him to the park and he put a piece of glass in his mouth and tried to eat it. *Autismo.* That's what the doctors say it is."

I had no idea if Javier knew what I meant. Most people didn't.

"But, Bárbara, you told me he was learning Chinese."

"He was."

"He's adjusting to the move."

"That's what we thought, but it's gone on for too long now."

I brought the children to Elmhurst a few weeks later. Jack was a year old by then and walking. Roselia admired him and gave him the extra time she always bestowed on the littlest children. But I could see that Danny was her mission. I was weary of would-be miracle workers; more than one well-meaning friend had said, "Give him to me! I'll get him to talk." They couldn't do it and I knew Roselia was not going to, either. But to preserve sanity I had learned to hope for, and celebrate, small victories. Roselia, I thought, might get him to at least smile.

She grabbed his hand and he went willingly. She brought him back into the kitchen, where they circumscribed a small, cool triangular world with their bodies and the open refrigerator. I peeked at them from the doorway, but I was not being invited, by either one of them.

Roselia took a banana, broke a piece, and put it in Danny's hand. *"Ay, qué lindo!"* she cooed at him. *"Danielito. Guapito."* Danny raised the banana to his mouth, and although he did not react in an obvious way, what I saw, or maybe I imagined it, was a half smile very much like Roselia's.

"He knows what I am saying," Roselia announced to me. "He did not forget Spanish and he still likes bananas."

"It will come back bit by bit," insisted Javier, who was standing behind me, watching, too.

I distracted myself by examining their apartment. The Almontes had become consumers of household furnishings. They had bought two maroon sofas swathed in plastic, a wall unit with a television, stereo, china knickknacks, and pictures of Elizabeth, Mauricio, Cristian, and Julio, and a leatherette bar.

The bar had three bottles on its counter: Chivas Regal Scotch, Brugal rum from Puerto Plata, and *mamajuana,* a homemade concoction of roots, herbs, and bark—Javier, I knew, liked to drink rum that had been steeped in a bottle of *mamajuana.* Like many Dominicans he believed it acted as a curative and an aphrodisiac.

On the wall next to the bar hung a framed painting of Antonio and Demetria Almonte. An artist had copied it from an old government ID. Demetria wore her hair pulled severely back behind her ears. That and the stiffness of the poses made the picture look like a Latino *American Gothic.* The difference was that the elder Almontes had good clothing on. Demetria was in a lavender sweater with a pointed collar, and Antonio had on a white shirt, red tie, and gray suit jacket. Those must have been their only good clothes.

A poster of Albert Einstein hung on the outside door of the second bedroom. I wondered if Mauricio could have done that.

Javier had grown a vegetable garden in the backyard. I looked out the back door and saw that it was overrun with cilantro. But the apartment felt the same: run-down and smelling exactly as I remembered it from a musty combination of cooking oil, cilantro, lavender soap, and aftershave. A few times, during the years I was gone, I thought that I had smelled the Almontes. I would be stopped by an odor in a house or coming from a man or woman walking down the street and feel an emotional familiarity. The same thing happened when I passed a lit cigar and felt as if my father—who was rarely without one—had been conjured up from the dead. Those reveries never lasted long because they weren't real enough. Nobody's smoke smelled just like my father's, and it wasn't only because Philly Panetellas were out of fashion. The smell of my father's smoke was complicated by his personality and history, and so it was with the Almontes. The people and the houses I thought smelled like them, and like the apartment on Fortieth Road, were only approximations. I knew what it was they were missing—Taíno *yuca* bread baking, exhaust fumes from black Volkswagens, *habichuela* bubbling on a charcoal stove, Mauricio's gardenias, and Demetria's yellow and purple flowers.

I sat on the plastic-covered couch and inhaled. On the wall was a small woolen weaving I had brought them from Mexico when Danny was a baby.

The new furniture was a sign Roselia's need to go home was not as sharp. She was still folding and hanging clothes in another of the small factories that were still all around the neighborhood. But later, when we had a chance to chat, she told me that she was happy. It was familiarity that made Roselia happy, and now she had that in New York.

Javier had quit Paolo Construction and was working for

himself, as a contractor. There were more immigrants than ever in Queens, and homeowners and landlords were eager to renovate their basements, garages, and other unused spaces to make extra apartments to rent out to the newcomers. It was an old American story. The ones who came first made money from the next wave. In Brooklyn my grandparents rented from German Jews who came before them. Javier rented from the Greek woman and Frank Corona, but now he was building apartments for newer immigrants. Meanwhile, he was making money from Frank Corona; he was the handyman for the house on Fortieth Road.

Javier was delighted to be on the upward part of this cycle, although he made it clear to me that he did not approve of illegal immigration. "There are so many *ilegales* who will work for less," he said. Javier was also angry at himself for not learning enough English to take a test for a contractor's license. He would have earned more that way. Instead, he had to give some of his earnings to a friend who did have a license—and who filed for permits for Javier. But after almost a decade in America, he had earned and saved enough to buy many *tareas* of land, which now surrounded his old *casita,* where Cristian and Julio Santini lived.

"You should see it now," Javier told me as Roselia and Danny came out of the kitchen. "It's a *finca.*"

The day that I brought Danny to Queens, Mauricio had been there, hiding in the background of greeting and noise. I hadn't known what to say to him. When I had left for Mexico, he had been a shy twelve-year-old, a boy still in need of mothering. Then, I was able to talk to him about school and his friends, or just silly things such as whether he could make a new invention with a hundred attached straws. But I didn't know what to say to a shy teenager. Or whether he wanted to talk to me at all.

Danny was pulling on me and I was trying to leave when Mauricio stopped me and said that he had been looking for an article I had written a few years earlier about Mexico that had been published in the *New Yorker.* I didn't realize he knew about it. He said he had seen it but wondered if I had a copy because he was interested in Mexican culture.

This was different. Mauricio Almonte read the *New Yorker.* I'd known about International High School, but just vaguely. I had not really placed Mauricio there. From Hong Kong, I had still been sending him foreign currency, as he had asked me to do when I left for Mexico. Gifts to delight a child. But now Mauricio was getting ready to go to college.

He began to visit us at our house on Long Island. He was great with my boys and went ice skating with Danny and Jack at our local rink. (His skating had improved since that day at Rockefeller Center.) He always brought books to read and was making his way through D. H. Lawrence and anything by Jack Kerouac. He told me he wanted to be a writer.

"What does your father think?" I asked.

"My father says I should be a doctor. He says that he has dreamed that for me since Camú."

I had never heard that from Javier. He had never been so specific. All he had said, to me at least, was that he had wanted his son educated in America.

Mauricio asked me where I had learned to write, and I gave him the stock answer about just doing it. He looked at me as if I were not being helpful. He was right. So I told him about Albany, where I had attended the state university. I told him about my teachers and friends in the journalism department, about the school's New York State Writers' Institute, and about William Kennedy, the Pulitzer Prize–winning novelist who was the city's literary hero and the triumphant soul behind the university's writing programs. I had been in Kennedy's class before he was famous. But fame had nothing to do with his being a great teacher. "It was in Bill Kennedy's class that I learned I *could* be a writer," I told Mauricio.

It wasn't long after that conversation that Mauricio called me and said he had applied to Albany State. He wanted me to drive him up to see the campus. On the way, he demonstrated what a typical teenager he had become; he complained incessantly about his parents. He was particularly annoyed that Javier was buying land in Camú. "I don't know why he's sending all of his money back there. I don't know why my father doesn't just buy a house in Queens. This is where we live."

When we got to the school, Mauricio met with the people who handed out loans and scholarships to minority students. He toured the science department. He had told his father he was seriously considering pre-med. When he finished, I took him to the dormitory where I had once lived, Melville Hall on State Quad, part of a starkly white, Edward Durell Stone low-rise in the outline of a square. In the center was a large white tower. There were three more dormitory complexes like that.

"In the winter you can't see the buildings for the snow," I told Mauricio. It was an old, unoriginal observation, the first thing prospective applicants heard about Albany State architecture.

Mauricio grinned.

"It's also very phallic," I said. Another important to know fact.

Mauricio looked at me as though this was something he had already figured out. I was not sure this was the right place for him, a large, looming campus. My freshman year had been one immense lecture class after another. I was a city kid, too, and I had felt alienated there.

We walked through the dorms, peeked in some of the rooms, which were the same as I remembered: overheated, messy, frenetic. Mauricio talked to girls who invited us in. It was remarkable to me that he spoke to them, these strange older girls, as though it were no effort at all. He said he liked the dormitories. I think he liked the idea of sharing a room with someone other than Elizabeth.

On the third floor of the Humanities Building, we stopped at the New York State Writers' Institute. Tom Smith, the institute's fabled director, offered Mauricio a glass of red wine, and John Montague, the Irish poet who taught the spring semester in

Albany each year, joined us. I had mentioned John Montague's poem "A Muddy Cup" in the newspaper series, and on the drive up I'd reminded Mauricio that John's mother had emigrated from Northern Ireland to Brooklyn, where the poet was born. His mother had hated America and took John back to County Armagh when he was still a boy. I thought Mauricio might like to have a conversation with him. "He's very easy to talk to," I assured him. But faced with a "real poet," Mauricio became his old self, the quiet little boy I remembered, not the flirt in the girl's dormitory room. I realized, too, that he had not read any of John Montague's poems. Mauricio knew, better than I, to keep his mouth shut when he didn't know what to say.

That night Mauricio, still in his little-boy mode, ate dinner with me and some of my friends. He didn't say much during the meal, but when it was over I eavesdropped on a conversation he was having with Bill Kennedy. The two of them stood outside on a snow-covered street.

"I think you should decide whether you want to be a doctor or a writer," Bill Kennedy was saying.

"I was thinking I could be a doctor and write," Mauricio said hesitantly.

Bill Kennedy shook his head. "William Carlos Williams. He did it. But there are very few who can do both well."

That, I decided, was one conversation I would never describe to Javier.

Mauricio was not accepted at Albany State. His SAT scores were too low. Instead, he chose Fredonia and a pre-med program. All he would say to me was, "I like Fredonia." He did. But by the end of his sophomore year, he had become a secondary education major. By the end of his junior year, he was an English major.

I had been back in New York about a year when Cristian flew up for a visit with her family. She brought her son Julito, who was the same age as my Jack. I offered to pick them up and bring them to Long Island for the day. It was summer and hot. We could go to the beach.

At the apartment on Fortieth Road, Javier answered the door. I followed him to the living room where Cristian, her thick arms popping out of a sleeveless shirt, greeted me with a hug and with giggles. I was struck not so much by her size—she was hefty, not obese, no matter what her sister said—but by the way, at twenty-one, she held herself like a mature, confident woman. What I remembered was a pretty, silly teenager in tight jeans; the last time I had seen Cristian she had been a junior at John Bowne.

"I didn't have time to cook anything," I said when we were all in the car. This time I giggled. My lack of domestic skills was, by now, legendary in the Almonte family. "Maybe we can take the kids to McDonald's."

"I know, Bárbara," Cristian said. "It's okay." Then she put her head down. "I have to reduce anyway." It was the first—and the last—time I heard her apologize about her weight. There was something odd about the serious, humble way she said it, which was not at all like a typical Dominican, who would laugh off such a matter. It was as if she was parroting things her family said, but I had the feeling that what they were really nagging her about was her life with Julio.

I had heard all about Julio from Javier and then from Elizabeth and Mauricio, and they all kept telling me that I had met him before, but I didn't know what they were talking about.

"So who is this guy anyway?" I asked Cristian.

"You don't remember him from the first time I went to the United States? You don't remember him from the airport?"

"No."

"You said to me, 'Cristian, who is he?' He was inside, in the immigration part. He was sitting there. And you said to me, 'Who is that, Cristian?' And I said to you, 'A friend.' "

I didn't ask any more questions that day. Mostly I was running after my own two sons. Jack was a particularly busy toddler, and Danny had to be watched all the time; his odd, sometimes dangerous activities had to be quickly intercepted. He had not regained his speech, but there was evidence that now, at age four and a half, he had taught himself to read, so we had glimmers of hope about his intelligence, if not his behavior. Roselia had known something. Cristian watched as I held on to him in parking lots, stopped him from grabbing strangers' hamburgers, changed his paper pull-ups, and walked with him on the beach, extracting seaweed out of his mouth every few minutes.

Julito, in comparison to my boys, was docile, all large brown eyes watching the action. He seemed, though, to feel an immediate kinship with his new American friend *"Yack."*

"Ay, Bárbara," Cristian said. "Two children looks very difficult."

I renewed my friendship with Elizabeth, as well. I went to lunch with her and her friends, to hockey games, even to Chippendales. Shopping with Elizabeth was the best though; it always had been. On one of her lunch hours we went to Ann Taylor. "There's something I need to try on," she said. She took a pair of navy silk pants off the rack, and I followed her into the dressing room. I saw the price tag, $125, and I remembered Robbins Department store on Junction Boulevard. I remembered twelve plastic heart earrings in different colors for a dollar.

"Are you going to buy them?" I asked. "No, John," she said, talking about her boyfriend. "Maybe he will buy them for me."

37

1993

In the fall, I decided to go back to Camú.

I had not been there since 1986, and, in keeping with Marta's prophecy, I had signed a contract to write a book about the Almontes. I needed to see Camú again, and what made the idea of a trip so compelling was that Javier would be returning as well. I had never been in Camú with Javier.

Javier went back to the *campo* often. But this trip was special. His fiftieth birthday was coming up, and he was determined to be standing on Juan de Nina soil for that.

There was also, finally, a vehicle involved.

Javier had a car, a used Honda. But that was a practical possession. He used it to go to work and to see his relatives in New Jersey. The Honda was not his baby. Javier's baby was a sleek black pickup truck.

Javier had sent his pickup truck back to Camú. He loved that truck as if it were an exceptionally smart child; he loved it enough to want to send it away to a better place. In Queens he worried that it would be stolen or damaged although he kept it locked in a neighbor's garage and rarely drove it. So he sent it to Camú, reasoning that Julio Santini and Cristian could drive it. Now he wanted to go back and check on his truck. He also wanted to make sure Julio Santini was driving it home to Cristian, not some other woman.

Javier and I talked about the trip at the kitchen table in the apartment on Fortieth Road, while my two sons played around the small patches of cilantro and corn he had planted in his city backyard.

I arrived in Puerto Plata on the day after Javier Almonte's fiftieth birthday and walked off my plane into the hot, open air. A sign explained that the airport's poor appearance was due to construction. I remembered the way this airport used to be—a sticky confusion in which planes were regularly delayed and baggage was lost—and wondered if construction could make it any worse. Men were playing bongo drums and maracas, but I couldn't hear them over the drilling. The musicians had a jar with an American five-dollar bill sticking out of it. But no one from my flight was adding to it.

Inside it was dark. Either there was no electricity in the terminal or all the lights were off. At customs, a man approached me and said in English, "Give me a tip and they won't check your bags." I didn't and was waved through customs anyway. Elections were coming up, and Balaguer, now eighty-seven, was running for reelection again. But if he had a sign up taking credit for any of this, I didn't see it.

In the crowd outside, I spotted Javier's balding head and his band of gray hair. He was dwarfed by a man whose stomach was his most prominent feature. Julio Santini. I hugged Javier, shook hands with Julio, who seemed happy to see me, and we walked together to Javier's truck, its black paint gleaming in the Puerto Plata sun. Julio drove, but Javier was obviously the proud owner; he was Víctor in the passenger seat of his own tractor. I sat between the two men. Julio was carefully groomed. He wore a new polo shirt, smelled from aftershave lotion, and his hair was combed with oil. We traveled toward Puerto Plata, turned off the main road in the direction of Camú, and turned again at the Bar Osiris, where Javier had courted Roselia. Children saw us and came to run alongside the truck. It looked the same to me.

"Are there phones here yet?" I asked Julio.

"Bárbara," Javier said, "Camú is just the same."

We didn't go as far as the turnoff to Fian's, as I had thought we would. Instead we took a road I didn't remember, directly up to Javier's old *casita*. It was still there looking the same. Cristian was waving to us from the road, Julito at her side. I got out of the truck and we hugged.

"You like, Bárbara?" she asked, speaking English as a welcoming gesture. The *casita* looked the same, but behind it was a large animal pen, which Cristian later told me held 150 pigs. Chickens and roosters, more than I had ever seen when this was Roselia's home, circled nearby.

As Cristian showed me around the *casita* and its expanded environs, she seemed as comfortable as I had ever seen her, with the way she looked and where she was, as though this was the natural way for a mother and wife, a woman with responsibilities, to grow.

"Where is your new house?" I asked. I was anxious to see how Camú did a suburban tract house, which was what Javier and Cristian had led me to believe they had built.

"Behind there." I followed her in the direction of Fian's house to what seemed like another construction site, although it was a lot quieter than the airport. There were a few walls made from *bloques* and a lot of rubble.

"It's not finished."

"No," she said, smiling. "It will be. We're doing it bit by bit."

She guided me through the unfinished rooms. "This will be the kitchen. Indoors," she said proudly. "That will be Mami and Papi's room, and this will be for Julito." We stepped over pieces of concrete and buckets of cement.

"This is all that's finished," she said. She took a key that hung on a ribbon around her neck and opened a door. I did not remember anyone from Camú ever having a key. The master bedroom was a small but pretty room painted a bright blue. Julio had built a closet with light oak doors. There was a bed with a frilly bedspread and Julito's crib. The bathroom was tile, white tiles with blue marks splashed on them to depict water. I told Cristian I was impressed. I wondered where in Camú I would sleep this time.

I knew that Javier had to return to New York in the morning. Our plane tickets and schedules had not coincided as well as we had hoped. But I really only needed to see one thing with Javier: the spot in Juan de Nina where he had grown up. We got into his truck but stopped, first, to see Fian, who hugged me as she had the first day we had met, as if I had never left, as if visiting her after a seven-year absence was the most natural thing in the world. She told me that Víctor was sleeping—he had suffered two strokes in recent years—and that I would be able to see him later.

Javier drove to the hill that went up to Juan de Nina, the one he had climbed when he was a young Taíno hunter who dreamed of flight. To the right of us was the river Camú. A young woman was doing her laundry in the river with a washboard. I had heard from Mauricio that there was a washing machine in Camú now. But only one, and people "rented" it from its owner.

The woman walked over to me. "Bárbara?" she asked.

I didn't recognize her, but she told me that she was Lucia, one of Lilo's daughters, and that she had been called for her *cita* and would be in New Jersey soon. Another notch for Marta. Lucia went back to her pile of clothes, her brush and soap powder. The river was so dry that white rocks rose high out of it, like stepping-stones. This river would be a cinch to cross.

"When I was a child, it was an immense fountain of water," Javier said. "Nobody could get to the bottom. You couldn't dive down. There were big trees and we would dive from the trees. Do you see those empty spaces? There used to be trees there. There were other kinds of trees here. We don't know how to keep our resources. In America they do. When I saw Fredonia, I saw that. The country that doesn't preserve its trees dies."

We walked up the hill together. Javier was no balder than when I had met him, but over the years his hair had grayed. He walked like a young man, though. He put his hand gently around my shoulder, almost flirtatiously, which was the way Javier was with me, as if that was his duty.

He looked out to the *cordillera* the way he told me he had as a boy. And then up to the spot, now empty land, where Demetria and Alemán had their *casita,* raised their children, lived their lives. There were no houses standing nearby. I could see a few in the distance. Lilo's old house was there, but abandoned. There was almost nothing left of Juan de Nina.

"This is the place that gave me life." Javier was looking at a spray of yellow flowers. "Fifty years ago. This is where my brother Mirito died."

"We called these yellow flowers *mantequillas,* and there were purple ones, *moradas.* The mango tree was much larger but Víctor cut it. Now it's growing again."

He tore a piece of paper from my notebook and drew a map

of where all his neighbors' houses used to be, little blocks of a village that no longer existed. The floods had driven a lot of people away, as did the lure of jobs in Puerto Plata, Santo Domingo, and for a lucky few, in the United States.

"It's very quiet," I said.

"*Ay*, Bárbara, there used to be a lot of noise here. Especially in the morning. The roosters crowing, people waking, getting ready to walk down the hill and cut sugarcane or work the fields. It was a very healthy life. But we did not own enough of our own land."

We walked down the road and Javier stopped for a minute at a house that still stood. He smiled.

"I knew a girl here once," Javier said, laughing. "But Roselia took care of her."

When we returned to Camú, Víctor was awake and sitting in his breezeway. He was wearing a plaid bathrobe over his boxer shorts and was exercising his hand, trying to make a fist. He looked old, weak, shorter than I remembered.

"*Ay*, Bárbara," he said when he saw me.

Later, Javier told me he was the one who now paid Víctor's medical bills.

That night Julio Santini went to sleep somewhere else, at his mother's in Puerto Plata or at the other house he had in Camú. I slept with Cristian in her new bed in her new bedroom that would one day be a house. We were like girlfriends again, or sisters, as we'd been the night before her mother and sister left for America, when she and Elizabeth moved over to make room for me. This room, though, had air-conditioning and a small black-and-white television. We watched *Punto Final,* a late-night Dominican talk and variety show, before we fell asleep.

Javier had stayed in the *casita.* In the morning I went to see him as he was packing. He had a revolver in his hand, but instead of packing it he put it in a drawer.

"We used to not lock our doors here," he said. "Some of the houses didn't have doors."

"But you had Trujillo then," I said.

Javier grunted. He put a roll of American cash into his pocket.

Julio and I dropped him off at the airport. We were getting back into the car when someone told Julio that he would swap an apartment in Puerto Plata for the truck.

I laughed.

"He's serious," Julio said. "But why would anyone want to live in an apartment? People here are used to the *campo.*"

He explained that the government had built a new housing project in Puerto Plata and was giving away apartments to political favorites, of which there were many. The next morning I went out with Julio Santini, to see his land and his cattle, some of which was really Javier's land and Javier's cattle.

Julio Santini wanted his wife and his bed back the next night, which was understandable. I went to sleep at Fian's. Despite my protests, she insisted I take her room, the nicest one in the house. The double bed had a ruffled peach bedspread and there were curtains to match. Fian sent one of her teenage grand-daughters in to sleep next to me, so that I wouldn't be lonely or frightened by the sounds of animals. I protested—what I really craved was privacy—but Fian insisted that I needed company.

The next morning, to avoid showering at Fian's—the garbage can was still in the shower—I walked to Cristian's. She had hot water, if the power was on to work the pump. I did shower at Fian's once that week, though, and the garbage can was not the worst of it. The showerhead emitted only a thin stream of cold water. I may not have understood the function of the garbage can, but I could not have agreed with Mauricio more—that shower alone was cause enough for emigration.

Each evening I sat on the porch with Fian, who was still tak-ing care of a few of her grandchildren. Often her children came to visit, and one night Tío Julio arrived with his wife and two children. He was not, he told me sadly, working in his profes-sion. Instead he was driving a taxi in Puerto Plata. I wanted to talk to him about that, but not on Fian's porch. I also wanted to go to the capital to see the Faro, the multimillion-peso light-house monument to Columbus, which had not been built the last time I was in the Dominican Republic. I asked if I could hire him to drive me, and his eyes lit up at the prospect of such a good fare.

I slept poorly the night before Tío Julio and I went to the Faro. The pigs and roosters kept waking me, and then I heard what sounded like a woman's sighs. It became quiet. I heard those sighs again in my half sleep, and they woke me later. It sounded as if someone was having a seizure.

I opened the bedroom door. Fian was in the living room, holding on to her youngest daughter, Bethania, who was nineteen and still unmarried.

"It's okay, Bárbara," she said sternly. "You go back to sleep."

It seemed like only a few minutes later that Fian was knocking on the bedroom door. "Hurry up, Bárbara. Hurry up." She was laughing. "There's going to be a lot of traffic." She didn't sound as if she had been up all night nursing a sick daughter.

I dressed quickly and ran into the kitchen as soon as I heard Julio's cranky Toyota drive up the rocky path to his parents' house.

Fian was there alone. I knew I wouldn't see Víctor. He tried to enjoy what he could of his forced retirement by staying in bed at least until the sun rose.

"Drink this," Fian ordered. It was tea made with *yerba buena* leaves and other herbs from her garden and mixed with lots of sugar. The strong mint flavor woke me up.

"*Bendiga, Fian,*" said Julio, who had also come into the kitchen. He was wearing a white T-shirt that had NEW JERSEY, THE GARDEN STATE written on it. His sister Ramona had sent it to him.

"*Bendiga, m'hijo,*" Fian blessed her son. Then she got back to business.

"You have to hurry because it will take you half the time if you go now, before the sun and the traffic. You could have gotten there in two hours if you had left a few hours ago. Now it'll take at least three. The longer you wait, the longer it will take."

Julio had warned me about the traffic the night before, but it had more authority coming from his mother, even though Fian only left her house to walk to her husband's land. We got into the Toyota with its failing upholstery and rattling windows. Julio had bought the car and the rights to a route with his savings and money borrowed from his father. In the morning chill we needed jackets, but it would be sweltering before noon and there was no air-conditioning in the car. Julio definitely wasn't taking many tourists on long trips. We drove slowly down the unpaved road outside Fian's house, and its big rocks scratched and banged against the underside of the car.

"Okay. Okay. Okay," Julio muttered to himself.

Haltingly, we drove by a few huts, the cockfighting ring—Javier's *gallera*—and a few small drink stands. We were approaching the main road, which was still haphazardly paved, although it had recently been resurfaced. Fian had told me that she liked President Balaguer because he had fixed the road. Víctor, too, had said that the best thing about Balaguer was that he had fixed the road. The old farmer who had hardly ever left the *campo,* even when he was young and vigorous, said he felt the repaving made it easier for people from Camú to reach their jobs at the resorts. On the road a billboard announced to voters, BALAGUER DID THIS!

If you turned right onto Balaguer's new road, it was a quick jaunt to Santiago, the country's second city, an efficient way to get half the distance to Santo Domingo. Julio turned in the other direction and we rode into Gran Parada, another *campo* town, which was where Javier's sister María had lived when she was married. Gran Parada was a bit more cosmopolitan than Camú, a bit closer to the beaches, clubs, and action of the resorts.

"That's my house," Julio said, beaming.

"The blue one?" I asked, pointing to a *casita,* a tiny hut painted a traditional Dominican turquoise. It had a thatched roof. "It's pretty."

"*Gracias.*"

"It's palm," I said casually. Then I wished I hadn't mentioned it.

"*Sí,*" said Julio, and he looked down at the steering wheel.

"Okay, I did come home from school expecting to work for Víctor, to manage the farm," he told me after he had driven quietly for a while. "Then he got sick and sold off about a third of his land and stopped growing cane. He abandoned it completely. Do you know why? Okay. The mill in Montellano was taking more than a year to pay him. They were paying him more, but what good was it if it was taking a year to pay? So now Víctor and Fian have cows and they're mining sand and rocks from the river, and they don't think they need any help. Do you know how many workers they have? Okay. One worker for a thousand *tareas* of land. My mother does the rest. I keep telling them they should give me the land. I have the degree. Give me the land and let me do something with it. They have the cows. I would plant something else. Diversify. I argue about this with them all the time, but they won't do it."

We passed a truck stop, a place of simple meals spiced with cilantro. Rice, beans, plantains, chicken. A chunk of *dulce de leche* for the road. I was hungry, but Julio didn't stop.

The traffic was starting to build and the fumes were increasing, too. Latin American fumes from too many old cars with too few emission-control devices. We were on the Carretera Duarte now—a highway named for the George Washington of the Dominican Republic. I remembered it as having only two lanes, but there were now three in some spots. "It's the Autopista Duarte now," Julio corrected me. The Duarte Expressway. We were crawling, but even when we hadn't been, it was apparent from Julio's driving that this was not the destiny he had planned for himself. Typically, his countrymen were aggressive behind the wheel, happy only when they owned the road. Julio was meek, tentative. He had to concentrate on where he was going. He didn't like passing other cars.

Julio felt stuck. He couldn't leave and he couldn't make his life any better. Some of this was his own lack of nerve, his need to wait until someone handed him a visa. But while he waited, he was stuck in a country in which success was ultimately determined by *relaciones*—connections. And more often than not it was the people in the upper classes who had the best *relaciones*. Education and determination could only get you so far, only protect you to a point. Julio knew that whatever he did now would be measured against the success of Mauricio's emigration. "Mauricio is going to be a professional," Julio told me, "and I am going to drive a taxi."

I slept, and when I woke, we were in Santo Domingo. We had left at six and now it was after ten. Julio was not as familiar with the capital as he had claimed and didn't know how to maneuver his car through the unruly traffic. I thought we might be near the U.S. consulate, so I asked Julio if he could figure out how to pass by there. We did and saw the same concrete wall with openings designed to deflect bullets, the same long lines of visa applicants outside.

"Okay. Okay. Mauricio doesn't write," Julio said. "Never. Neither does Elizabeth. I used to take Elizabeth to school. Ask her. Okay. She had to ride in the back of a pickup truck in the morning to get to school. I used to take her on my motorcycle so she wouldn't get her uniform dirty. Okay. Ask her. I remember Mauricio as the baby I used to bathe."

We drove to the Faro. What we saw as we rode up to the monument was a large white building, a gleaming, foreboding mausoleum. There were no visitors, no cars, no signs, no direction on where to park or enter. Columbus had more company when he stepped on the shore of his first Caribbean island. The Faro was haunted—if a white edifice shining in the sun can be haunted.

We decided to see something else first and went to Santo Domingo's Malecón. Across the road is the old section of the city, where colonial buildings are preserved. We walked up to the Alcázar, which had been home to Columbus's heirs. It was built by his son Diego, who returned to Santo Domingo in 1509, three years after his father's death. Diego had been named viceroy and governor general and was determined to live in a manner that would, in appearance at least, restore his father's lost glory.

The word *alcázar* means castle or fortress. The Alcázar looks more like the latter, a staunch rectangle of limestone blocks, built with Italian influences. The front has a portico of Roman-Doric columns. In the back is an expanse of garden, a view of the Ozama River and the Faro. Diego would probably have liked that, although critics of the new monument are quick to point out that Columbus managed to find the New World without the help of any lighthouses. Pamphlets distributed inside the Alcázar note that "Indian slave labor" was used in the construction of the residence. Official guides and textbooks in the Dominican Republic are often like this. They admit that atrocities occurred without going into too many details or voicing too strong opinions.

Inside, the rooms are open to the public.

"What's here from the original house?" I asked our young guide as she showed us some furniture.

"The walls," she said.

The Alcázar was pillaged by Sir Francis Drake, who captured Santo Domingo in 1586. It descended into disrepair and was even used as a stable until 1957, when Trujillo had it refurbished. It is one of this country's jewels, both architecturally and historically. Although there are no original pieces, it does contain numerous others from the period. It isn't a very good museum. Nothing is identified. Visitors are at the mercy of unenthusiastic guides who apparently got their jobs through *relaciones*. A curator would cost a lot less than a Faro. Julio was bored. He was worried about his car parked on the street.

We left and drove back to the Faro. Other cars were there now. In the parking lot, an officer directed us to a spot.

"If you leave your car here, I can watch it."

I gave him some pesos.

When the Faro was built, Columbus's remains—or what are said to be his remains—were moved there from the cathedral. They are guarded by a succession of serious-faced young sailors in white suits. The Faro is 800 feet long, 150 feet tall. The guides who show visitors around say it cost 136 million pesos or about $10 million, although unofficial estimates range from seven to twenty-five times higher. During its construction, many residents of a nearby neighborhood were evicted or awaiting eviction. President Balaguer had pledged to resettle them in better housing. But in 1992, when the Faro opened, a number still had not been resettled. Many refused to move. A block wall went up between the neighborhood and the Faro, and many said it was to the hide the poverty from the legions of foreign tourists who were expected. Throughout Latin America there are hundreds of neighborhoods like the one that borders the Faro. But none so close to a new multimillion-dollar monument.

We walked up the steps of the sphinxlike Faro, overwhelmed on all sides by white blocks with quotations from the Bible and the philosophers, including one that reminds any potential Taíno sympathizers, "This land belongs to the Christians." We paid five pesos each to enter. Inside it was as light and modern as the Alcázar is dark and old. Julio, who had been so talkative in Camú and fidgety at the Alcázar, was silent with wonder. His eyes were larger than they had been over my offer of dollars for the fare as we passed by the new gold and marble Columbus tomb at the front entrance. He didn't mention his car once. Instead he read over the historic details and examined the lighted map showing Columbus's four voyages. We walked through halls filled with exhibits donated by other countries to commemorate the quincentenary. Many were modest, with copies of pieces of art. Still, it was more museum than any schoolchild from Camú or even Puerto Plata would see and certainly a lot more organized and professional than the Alcázar.

Japan had donated a huge Sony screen flashing pictures of snowy mountains. Julio had never seen snow, and he lingered awhile. He might as well have been at Tokyo Disneyland. This is what Balaguer must have known when he insisted that the Faro be built, no matter how extravagant it seemed. The Alcázar was not enough to take people's minds off their problems.

We had a guide at the Faro, too. A young man. When Julio spoke, it was to ask him how he got his job.

"Por relaciones," said the guide. Connections.

Soon we left to drive back to Camú. We went by the truck stops again, and again we didn't stop. Julio ate like a Taíno, too.

A few days later he came to see me at his mother's house. He excused himself, went into the bedroom where I had been staying, and rummaged through a closet. He came back with a thin paperback: *Historia de mi Patria—4 grado. History of My Country—Fourth Grade.* "This is how I learned about Columbus," Julio told me.

On the cover there is a painting of a Taíno peering through palm leaves at three caravels, presumably the *Niña,* the *Pinta,* and the *Santa María.* We only see the Taíno's back and it is impossible to tell whether the tension of it and the straining of his neck come from curiosity, terror, or a combination. Terror, of course, would have been more prescient.

The textbook with the Taíno on its cover was published in 1968 and is 104 pages long. It has about a dozen pages on the Indians and on the settlers' relations with them. It is diplomatic, suggesting that teachers have students look at both the accomplishments of the *conquistadores* and the way "some of them were cruel to the Indians and some were generous." It is scant with details about both the cruelty and the generosity.

The spine of the book is broken, and inside, on the title page, it says in a childish cursive, "This Book Belongs to Mauricio

Javier Almonte." Cristian's name is in the book, too, and so are
the names of several of their cousins.

Samuel Eliot Morison described the Taínos as being "fairly
advanced." They lived, he wrote, "in huts made of a wooden
frame and palm thatch."

My husband and children met me in Puerto Plata the next
week.

Danny, who was six, loved the *campo*. He hiked happily to
the outer reaches of what was left of Víctor and Fian's fields,
walking arm in arm with one of her grandchildren. I had not
seen him so communicative since he got sick.

Jack, three years old, wanted to know why there was no
McDonald's. But he liked the rides Julio Santini gave him and
Julito in Javier's truck.

Fian wanted us to take Danny to see Fransica. "Maybe she
can get him to talk," she said.

I had always wanted to meet the *bruja* of Camú. But I wasn't
sure this was the way to do it. On the other hand, as parents of
an autistic child, we tried any promise of magic that came our
way. Some of the things we had done with licensed physicians
and therapists in New York were more unlikely to work than
the spell of a *bruja*.

I knew Danny understood what I said to him now. I told him
about Fransica, and he jumped up and down, which was one of
the things he did to indicate that he was interested.

I told him that she would not be able to cure him. That he
should view this as an educational experience, a look at the way
the people of Camú lived.

I touched his right hand. Without letting go of me he moved
his hand away from his body. Under a system we had devised,
that meant yes.

We walked up a road by Cristian's house, and on the way a
guagua turned and let off about twenty people, who were also

going to see Fransica. Up the hill, outside a complex of palm huts, a line of about thirty people was waiting to see her.

Fian had told us we should not wait. Just let her know that we were there.

We knocked on her door and she ushered us in. Fransica was a small, pretty woman in a pink dress—a younger, trimmer version of Fian. She sat in front of an altar that was packed with statues and trinkets. A porcelain statue of Dr. Gregorio Hernández—the legendary Venezuelan physician and humanitarian—loomed over the table. Dr. Hernández, famous throughout Latin America, was dressed in a crisp, black suit and a bowler hat that made him look like Charlie Chaplin. He had a string of rosary beads around his neck. Dozens of smaller statues of the doctor were also on the altar, mixed in with pictures of Jesus and a variety of saints. Behind Dr. Hernández there was a tapestry of the Last Supper. Votive candles and bottles filled with colored water were on the table.

"Whiskey bottles," whispered my husband into the tape recorder he was holding for me. "Whiskey bottles. One, two, three, four, five, six pints with different-colored liquid in them. A bottle of Finesse shampoo. Half a dozen candles. A dozen paintings of Jesus, a guy with a hat on him."

A little boy was in a chair next to Fransica. His mother stood beside her.

"Has this child been to a doctor?" Fransica asked. That, I suspected, was for our benefit.

"No," the mother said.

"The first thing I want to tell you is you should take him to a doctor."

The mother nodded, surprised.

"Listen to the way your body feels," Fransica said to the boy. "You have a lot of pain in your back, a lot of pain in your shoulder. A lot of pain in your teeth. Your knee. Where in your body do you feel the most pain?"

"The most pain is in my head."

"The head, you are suffering a lot because of your head. We are going to cure your head." She put her hands around the circumference of his head.

"Sanctify your body in the name of God, in the name of the Holy Ghost, in the name of the Virgin Mary. In the name of all the saints. Oh, my Father, it is said that with your help I can used my hand to pass over this body and to take the pain from this head. Oh, Lord Jesus, how you can cure so that no pain is felt neither in the days or in the nights. How good that we believe in Lord Jesus and that when we feel the hands of saints working, we know that we will no longer feel pain. Put your hand in the name of God, the Father, the Son, and the Holy Ghost. The Father, the Son, and the Holy Ghost . . . the Father, the Son, and the Holy Ghost . . . Get one bottle of this water in the name of the Holy Ghost. And take three drops of it in the name of San Gregorio Hernández."

She did not take money from the mother. But I knew that people paid her.

With Danny, Fransica worked quickly. That was the key. He had almost no ability to concentrate.

He sat in the chair and she put her hands on his head. He squirmed, but she squirmed with him. "Cure your body in the name of the saint. Your little body in the name of God. In the name of the Holy Ghost. And in the name of the love and tenderness of Christ. Lord Jesus, you know that this child was born healthy. If it is possible, return to him his ability to speak, then let him speak. . . . Leave us now in the hands of the Holy Ghost."

I couldn't have said it better myself.

Fransica gave us a little statue of Dr. Hernández, instructing us to keep it near Danny, and a prescription for holy water we could buy at a pharmacy in Puerto Plata.

Fransica then turned to me. "Now you know," she said.

I asked her if I could give her some money, but she refused.

"A hug for her, Danny," my husband said.

And Danny hugged Fransica.

★   ★   ★

A few days after we returned home, Elizabeth called to say that Bethania was in the hospital. She told me the whole story, some of which I had already heard in the *campo:* Bethania had suffered from epilepsy for years and had controlled it with medication. But now she was nineteen and Fian had convinced herself that the medicine would make her daughter sterile. She had taken Bethania off it and put all her faith in Fransica the *bruja.* Fian's other children had been trying, desperately, to get Fian to give Bethania her medicine before something bad happened.

Everyone, in New York and Camú, was angry with Fian. Javier almost got on a plane back there to "have a conversation" with her. But as wrong as I knew Fian was, I couldn't help feeling a new kind of kinship with her. I put Dr. Hernández in Danny's room.

ENDING

Tía Marta is resting on the couch and says to end the story with Javier. "It is true that without me there would be no story. Two dozen people are now here because of me, and there will be more. *Ay.* I think it's two dozen. I can't count them anymore. I am La Cabeza. But Javier is the storyteller. He is the one who remembers what happened."

"Everyone should have their own opportunity to end," Javier says. "Bárbara, I am sure, has an ending of her own. As for me, I have one more thing to say. I was Almonte from the land. I am Almonte from the land. But the land had to be mine. Not Víctor's. Mine. Because when you work the land for somebody else, you don't get anything out of it. But when you work for yourself, you do. I always liked the life of the countryside. It's a sane life, a pure life. In the country you breathe pure air. In the country you have trees. You know what purified the air, what purifies the air a hundred percent? It's the trees.

"What are you asking? Would I go back to Camú to live? I don't know. Cristian's house still isn't finished. Frank Corona has a house in Santiago, but he has a house in Florida now, too. *Ay,* Bárbara, that is beautiful. I could retire in Florida, too."

When Roselia comes home from her factory job, she is asked how she would end the story. She has to pick up Julito, Cristian's older boy who lives with her now so he can go to an American school. He is at the baby-sitter. His mother lives in Camú, but he is doing well at P. S. 19. When asked how she is coping with the boy, Roselia says, "It is easy. I already know how to do it." Knowing where to end is not as easy. "*Ay,* Bárbara," Roselia says. "I am too tired to know where to end. Ask Javier. Wherever he wants to end. *Y sus niños?* 'Your boys?' How are they?"

There are still no phones in Camú, so we cannot call Cristian to ask her where to end. She has left Julio Santini twice now, and twice gone back to him. Probably she would say, "I told you this was about love, not immigration."

Elizabeth, long broken up with her boyfriend John, ends with the condominium she has bought in Valley Cottage, New York. It is an hour's commute from the World Trade Center, where she still works. "If only you had ended a few months from now. I will have my bachelor's degree in science and management from Nyack College by then," she says. "But I love my condominium. It is all woods behind it, like Camú. I love it here. It is quiet. Papi loves to come here. No, he doesn't fix anything. It's new. There's nothing to fix."

I want to end with a book I rediscovered among my mother's possessions, a Yiddish book published in the Bronx in 1937 by the First Felshteener Benevolent Association. It is a group memoir that includes a chapter by Ozzie Siegel, my grandfather. My grandfather called his chapter "I Searched for My Child in Fire and Flames," and wrote about the day he spent looking for my mother, expecting her to be dead. My grandfather died before I was born, and since I had never heard him tell my mother's "haystack story," I asked a friend to translate the chapter for me. It is almost the same story, although according to my grandfather my mother was not quite as noble or unspoiled as she had claimed. In fact, she sounded more like Elizabeth. Or like me.

The book also has a map of Felshteen, a crude ink drawing that shows every building, every house. When I saw it, I was reminded of the map Javier drew for me of Juan de Nina, when we returned for his fiftieth birthday. When a village was yours, the memory of every little house is important.

I suggested that Mauricio end with his last trip to Camú, the one he needed to sleep off for a week. When he woke, he said that he could not go back there to live. But he would go back there often. Another book about the Almontes will, I hope, be written by him.

"I still think," he says, "that I should end with a book about your family."

ACKNOWLEDGMENTS

Mauricio Almonte has inspired me since he was eleven years old. As an adult, he was an invaluable adviser and researcher. Javier Almonte shared stories, wisdom, and practicality, and Roselia Almonte embellished all that with her quiet, vital insight. Cristian Almonte generously told her own story, while her sister Elizabeth was slow to anger no matter how much was asked of her. Marta Gordon—Tía Marta—related whatever was most difficult. She is a woman of action, a quintessential immigrant, and the true head of the Almonte family. The Almontes are courageous people—and courageously honest. I thank them, as well as their relatives, their friends, and their ghosts, all of whom helped to make this book. Special among the Almonte relatives is Flor María Seecharan (née Gómez), the first family member to trust me. To Flor, her kind mother, Tía María, and their family, I express my gratitude.

My own family bolstered me so that I could write. This book is dedicated with great love to my husband, Jim Mulvaney, the best of bolsterers, as exceptional an editor as he is a mate and father. Our sons, Dan and Jack Mulvaney, were ages five and two when I began this book, and nine and six when I finished. They are caring, patient boys of stamina—and dutiful listeners. Jean Strole and Cristina David took care of them and taught them to be even better. Eileen Mulvaney, Patrick Mulvaney, and Jim Mulvaney, Sr., helped me to understand immigration from yet another perspective, that of the Irish. Ted Fischkin was the first storyteller I knew. Doris Siegel Bernstein, our family's last living survivor of the Felshteen pogrom, remembered the *shtetl* for me; Mollie Siegel Brown remembered the *shtetl* stories. The spirits of Ida Siegel Fischkin and David Fischkin drove this book from beginning to end.

New York Newsday survives in spirit as well. Don Forst had the idea for a newspaper series on an immigrant family. Bob Sales suggested he assign that series to me. Jim Toedtman,

Brooke Kroeger, Peg Finucane, and John Van Doorn were my able editors. And the Livingston Awards kindly honored our efforts.

Many editors and friends helped me to turn what was a newspaper series into the book *Muddy Cup*. David Chalfant, my beloved agent, was the first to see it; Carrie Chase shepherded its early stages; Hamilton Cain at Scribner adopted it, improved it, made it whole. William Kennedy, first, most enduring, and best instructor, was ready, as always, with advice and support. Sands Hall, of the Squaw Valley Community of Writers, led me to important revisions. John Montague permitted me to borrow his poem; this book could have no other title.

Muddy Cup thrived thanks to the assistance of the Dominican Studies Institute of the City University of New York. The Institute's programs and seminars provided me with historical and cultural perspectives of the Dominican Republic, unmatched and unavailable anywhere else. I am grateful to the the the Institute's director, Dr. Silvio Torres-Saillant, for sharing his scholarship.

For additional assistance and encouragement I thank Rebecca Allen, Joe Ames, Linda Miller Ames, Natalie Bates, Max Byrd and the workshop he led at Squaw Valley, Jenn Chen, José and Manuela Duarte da Silveira, Sandra Draper, Guillermo Garcia, George Gerardi and Alberto Munera of Hermandad, Dina Heisler, Patrick Kelly, Dianne Klein, John McGovern of the Suffolk County, New York, Police Department, Lois and Kevin Pilot, Bert Rosenberg, Meghan Sercombe, Paul Vitello, and Ruthellen Weiner. Wendy and Dr. Gary Kaplan provided Yiddish translations. Dr. Robert Shapiro advised on *shtetl* history. Bruce Gilbert's photographs of the Almontes have always helped me to see them.

I have quoted from various books, all of which were helpful in providing historical perspectives and information beyond those individual citations. Robert D. Crassweller's book, *Trujillo: The Life and Times of a Caribbean Dictator*, was a source of numerous anecdotes about Trujillo and about the Catholic Church in the Dominican Republic.

I thank Franklin W. Knight for alerting me to the existence of the 1921 State Department memo on Haiti and the Dominican Republic in the second edition of his book *The Caribbean: The Genesis of a Fragmented Nationalism*. Tad Szulc's book *Dominican Diary* helped me understand the 1965 civil war, as did an article by Michael J. Kryzanek. I am also indebted to books, poems, and stories by Julia Alvarez, Junot Diaz, Pedro Mir, Frank Moya Pons, and Viriato Sención, articles from the *New York Times* and the *San Juan Star,* and the books *Timetables of Jewish History* by Judah Gribetz and *Ellis Island* by Wilton S. Tift.